SELF-HYPNOSIS

A CONDITIONED-RESPONSE TECHNIQUE

LAURANCE SPARKS

Published by
Melvin Powers
WILSHIRE BOOK COMPANY
12015 Sherman Road
No. Hollywood, California 91605
Telephone: (213) 875-1711 / (818) 983-1105

Library of Congress catalog card number: 61-18529

Wilshire Book Company edition
is published by special arrangement
with Grune & Stratton, Inc., N.Y.

Printed by

HAL LEIGHTON PRINTING COMPANY
P.O. Box 3952
North Hollywood, California 91605
Telephone: (213) 983-1105

Printed in the United States of America (B)

ISBN 0-87980-139-5

CONTENTS

ILLUSTRATIONS

IN APPRECIATION

The author wishes to express his sincerest gratitude to:

Dr. Duncan A. Holbert, for his friendly receptivity, his patience, and his generosity in sharing his wisdom.

Dr. Lewis R. Wolberg, whose excellent works for years have been an inspiration, for his guidance and constructive criticism during the preparation of this book.

Dr. Henry M. Stratton, for his encouragement and many wise and helpful considerations.

Dr. Marvin T. Roberts, for his sage advice and for his cooperation in many phases of this work.

Dr. Joseph Wolpe, whose book *Psychotherapy by Reciprocal Inhibition* contributed considerably to the formulation of many concepts presented in this book.

Dr. James E. Yates, for many informative discussions and helpful suggestions over a period of many years.

To my wife

PAULINE

ACKNOWLEDGMENTS:

Figure 2.: Reprinted with permission from Boring, E. G., Langfeld, H. S., and Weld, H. P., *Foundations of Psychology*, John Wiley & Sons, Inc., 1948.

Cover design: Miller McDaniel

Line drawings: James Forsberg

FOREWORD

SINCE THOSE DISTANT TIMES when humanoid evolved into human, Man has distinguished himself from all other forms by his insistent determination to adapt his environment to his own ends. From those ancient times until today, Man has been consistently fearful and timid. Because of these characteristics, his principal preoccupation has been in the accumulation and control of physical power greater than his own. The digging stick gave way to the flint adze and this in turn to the bronze spear point and then the wheel. The Phoenicians captured the wind for their blue-hulled ships and roamed the seas to the Arctic and below the Equator.

The historical progress of Man has been recorded principally in terms of his growing control over the physical aspects of life and environment. In his efforts to accomplish these ends, the Sciences were born. The early Greeks and Egyptians organized their control of physical force in mathematics, physics and astronomy. Working in a natural world, it was inevitable that medicine as an important and separate study should take form. Throughout the history of medicine, we have witnessed the same preoccupation with the physical aspects of the patient. Trephination was skillfully performed before the physician could write. Man's earliest scribblings are full of erudite prescriptions, advice concerning the care of amputations and how to best cut for the stone!

The importance of the mind and how it works was scarcely referred to, and then only in terms of its pathological states. The early sufferers from mental disorders were treated by hanging in chains, by dropping into the snake-pit or by some other shocking physical approach. Certainly more has been learned about the structure and function of the human mind in the last 50 years than had been learned in all of the preceding time. There are still huge areas of ignorance in our understanding in this area. Our overflowing mental hospitals offer tragic testimony to our limited knowledge.

Even the individual who is healthy in mind and body is still much more preoccupied with the state of his physical self than with the state of his mind and emotions. He periodically goes in for setting-up exercises, worries about his golf score, buys vitamins and organic foods, inspects his tongue daily and is concerned a great deal more about the wrinkles in his face than those in his cerebrum. The capacity of the body in terms of its muscles is familiar and has long been used to efficient function and discipline; we take the mind for granted!

Mr. Sparks has described in this volume the general theory and techniques for use in learning or teaching the art of relaxation, concentration and discipline of the voluntary mind. In its simplicity this is what self-hypnosis achieves. The method described in the text involves the use of symbols to reach the state of hypnosis, and symbols are further used to reenforce suggestions which are given for therapeutic purpose. The symbols chosen are familiar to the patient so that each time the symbol is perceived the related suggestion is thereby strengthened by reenforcement, and the effect is further gained in the primary purpose.

This is all familiar ground; we respond to symbols of all sorts in every daily activity. In this technique for self-hypnosis the use of symbols is made more effective by applying the well-known psychological principles of conditioning and reenforcement. However, in the hypnotic state with complete relaxation and concentration on the part of the subject, conditioning and reenforcement are so much more effective that at times it seems almost miraculous. This volume is therefore a serviceable and workable guide for any serious individual who recognizes that many functions of the mind can be improved by an organization of technique and discipline. We are all familiar with individuals who can wake themselves up on time without benefit of Ingersoll, or who can study and "concentrate" while the radio is blaring and the kids are chattering. These are all unrecognized examples of what "self-hypnotic" techniques can achieve in an entirely unorganized and undisciplined situation. Self-hypnosis in essence, then, involves "setting-up exercises" for the mind.

I wish there were another word to use besides "hypnosis"; the term is loaded semantically, and for many of us it suggests a lot of theatrical foolishness that characterized its infant days.

I have been using the techniques described herein for the past four years with carefully selected patients from my practice of allergy and dermatology. Under Mr. Sparks' tutelage I developed my own approach, and the results have forced me to discard my initial skepticism about hypnosis as an "ethical" medical technique. One of our first patients was a 48 year old man who presented himself with acute dermatitis involving 80 per cent of his skin area. He had been referred by a specialist from southern California who had treated him for eight years without benefit. I treated him for two years by traditional methods, and the patient remained so severely involved that he was unable to work. He was taking steroids, antihistamines, tranquilizers and multiple topical applications. Under hypnosis, material was elicited which was used to help diminish his anxieties; with self-hypnosis he was able to control the itching and to reenforce his acceptance of new values and of a new role for himself. After six weeks his skin was entirely clear, and he has been working now for two and one-half years and has taken no medication whatsoever.

Using self-hypnosis an attractive school teacher overcame a disfiguring facial grimace. This tic-like mannerism had been present since she was twelve years old and had so affected her personality development that she was a shy and withdrawn individual. In a self-induced hypnotic state, she would repeatedly see herself in a mirror, talking, laughing, and all without the unhappy handicap. She would practice using words which, in the waking state, triggered this tic, and within four months every trace of the grimace had disappeared. There has been no relapse after more than two and one-half years.

These illustrative cases are not unusual but are typical of what can be accomplished by a well-motivated patient under the care of a physician who is willing to work with him. Frequently, more sophisticated techniques of hypnosis are utilized, but a patient who understands self-hypnosis and can use it is happier, more comfortable and secure because he has learned that aberrations in his emotions and attitudes can aggravate his illness, that anxiety is always detrimental; and he has also learned that he has a measure of control over these things by using self-hypnotic techniques intelligently and under competent guidance.

All those who are really familiar with hypnosis and self-hypnosis recognize these phenomena as natural and productive but valid only within their limitations in the broad field of medicine and psychology. Hypnosis is no cure-all. Although hypnosis works well for anesthesia and obstetrics in about 20 per cent of the cases, an additional 20 per cent obtain practically no benefit. In approximately 60 per cent, results may range from a slight increase in ability to relax, to a partial development of anesthesia.

Anxiety-ridden, unstable patients should definitely be under the care of a physician. No one should sanction experimentation in this field without knowledge, serious purpose and a sense of perspective. However, the intelligent use of self-hypnosis offers much to the individual in whom increased efficiency in concentration, relaxation, self-control and learning capacity is important.

The busy physician, worried about his ulcer or his atheromatous coronaries, would do well to learn this technique for his own use; ten minutes a day is equivalent to at least four hours of refreshing sleep and ten years of additional productive life.

–*Duncan A. Holbert, M.D.*
Santa Cruz, California

PREFACE

THERE ARE many benefits to be derived from the learning of self-hypnosis. Typical conditions responsive to the method are listed in the two groups below.

The reader who intends to utilize self-hypnosis for any therapeutic purpose is strongly advised to consult with a physician or psychiatrist to determine whether or not the habit patterns, symptoms and conditions for which he is seeking relief require more precise diagnosis and extensive treatment. In such an event self-hypnosis may still prove to be a valuable adjunct when used as directed.

Group One consists of relatively minor problems for which relief is often readily available through self-hypnosis.

Group Two includes manifestations of more severe conditions, the total management of which should be under the direction of a physician. The techniques to be described may then be facilitative to other recommended procedures.

GROUP ONE

Improvement of intellectual potentials, including: (1) concentration, (2) retention, (3) recall, (4) creative imagination, (5) constructive thinking and (6) verbal, graphic and artistic expression.

Bolstering of personality resources, such as: (1) self-confidence, (2) assertiveness, (3) motivation and (4) goal determination and achievement.

Correction of disturbed habit patterns, including: (1) excessive smoking, drinking and eating, (2) procrastination, (3) incapacity to rest and relax, (4) insomnia and (5) mild compulsions and obsessions.

Alleviation of mild anxieties related to: (1) feelings of inferiority, (2) shyness and stage-fright and (3) environmental pressures from difficult vocational, marital or other life-situations.

GROUP TWO

Alleviation or elimination of pain for: (1) dental procedures, (2) surgical, obstetric and orthopedic procedures and (3) relief in cases of intractable symptoms.

Control of miscellaneous conditions, such as: (1) anxiety, tension and fatigue, (2) obesity, (3) excessive drinking, (4) obsessive and compulsive reactions, (5) enuresis, (6) nail-biting, (7) phobic reactions, (8) psychosomatic symptoms and (9) abnormal behavior patterns.

These groups of problems are extremely abbreviated. The intent in listing them is to give the reader some idea of the types of conditions that may be reasonably expected to be influenced. Too much emphasis cannot be placed, as mentioned above, on the advisability of obtaining professional assistance before proceeding to utilize these techniques for reasons even remotely connected with conditions listed in group two.

It is entirely possible for symptoms to be alleviated or eliminated even though the underlying causes continue to exist. This could lead to serious consequences, such as concealment of a remediable condition that could develop into one of a more serious nature due to the delay in obtaining proper medical attention.

Contrary to the opinions expressed by a few professional people, the author is firmly convinced that it would be difficult to find a safer modality than hypnotism. The current material being published on the so-called "dangers" of hypnotism and the warnings regarding its use are not at all substantiated by the facts.

Since the early part of the seventeenth century such men as Braid, Esdaile, Mesmer, Elliotson, Bernheim, Bramwell and, more recently, LeCron, Erikson, Wolberg, Weitzenhoffer and many, many others have reported literally thousands of cases in which hypnosis and self-hypnosis were used with not one single incident of harmful result being observed.

It would seem, therefore, that any untoward effects have occurred rarely and that these negative results were due not to hypnosis but to the lack of understanding on the part of the practitioner of how to utilize himself and his techniques constructively in the therapeutic situation.

A person entering the hypnotic state tends to behave according to what he has been led to believe is appropriate behavior for a hypnotized subject. Proper guidance and "mind-set" before and during the trance obviate the spontaneous and bizarre behavior reported by those hypnotists who do not take the trouble to instruct and inform their subjects intelligently.

The facts strongly indicate that no harm can befall the hypnotized person *even if it is suggested* that harm occur. This is because the individual has built-in safety mechanisms that serve to protect him against ill-advised suggestions, inferred or direct, and against misuses of the hypnotic methods.

Some of the preceding remarks regarding the advice to proceed cautiously, yet minimizing any possible dangers, may seem contradictory. The simple explanation is that, in dealing with a modality so intimately associated with human emotions and conditions, it is best to consider every eventuality and exercise every reasonable precaution.

Although it is possible for a person to develop self-hypnosis without assistance, it is much easier to do so with the help of another individual. This person, most ideally, should be skilled in hypnotic techniques and qualified in the area to which the techniques are to be applied.

It is essential that a period of time be devoted each day to practice until certain responses are adequately established as described in the text. This may be from 15 minutes to one-half hour daily for 8 to 16 weeks or more, depending upon factors of individual problems, motivation and ability.

Most every person who can read, understand and follow the text can expect some positive result, such as improved ability to relax at will. Approximately 20 to 30 per cent can reasonably expect to achieve exceptionally good results. The others can expect benefits of varying degree. Some people react very quickly and easily. Others require considerable time and effort.

Unfortunately there is no known way to predict results for a particular individual. Only by trial can results be evaluated. The ability to relax, however, is well worth the effort to most people. Anything further should be gratefully accepted as a bonus.

If and when you decide to proceed, you should arrange appointments with the professional person who is to help you for at least one hour once or twice each week, plus practice time for you alone of 15 to 30 minutes each day or evening. In the event you are able to proceed alone the daily practice periods will suffice.

During the time you are receiving assistance it would be helpful for the other person also to have a copy of this book.

Over the years these techniques have been utilized with a very high incidence of success in the induction of hypnosis and in the development of self-hypnosis by professional people themselves. Doctors, including those specializing in psychiatry, and people in other allied professions are notably poor hypnotic subjects. This concept of developing hypnotic abilities through a series of conditioned responses apparently overcomes many of their resistances and appeals to them not only as an effective and convenient method to utilize in the treatment of their patients but also as a means of increasing their own abilities.

It is the sincere hope of the author that this book will help the professional worker and the lay public to better understand hypnosis and the possible benefits to be derived from its judicious use. Although it is certainly not the panacea that many people seem to be attempting to substantiate, hypnosis should no longer be thought of as mystical, supernatural or occult and surely not as anything to be feared, especially in the hands of those with ethical experience in its use. It can be of considerable value in many ways. Let us not over-emphasize these values nor magnify, out of all reasonable proportion, our conclusions as to results—beneficial or otherwise.

—L. S.

Figure 1. Color for experiment in retinal fatigue.

CHAPTER 1

SOME PRINCIPLES OF CONDITIONING

EARLY in this century the Russian physiologist, Ivan Pavlov, became famous because of his experiments on the digestive functions of dogs. One of his incidental findings, the significance of which became more apparent later, had to do with the observation that dogs could be trained, or conditioned, to salivate (drool) at the sound of a bell.

The importance of this finding, relative to human behavior, is that it has since been shown that human beings too can be conditioned to respond to a stimulus in a different manner than would ordinarily be expected from the particular type of stimulus being applied.

To explain further, it would not be at all unusual to expect a dog to salivate when exposed to the sight or odor of food, especially if the animal were hungry and the food just beyond his reach. For the dog to salivate, however, when there is no food in evidence, but only the sound of a bell ringing, is rather unexpected—unless, of course, the observer is familiar with the processes of conditioning responses.

This and many other types of behavior can be brought about by repeatedly exposing an animal (including a human one) to a stimulus that will evoke the desired response while, at about the same time, the animal is also exposed to the new stimulus that is desired to also bring about the response. This new stimulus would be comparable to the sound of the bell mentioned previously. It would not ordinarily evoke the response that is being conditioned.

It is important that anyone interested in developing self-hypnosis by these techniques be thoroughly familiar with these principles. Such knowledge is essential not only to developing the technique but to utilizing intelligently the information in subsequent chapters regarding the application of the technique to various problems and conditions.

In view of this, several additional examples of conditioning responses in animals will be described and the relative importance of the application of these principles to human behavior explained.

Let us first consider the effects of different types of conditioning on an ordinary domestic cat—a cat that is friendly, healthy and reasonably content with life in general.

Suppose our cat is placed into a large cage where he has ample room to move about and is fed each day from a box placed in a particular corner of the cage. If the feeding occurs at approximately the same time each day, it will soon be observed that the cat is appearing to show increased interest in that particular corner at about that time each day. He will tend to drift toward that corner and hang about with an air of expectancy. His manner in approaching the feed box may be leisurely if the food is adequate, or it may be hurried if the amount is skimpy.

Now, if the food supply is purposely kept below a satisfactory level, and if a bell is sounded just prior to feeding time each day, the cat will invariably be in the feeding corner promptly at feeding time. The process of conditioning is beginning to operate. The cat will soon respond to the sound of the bell at any time of day or night, whether food is presented or not. The response of getting to the corner at the sound of the bell can be more firmly conditioned with the application of a noxious stimulant. Suppose we place a metal grid upon the floor of the cage through which a mild electric current can be administered to the feet of the animal. If, shortly after the bell is sounded each day, the electric shock is applied until the cat goes to the feeding corner, his response will soon take on the appearance of great urgency. After a very slight amount of this type of conditioning the cat will be motivated literally to flee to the corner each time the bell sounds . . . even when no shock follows the sound of the bell. At this point the cat is responding to the sound of the bell only, with responses more appropriate to being shocked. These may seem like rather extreme measures to use on a poor, dumb animal that was formerly so friendly, but this type of experimentation has led to significant increases in knowledge regarding human behavior and so, perhaps, may be pardonable. When you consider the amount of time, money and energy being spent by the nations of the world on attempts to reach outer space and contact other beings when we have not as yet learned how to get along with ourselves, such investigations seem not only warranted, but essential.

Conditioning of this type can be carried to much more extreme consequences for the poor cat. He can be made neurotic or even, in all observable ways, psychotic.

Suppose the cat, after being thoroughly conditioned to respond to the bell by going rapidly to the feeding corner, is equally well conditioned to respond to the sound of a buzzer by going with equal urgency to the opposite corner. What happens when the bell and buzzer are sounded simultaneously? The cat is now in a sorry plight! He has reached a point of difficult discrimination. He is torn between two urgent responses. If the conditioning is continued and the electric shock applied to all areas of the cage during the sounding of both bell and buzzer, giving the cat no way to avoid the objectionable stimulus, he will very quickly become nervous and, soon thereafter, neurotic.

By increasing the intensity and frequency of the conditioning stimuli, one can cause the cat to express the behavior of a raging beast. He loses interest in food and, upon simultaneous sounding of the bell and buzzer, he snarls and quivers and ceases to perform any act usually expected from a normal cat.

This adverse condition can be made, to all intents and purposes, permanent. What was formerly a mild, friendly animal is now a psychotic bundle of nerves and flesh. He will lose weight from refusing to eat. He will quiver and arch his back at the least provocation and make little or no rational response to any attemp to touch or feed him.

Unless steps are taken to desensitize, or de-condition, this animal, the chances are great that he will never recover. He will continue to react in the abnormal manner described to any stimuli associated even remotely with the environment in which the conditioning took place. If, however, he is placed in a different environment, as much unlike the conditioning cage as possible, there is good possibility for recovery. If he can be brought to the point of eating again, and the stimuli of the shock, bell, and buzzer are carefully avoided, the cat may evidence an increasing interest in food and eventually calm down.

After normal eating habits are resumed the cat can gradually be made hungry again so the appeal of food becomes strong and will dominate other responses. At this point the sound of the bell occurring faintly during eating time will evoke only slight anxiety which will diminish rapidly. By gradually increasing the volume of the sound at each feeding, the anxiety responses to the bell can be completely extinguished. The same procedure with the buzzer will eliminate anxiety connected with that and, by gradually exposing the cat to environmental stimuli increasingly similar to the original cage, he may be brought back to his normal, friendly self once again.

Now that we have seen how the process of conditioning can be applied to bring about both negative and positive responses in animals, we can proceed to a consideration of what similar processes may have to do with human behavior.

Let us suppose that, for experimental reasons, we wish to condition a person to blink his left eye each time he hears the word "red". In humans, as differentiated from other animals, it has been found that an idea or mental symbol is, at least to some degree, as effective as a sensory stimulus. In other words, an idea tends to generate actuality of what the idea represents. What we wish to determine is whether or not such an idea, or symbol, can bring about a predictable response.

We would first seek some way to cause our subject to blink upon application of a controlled stimulus that would not harm him in any way. This might be a puff of air directed at his open eye through a tube, such as an ordinary drinking straw. This stream of air would be considered the unconditioned stimulus (U S) as it is predictable that it will evoke the desired response. After determining the amount or intensity of air needed to force the subject to blink every time, we could then speak the word "red" (the conditioning stimulus, or C S) and follow it closely with the puff of air. It has been found that conditioning is more efficient when the conditioning stimulus precedes the unconditioned stimulus by a short interval. After several trials it will be found that mention of the word "red" will cause the person to blink even though the puff of air does not follow. Sometimes only eight or ten trials will be sufficient. If not, another ten or so will almost certainly do it.

Conditioning in this manner will not be permanent. It would be necessary periodically to reenforce this conditioning or to find some way to "generalize" it to something to which the subject is frequently exposed. So far we have conditioned the response to a sensory stimulus, the sound of the word "red". We can complete what we started out to do by asking the subject to think of the word "red" on each trial, just preceding the application of the puff of air to his eye. He will soon respond correctly just to the thought itself. Instead of the word "red," we might use the thought of an item of food, or an action such as picking up a spoon. The more intense and the more frequent the application of the unconditioned stimulus, the more firmly established will be the response to the conditioned stimulus.

Conditioning to stimuli in addition to the original ones used is called generalization. This may sometimes occur unexpectedly. If one of these stimuli is something the person does, thinks of or is exposed to periodically, the response can be automatically reenforced and made relatively permanent.

On the other hand, if the conditioning stimulus is frequently applied without the unconditioned stimulus, the response may diminish and eventually disappear.

In this manner a person can be conditioned (or condition himself) to respond to a mental image, or symbol, with thoughts, feelings or actions that are desirable. Also, desirable responses so conditioned can be made to dominate or replace undesirable responses that have been previously evoked by the same, or similar, stimuli.

In everday life people are exposed to conditioning stimuli. Starting at birth, and from then on, those stimuli that occur in close proximity to the inevitable unconditioned stimuli are constantly conditioning, generalizing and extinguishing their responses, both negative and positive ones. In any given individual many responses are only lightly conditioned and quickly become extinct. Many others, of course, are intensely conditioned and, unless there is equally intense exposure to negating stimuli, may remain always as part of the personality structure.

Between these two extremes lie an infinite number of responses and response patterns undergoing infinite degrees of change and reenforcement. Fortunately, most of these are positive, or desirable. That is, they are major factors in survival, learning and enjoyment.

The negative ones are major factors underlying emotional trauma such as unadaptive anxiety, tension and fatigue.

Many investigators believe conditioning to be involved in every human sensation or expression. This may well be true.

Let us now take a hypothetical human being and see how the principles of conditioned responses may apply to a variety of situations and behavior patterns over a period of time.

Our subject could be a little girl, three or four years old, living with her parents in a typical American town. In her learning to read and talk let us consider what often takes place. Perhaps the little girl has a picture book of animals with their names spelled out in large letters. She is repeatedly shown the picture of, for instance, a cow, and the word "cow" is spoken simultaneously. Each time an appropriate occasion arises, an actual cow is pointed out to her and, again, the word is repeated several times. After sufficient exposures of this nature she responds to the sound of the word with a mental image of the printed word, the picture of the cow, or of the actual animal. She becomes conditioned, in a generalized way, to respond to any of these stimuli with mental images of each or all of the others. This becomes a continuous process of reenforcement, and the little girl finally "learns", through conditioning of responses, the relationship of words (symbols), both printed and spoken, to pictures and objects.

Learning, then, is a process of conditioning responses.

Many psychologists believe there are three methods by which we learn: rote, or memory learning; trial-and-error learning; conditioned-response learning.

It is beyond the scope of this book to discuss in detail each of these methods. It is worthwhile, however, to point out that stimuli and responses are involved in each of these methods and that rote and trial-and-error learning are quite probably explainable as conditioned-response learning too. It may be, as the writer and many other investigators believe, that all learning results from conditioning of responses. It seems very likely that learning may be said to have occurred when a stimulus-response sequence becomes interchangeable.

When the little girl has learned the word "cow" each of the symbols connected with the concept of "cow" have become interchangeable as stimulus and/or response. The sight of a live cow acts as a stimulus to evoke a response of imagery of the printed word. Here a sensory image is the stimulus and mental imagery the response. It is evident that a sensory image of the printed word (or a mental image for that matter) will now evoke imagery of the cow. We now have a characteristic of "interchangeability" of stimulus and response.

In learning the complete concept of "cow" this characteristic must be extended to include the sound of the word, the picture of a cow and expression, by the child, through pointing, speaking, writing and drawing. Before such learning takes place the stimulus value of the printed word is practically nil. It is in the same category as a nonsense syllable and only takes on meaning to the child as it is conditioned, first as a stimulus, then as a response and finally as an interchangeable stimulus-response.

Generalization begins when symbols that are not contained within the original concept are associated with it. For instance, when the word "milk" is associated with any of the symbols in the cow concept it will not only serve to reenforce each of those symbols but will become established in another constellation of symbols such as those associated with "bottle", "white", "food", etc.

Here, then, is a reasonable basis for considering conditioning as the underlying process of learning and also of retention.

The reader will better appreciate the function of stimulus-response interchangeability by going through the following exercise himself: Analyze what goes on in your mind and in the muscles of your lips and vocal chords as you read the following description: A...white...furry ...animal...with...pink...eyes...and...long...ears.

Did you form an image in your mind of a specific animal? And did you say the name of this animal to yourself? Now see what happens upon reading the name of this animal...RABBIT. Perhaps you said the name to yourself and noticed that your lips moved slightly while doing so. If you repeat the word, you will also notice a difference in tonicity of your vocal chords. Most people can recognize this easily.

Do the same thing with several words such as "tree", "car", "house", etc. Try it with words other than those denoting objects and things: "sad", "gay", "laughing", "baseball", "fast", etc.

Talk with someone who knows some foreign language with which you are not familiar and ask them to choose some word in that language and write it down for you without telling you, at first, the meaning or the sound of it. Notice how little associative value the word has as you look at it. Then ask to hear the sound and consider your reaction to repeating the sound as you continue looking at the written word. Finally, ask the meaning of the word and observe your reactions then. As you go through these steps it will be clearer to you how learning takes place and you can see for yourself how conditioning plays the major role. You might see how long it takes and what processes you go through in order to learn the word sufficiently to write, speak and define it a week or so after you have had no assistance.

The writer, in searching through various texts, has never found mention of imagery as being associated with the Pavlovian-type experiments on dogs. It does seem rather conclusive, in light of the above observations, that the sound of the bell is not the direct stimulus for evoking excessive salivation but is, instead, the stimulus for evoking imagery of food. Such imagery is then the stimulus that evokes the salivation.

It should be understood that mental imagery is not limited to visual perceptions. Although these are undoubtedly the most common, imagery of sound, odor, taste and tactile sensations such as touch, pain, pressure, tickling, etc., is also evocable.

In dogs the imagery evoked is quite possibly that of odor, as dogs do not discriminate as to color. A dog can recognize the difference in certain colors, but this is due to variations in brightness rather than hue. It is also highly unlikely that dogs can conceptualize to any great degree. This becomes apparent when even well-trained dogs are shown to have little or no appreciation of the reason for their responses to certain stimuli. The writer once had a dog, "Duke", who would immediately flop over and "play dead" upon the command (usually given in the form of a question) "What would you rather be, Duke, a salesman or a dead dog?" Duke had been conditioned to perform this amusing response to the stimulus "dead dog" by rewarding him with tasty bits of food each time he responded correctly. It mattered not at all to him what the words were immediately preceding this stimulus. To the great consternation of salesmen, doctors, artists, etc., and to the amusement of observers, Duke would appear to have a preference for "death" rather than be classified in any of the aforementioned professions. It was, however, actually up to the sadistic whim of the writer, rather than through any discriminatory power or ability of Duke's, as to what was to be inferred from his behavior. He would flop over with equal facility to "If you couldn't be a salesman, would you rather be a live or dead dog?"

Duke's training had been accomplished through a considerable amount of conditioning and several pounds of dog food. When Duke put on his little act, and while he was lying on the floor, imagery, probably of an olfactory nature—the imagined odor of a forthcoming tidbit, kept him pinned down rather than the "shame" of being or not being a salesman.

These same principles are involved in the development of behavior patterns in our hypothetical little girl. She, however, due to her infinitely more complex neural system, is able to retain and associate more ideas. She can conceptualize to a far greater degree than the dog or any other animal. When she is punished for certain types of behavior, or when she is rewarded for other types of behavior, she learns to respond with appropriate approach or avoidance patterns.

It should again be mentioned that the intensity and frequency of the conditioning stimuli are directly proportional to the intensity of response. When the reward is great, or the punishment severe, the response is more thoroughly conditioned.

It is beyond the scope of this book to detail the principles of child care. It should be made clear, though, that when a child is spanked for being "bad" the pain of the spanking soon becomes associated, in the mind of the child, with the performance preceding the spanking. The child soon learns that to perform the act invariably leads to a painful result and will be less inclined to perform the act thereafter.

Of course if the child performs the act occasionally *without* being punished, this will have the opposite effect in proportion to the degree of satisfaction the child derives from the performance itself.

There is a very notable exception to this, but it does not in any way obviate the principles involved. This is the situation in which the child continues to perform the objectionable act in spite of being punished every time. When this happens it simply means there is a stronger stimulus at work. This may be the desire for attention. When the child is not getting the attention it feels it needs, the punishment may actually be a "reward". If the only way a child can find to get attention is by doing something he was told not to do, the reward of attention may far exceed the effect of punishment, and the objectionable performance will be repeated.

In order to condition a child to "good" responses it must be rewarded adequately for good deeds as well as punished for "bad" ones. When factors of attention and affection are involved, what may seem like reward and punishment to the adult may be considered just the opposite in the mind of the child.

To continue with the possible effects of conditioning responses on our hypothetical subject, we might consider how the child learns to avoid painful or dangerous situations.

Perhaps, somewhere in the child's environment, there is a large, black stove. It should be clear that the size of the stove, or any object, may seem different to the child than to an adult simply because the child is smaller than the adult and observes everything from a different angle. What may seem average or normal to the adult often appears tremendous to the child. Also, things we do not know about or do not understand can be magnified in their importance. Fear of the "unknown" is an experience common to most of us, adult or child, but in most circumstances there are more objects unknown to the child than to the adult.

Now, the child may often be told that the stove is "hot", that it will "hurt" if one touches it. Not yet having experienced the sensation of "hot" the child has not learned that to touch hot things may be painful. The tendency of the child is to explore and discover things for himself. This may lead him to wish to touch the stove in spite of any warnings, especially if he feels he will attract attention in so doing. Once he touches the stove it may happen to be cold, in which case he undoubtedly has an unpleasant surprise in store for him. In the event of the stove being hot, the painful stimulus may be so severe that he is conditioned, once and for all, to avoid touching it again. He may also have learned to respond with avoidance upon being warned about other hot objects. On the other hand, he may try touching several times before the avoidance response becomes conditioned. If someone has observed this process and mentioned the word "hot" each time, the child will soon have learned to avoid other hot objects when warned that he should do so.

Let us see how this can lead to situations which affect the child in later life.

Suppose the child accidentally falls against the stove and is severely burned. This may so strongly condition the child that he cannot be made to go near the stove again. The stimulus of the big, black stove may become generalized to the extent that the child also avoids anything big and black. Conditioning may also occur from other stimuli present at the time: the color of the walls, the sound of the teakettle, the odor of food, even the people in the room. In later life the child may have grown into an adult who feels anxious upon seeing a big, black automobile. This may be true even though the incident of the burn has long since been forgotten and fear of stoves extinguished. Avoidance and anxiety-responses may have been generalized and reenforced so that now the only one left, connected with the original incident, is a dislike for a particular color. This reaction, however, may be a mystery to the person, and anyone else involved in the original incident, as to what caused it.

The original avoidance response may be diminished over a period of time as the child learns he can go near a hot stove without touching it and without pain. When the avoidance response was at a high level, though, the effect of the stimulus-object may have been generalized to other things of a similar size, shape, color or sound. The avoidance reaction then could have been continuously reenforced over the years so that in adult life the person becomes nervous, anxious, or depressed upon seeing any big, black object and yet has no fear at all of the stove that originally conditioned the response.

An adult may dislike, or may express a more violent reaction to, certain colors, sounds, persons or situations without being able to understand or explain why. This would undoubtedly be due to his having once been conditioned by events impossible to recall.

We can look into some possible reasons why a grown person may have a fear of confinement, as when riding in elevators, and yet have no recollection of ever having been frightened by such a situation. One possibility, which is not intended to apply to any specific case but only to serve as an illustration, could start with the father of a small child playing a game with him on the kitchen floor. Perhaps the family had just received something delivered in a large paper carton and the father had placed the carton over the child and was lifting it up periodically, peeking at the child and then dropping it over him again. A game of peek-a-boo. Lots of fun and a pleasant pastime for both. But suppose the doorbell rings and the parent forgets, momentarily, about the child while he rushes to the door. He probably feels that the child will be safe for a few minutes, or he may not even consider this at all. Meanwhile the child is waiting for the carton to be lifted again, and when it isn't he soon gets tired of waiting. He may attempt to lift the carton himself, but he can find no place to grasp it. In his struggle his feet may touch one end of the carton, his hands and arms the other. He may feel confined...trapped. No animal or human can bear this feeling. The harder he tries to escape, the more helpless he feels. He becomes frightened, perhaps to the point of hysteria. The father, when he finally returns, may realize part of what has happened, but he may not think of the intense impression it has made upon the child. If the baby does not stop crying immediately, he may spank him in an effort to break the hysteria. This, of course, only reenforces the event as more traumatic in the mind of the child.

In the years following, other events may occur further to condition these feelings while the original event is slowly forgotten. At some future date the child may be riding in an elevator that suddenly gets stuck between floors. Perhaps the lights go out too! His reaction may be a mild expression or feeling of nervousness or it could range through increasingly violent responses to one of near-panic proportions. He quite likely would be unable to explain his emotions or behavior, even to himself. He may wonder whether or not he is a coward. He may, on the other hand, pass it off lightly. Yet again, he may continue to fret about it. The point is, an adult may often behave in a manner that results from previous conditioning even though there may be no awareness left of the original conditioning episode. This is true of positive as well as negative responses, adaptive as well as unadaptive; constructive or destructive behavior patterns, all in various ways conditioned by previous events and experiences; responses conditioned to the never-ceasing stimuli, internal as well as external, to which we are all exposed.

Many human ailments—fears, anxieties, guilt and pain—are conditioned in the same way. So, too, are our pleasures born. Tears are not the only fruit of this strange harvest. The seeds of laughter, friendship, pride and compassion are also sown and nurtured by processes involving conditioning.

What interests us more, perhaps, is that such responses not only are conditioned, but they can also be deconditioned, altered or strengthened. Responses of a negative nature can be replaced with responses of a positive nature. The entire personality structure can be rebuilt.

Some desirable alterations may be easy to accomplish, some difficult, some apparently impossible. We never know until we try.

CHAPTER 2

DEVELOPING MIND-SET

U NFORTUNATELY, the history of hypnotism is such that simple mention of the word evokes images of magicians, crystal balls and turbans. It is true that hypnotism in one form or another has been practiced for thousands of years and incorporated into the rituals and rites of all sorts of mystical cults, societies and religions. Even today the basic principles are found to be among the underlying factors in most of our religious concepts, but so are many other psychological truisms that we are inclined to accept as fact with no thought of their being mystical or supernatural at all.

During the period from 1830 to the early 1900's an increasing number of medical doctors were using hypnosis in ever-widening areas of medical treatment. Thousands of cases were recorded in which hypnosis was used successfully in the performance of painless operations ranging from lancing of boils to amputations of limbs and the removal of huge scrotum tumors which ordinarily are considered extremely painful.

Through the efforts of men such as Braid, Esdaile, Charcot, Bernheim and Bramwell, hypnotism began a gradual transition from the realm of mystical phenomena toward acceptance in scientifically-oriented areas of research.

With the advent of chemical anesthetics such as ether, hypnotism suffered a temporary setback. The new procedures could be used on everyone, were less time-consuming and required little knowledge of a psychological nature. Interest and experimentation in hypnotism declined until during the first World War when it was revived as a means of helping to combat "war neuroses". Unfortunately there was also revived an interest in the phenomena as a fascinating form of entertainment. And once again the medical professions ignored or were skeptical of their practical applications.

Finally, in 1959 at a formal meeting of the American Medical Association, hypnotism achieved the "official status" of an "adjunctive tool" in medicine, status recognized by the British Medical Society some years previously. So now there is general acceptance in scientific circles, and intensive research is once more being conducted. Hypnosis is now being practiced in more areas of human behavior than ever before. Today there are literally thousands of medical, dental and psychological procedures taking place in which hypnotism is an important factor. In view of these developments any tendencies toward skepticism or mysticism are quite unfounded and unrealistic.

Research in the field of conditioning-responses is of much more recent vintage. And the concept of utilizing hypnotic techniques to aid in the conditioning of desirable responses, and to facilitate desensitization of undesirable ones, is newer still. Whether hypnosis is being utilized to further conditioning procedures, or conditioning is helping to achieve the hypnotic effects, is only a question of semantics. The two concepts may turn out to be highly correlated or even identical. For the practical purposes to which these principles may apply, let us not, for the sake of clarity and expedience, become too embroiled in such differences or similarities (as the case may be).

It should occasion no surprise to learn that our responses are ofter. inclined to be negative in character. In many of us they may far exceed in number and intensity any pleasurable ones we can experience. If one takes the trouble to inquire of each person he meets during any given day, he will be fortunate indeed to find more than one or two who will not admit to some ailment or problem. Real or fanciful, mild or severe, the evidences of negative responses are multitudinous.

Strangely enough, however, all responses classified under "negative" are not necessarily undesirable. Many are extremely important to our continued well-being and essential to our continued existence. Anxiety, for example, may at first glance seem to be a response we could well do without. This is not true. Many anxieties are "adaptive". By this we mean that they serve a constructive purpose. The anxiety evoked by our perceptions of potentially dangerous situations leads us to protective or preventive actions. Anxiety associated with falling from an airplane undoubtedly led to invention of the parachute. Anxiety at the sight of a hungry lion would cause one to seek a safe place. Anxiety regarding a painful or strange sensation leads us to the consulting room of a physician. These are adaptive anxieties. They serve a useful purpose.

If, on the other hand, we become anxious at the sight of a friendly kitten or a particular color or anything that obviously can do us no harm, the anxiety serves no constructive purpose. It may result in unnecessary expenditure of physical or emotional energy. It is unadaptive. It may result in tension and fatigue. We should eliminate this type of anxiety if we can.

Anxieties also exist that seem to have no basis or that, in many people, seem to be caused by almost any stimulus. This is called pervasive or "free-floating" anxiety. This undifferentiated type often is felt in varying degree along with the "specific" type mentioned above. The individual may continuously feel a certain amount of anxiety that he cannot associate with any particular object or situation and also experience an additional amount under specific circumstances.

We will consider additional factors connected with anxiety later in the book. There are other negative responses having both adaptive and unadaptive qualities that are more pertinent to this present discussion.

As we go through life we are constantly faced with questions that affect us in various ways. Some intrigue us, some do not. Many people spend their entire lives seeking answers to questions that capture their interest. Many have found their answers while others have died in frustration, sometimes motivated by the identical question.

During childhood most of the questions with which we are confronted have to do with how and why things work in the way they do. Material objects incite more curiosity than do moral issues. As we mature we tend to examine our relationships with others, to seek answers to profound questions involving politics, theology, philosophy, infinity, eternity and a myriad of other ideas and concepts. Our attitudes and prejudices begin to form. We develop our beliefs and skepticisms and our neutral or willing-to-be-shown personality traits. The number and strength of these attitudes and traits not only are constantly changing in any given individual but are probably as diverse in pattern as fingerprints or other characteristics.

Although it is usually difficult to get most of us to admit it, many of our traits, beliefs and attitudes are based on erroneous assumptions. We often feel that if we see something, or experience it ourselves, we can accept it as so. Yet even when our conclusions are based upon our own experience, we are quite apt, unless we have knowledge of scientific methods, to be mistaken.

It is quite easy to show how unrealistic we are being when we attempt to rely upon our own perceptions. I would like to cite several examples illustrating this because belief and skepticism are such important factors in the success or failure of development of self-hypnosis. An understanding of the facts or fallacies we derive from our perceptions will help to alter existing belief or skepticism regarding the ideas and comments that follow.

RETINAL FATIGUE

If the reader will refer to figure 1 at the beginning of this book, he can demonstrate to himself how perceptions can change with no awareness on the part of the perceiver that such changes are taking place. Using a white card or small piece of paper, cover up about half of the colored rectangle and then stare fixedly at the line formed by the contrasting areas until your eyes feel slightly fatigued. A few seconds will usually suffice. Keeping your eyes focused on the same area, slide the white piece to one side, exposing the rest of the colored area. You will observe what appears to be an intensification of the color in the newly exposed area. Many people remark, upon doing this, "The color is much more intense!"

It is difficult for most of us to refrain from expressing this same deduction. But the truth of the matter is that the color has not changed at all. What has changed is the perception of the observer. This is only a temporary change, as will be evident upon looking at the color again. The whole area will now appear the same, indicating that another change in perception has occurred, returning it to its original state.

The explanation is rather simple. The sensation we call sight is the result of decomposition of chemical elements in the rods and cones, or recepter cells, of the retinal surface of the eye. This causes neural impulses to travel from the retina to the optical areas of the brain where the sensation of sight is perceived. During the perception of the color this process is going on, and the chemicals gradually get "used up". Without our realizing it, the area of our retina being affected is sending weaker and weaker impulses to our brain. The sensation of color perception is diminishing, but so gradually that we do not notice it until we expose a different area of the retina, in which the chemical elements are not used up, by removing the neutral piece of paper. We are then seeing the color in original intensity in one part of the eye, while the first area exposed has undergone a change. (Actually, because of the "all or none" principle of neurone firing, the change is due to frequency rather than intensity of neural impulses. For purposes of simplicity and clarity technical accuracy has been sacrificed.)

This process is called retinal fatigue. It is a well-confirmed principle accepted by all men of science. It substantiates the above comment that what we think we see is not always dependable as being truly representative of the facts. In this example we have evidence that our perception of color becomes altered, without our being aware of it, during the interval of observation. Only by shifting the gaze or blinking periodically will the chemical elements be replenished and color perception maintain some degree of constancy.

APPARENT MOTION

One of the most universal examples of perceiving motion when actually no motion exists is in the "motion" picture theatre. The smooth and realistic movements apparently taking place on the screen are really a series of slightly different "still" pictures being observed in rapid sequence. The projection machinery causes the film to move one "frame" or picture at a time. This picture is exposed to view for a fraction of a second; a shutter then covers it and the next one moves into its position. Although the film does move, very rapidly, it is not doing so while the observer is viewing it. The effect, genuine as it may seem, is not due to motion occurring before our eyes. So again, unless we are familiar with such things, our perception can be in error.

Many examples of this occur in our everyday life: the arrows that seem to be jumping back and forth on electrical signs; the alternately-flashing lights at railroad crossings; the apparent movement of the moon, on some nights, when it is really the clouds that are the moving objects.

There are literally thousands of situations, natural or contrived, that can create erroneous perceptions not only in our visual field but in all our sensory areas. The magician, the advertising and display men, all take advantage of these errors in our perceptions, and whether we like it or not, we must fact the fact that we are often wrong about many of the things in which we most deeply believe.

AMBIGUOUS STIMULUS PATTERNS

An example of a structured pattern designed to purposely effect perceptual changes is shown below in figure 2.

■ Your perceptual reaction to the patterns shown in figure 2 can be predicted.* If you will first stare for thirty seconds or so at pattern "A"

---

* Throughout this book the symbol "■" indicates matter directed to individual concentration and participation; general text matter directed to the "audience at large" is preceded by the symbol "□".

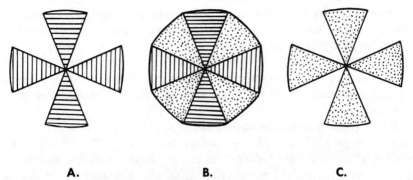

A.   **B.**   **C.**

Figure 2.   Ambiguous stimulus patterns.

and then look at pattern "B", you will see pattern "A" as if it were against a background of crossed lines. But as you continue to look, pattern "A" will become the background and the crossed-line pattern will become the figure. Once this change takes place, it will continue to reverse itself no matter how hard you try to keep it from doing so. If you will then stare at pattern "C" for thirty seconds or so you will find, upon looking at "B", that pattern "C" is first perceived as the figure, but again, the changes will take place automatically.

☐ Practically every book on general psychology contains examples and illustrations of ambiguous stimulus patterns and explains in more detail the various ways in which our perceptions can be manipulated.

The above examples will be sufficient, I am sure, to convince the reader that reactions can be affected and controlled to a predictable degree upon application of the proper methods for so doing. Belief can be changed to doubt. Doubt or skepticism can be replaced with belief. And belief can be increased to conviction.

Most of us have a certain amount of skepticism, especially about things with which we are not familiar. The "unknown" often evokes some degree of doubt or apprehension.

Feelings such as these can form the basis of resistance: resistance to accept changes of existing conditions; resistance to changing established beliefs; resistance to act in any manner contrary to the dictates of our perceptions, even after we may recognize our perceptions as faulty.

Here again we have negative responses playing a dual role. Some resistance responses are adaptive. They serve to protect us in situations ranging from those that might cause embarrassment, such as the resistance to appear before an audience shown by a person with stage fright, to those that might involve financial loss or physical harm. The last two are exemplified by resistance to purchase stock in an unknown company which, actually, may or may not be sound; and resistance to being the first to fly an untested airplane which, again, may or may not prove to be safe. The fact that some people do all of these things does not obviate the presence of resistance impulses. It simply means that the resistance has either been inhibited or that a more dominant response has been evoked.

Many people with severe cases of stage fright do speak or perform in front of large audiences. Many famous actors and actresses admit to being near a panic state before their cue to go on. They would not go on at all were it not for some equalizing, dominating factor. The appeal of applause, financial gain or the strong belief in the message to be conveyed are factors that could dominate the resistance responses of these people. Another very likely factor may be a conditioned inhibiting-response. That is, they may feel that once in front of their audience they will be all right. If the person believes this, it is apt to be so, but it has come to be for reasons far different than he would probably state. A fine actor dissociates himself, at least to some degree, once he goes into his act. There is little possibility that any physical harm or embarrassment will befall him. At each performance, as he asserts himself in his acting and finishes with feelings of pleasure and relief, he is conditioning himself to respond in a similar manner in the future. The anxiety experienced before the performance actually serves to exaggerate the relief responses later—by contrast alone.

When you start the actual development of self-hypnosis, a belief in the processes you use will be a major factor. Skepticism must be brought to at least a neutral level. We may not need all the techniques at our disposal. It may turn out that you are an excellent subject for this method. You may understand and utilize each bit of information and instruction easily and quickly. Then again, you may not.

We do not know until we work on it for a while. We have no way of determining it at this point. Whatever your opinion may be, it has as much chance of proving to be wrong as it has of proving to be correct.

There are a number of factors that are favorable to success, and, fortunately, we can take advantage of them. If you develop a high level of proficiency in self-hypnosis, this may be due to the operation of the factors I mention, or it may simply be that you would have been a good subject anyway, with few of these factors being responsible. In mentioning the negative possibility I was speaking of you as an exception. Considering you (if I may) as part of our present culture, the mathematical odds are very much in your favor. Success may not be quick nor easy, but the chances are that you can develop at least some significant degree of self-hypnotic ability.

The way we will inhibit any resistance to self-hypnosis (and you may have some of which you are unaware) will be to describe a series of experiments for you to perform. Each of these will be explained as we proceed, and each will become a little more complex than the preceding one. With each succeeding experiment your belief in yourself and in your ability to utilize this technique will grow. Your skepticism will diminish and, as you become more and more familiar with the phenomena you observe, which will be increasingly related to self-hypnosis, any apprehension of the unknown will disappear.

Conscious effort can help to some extent. For instance, by outlining a good schedule to follow and making up your mind to follow it, you can promote progress immeasurably.

You should plan to spend one or two hours on from one to two sessions per week. In between these sessions you must plan on at least a few minutes each day to practice what you have learned during the longer sessions. If someone is to assist you, it should be during the longer sessions, and plans should be made for an uninterrupted schedule of from eight to sixteen weeks. Rigid adherence to the schedule is mandatory. You can, if you wish, work alone on the experiments or tests, to be outlined in the rest of this chapter. Your assistant should read them too, but he will be of active help later on.

Read each experiment over and over again until you understand the principles involved and can remember the essentials without referring to the text. Once you have done this, you should perform the experiment a sufficient number of times to experience the effects intended before going on to the next one. Let each experiment build your confidence and belief in the technique and try to avoid any analysis or questions, since the latter will probably be covered later in the text. You should have no difficulty in performing each experiment, as each one has been thoroughly worked out over a period of years and with hundreds of people from all walks of life. If by any chance you do have difficulty in understanding or experiencing the intended effect, you should definitely consult with an expert before proceeding further.

THE PENCIL EXPERIMENT

The major principle involved here is sometimes called "mono-ideaism". This simply means "one idea". It will demonstrate to you that your voluntary actions can easily be inhibited by systematic thinking. When you are thinking of one idea without interruption, it is generally impossible to perform even a simple voluntary action, let alone a complex one. The value of this will be apparent when we get to our discussion on

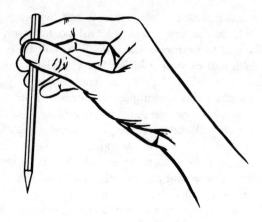

Figure 3.   Pencil experiment.

physical relaxation. When you can inhibit muscular activity with your thoughts, you can bring about relaxation with your thoughts.

■ Although this is called the pencil experiment, you can use any object of similar size and shape, such as a pen, spoon, or even a piece of paper. Select the object you intend to use and hold it between your thumb and first finger in a pendent fashion, as shown in figure 3. The voluntary action of dropping this object would be very easy to perform, would it not? You could simply open your fingers and it would fall of its own accord. Let us now see how equally easy it is to inhibit the neural system and block the impulses necessary for activating the fingers. Let us see if we can make it difficult or impossible for you to drop the object. This effect will, of course, last only while you are thinking as instructed. Meanwhile, make up your mind that for a few seconds you are going to do exactly as instructed.

Hold the object as described, with your hand in a position where you can easily look at the object and hold it steady for a minute or two. Stare at some point on the object and keep your eyes in this fixed position and try, as much as possible, to refrain from blinking. Now think to yourself, "I can drop it. I can drop it." Think these words repeatedly, exclusively, and *without interruption*. During the interval that you are thinking in this manner you can try to drop the object, but you will find you cannot! In fact, the harder you try to drop it, the tighter your fingers will grasp it. It is absolutely impossible for you to drop the object if you are thinking the phrase, as instructed, over and over without interruption. When you have done this several times, you will realize that thinking you can do something does not necessarily mean you can actually do it. Here you have been thinking very intently about a simple act of dropping an object but, while you are so thinking, you cannot do it.

In order for you to open your fingers a decision must be made as to *when* you want this to happen. To make such a decision requires neural activity to be instigated in your cerebral cortex. This cannot happen easily when you are thinking exclusively of one idea. Even the idea of the act that you wish to perform!

If by any chance you do drop the object, it simply means one of two things: Either you have misunderstood the instructions, or you are not cooperating. You must work on it further.

When you are satisfied that you have successfully completed the pencil experiment, go on as soon as possible with the next one.

THE SEMAPHORE EXPERIMENT

☐ This experiment involves what is known as "ideomotor" response. This means the innervation of appropriate musclegroups by an idea or mental image. Actually, there is more than one idea involved in this type of response. It might be better described as "concept-motor-activity". The major differences between this and the "mono-ideaism" response lie in the limitations placed upon the subject's thinking. In this experiment you will be given two concepts to think about, as there are two responses to be evoked. The principles involved are the same for both responses and could be explained singly. The fact that the responses are opposite serves to heighten the effect.

Instead of the muscles being inhibited, as in the previous experiment, they will be activated. This will occur because you will be able to think, pretty much in your own way, of actions taking place rather than being constrained to a single set of symbols that, in themselves, denote no activity.

■ You should be seated in a comfortable chair so that you can remain in one position for two or three minutes at a time. Your feet should be placed flat on the floor and you should be able to lean back against some firm support, such as a wall or the back of the chair. Make up your mind to do exactly as instructed for two or three minutes at least.

Read the following instructions thoroughly until you know exactly what you are to do without again referring to the text.

While in the position described, extend both arms out straight in front of you at shoulder height and with your palms facing each other. (See

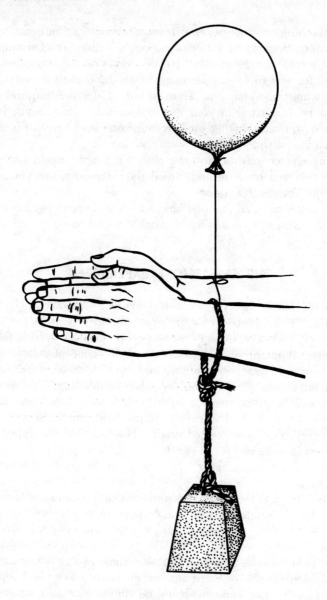

Figure 4. Semaphore experiment.

figure 4.) Close your eyes. Now, imagine as clearly as you can a balloon tied to your right wrist with a piece of strong string. Imagine that this is a big balloon filled with gas and that it is so light it is lifting your arm, higher and higher. Develop this image clearly. Think about the color (any color you choose) of this balloon, the size of it, the shape of it and the manner in which it is tied to your wrist. Think of your arm floating up, higher and higher. Let yourself enter into this scene completely. "See" your arm floating up higher with each breath.

Once you have this idea clearly in mind, think of a very heavy weight being attached to your left wrist with a strong rope. Imagine a piece of cast iron, such as a sash-weight, tied to your left wrist. Think of how heavy this weight is, the size and shape of it and the way it is tied to your wrist. Picture your left arm as being so heavy that you cannot hold it up. "See" it falling lower and lower.

Alternate between the two ideas for a few seconds with each. If you find yourself thinking of the actual position of your arms, try to get your mind back to the images of the weight and balloon. After two or three minutes...open your eyes. Your hands should be several inches apart, in the horizontal dimension, with your left hand lower than your right.

Normally, if you extended both arms in this manner they would both become heavy and you would experience great difficulty in maintaining such a position for more than a few seconds. In this instance, one arm reacts this way, but the other becomes increasingly lighter. Again, if your arms reacted in the manner described, go on to the next experiment. If not, you must practice until they do. Only a few inches difference denotes success. These few inches, however, must occur automatically, while you are thinking as instructed—not just by "doing" it.

THE PENDULUM EXPERIMENT

☐ Often called the "Chevreul Pendulum" phenomenon, this too is an example of ideomotor response. There is nothing particularly mysterious about it and you cannot, contrary to what many people think, predict future events in this manner. Neither the sex of an unborn child nor any other occasion of equal mathematical predictability can be foretold with any greater degree of accuracy by means of a pendulum. It very well may indicate the wishes, possibly subconscious, of the person holding the pendulum, but any further claims will try the patience of even the most gullible of scientific investigators.

A length of thread, string, light chain or ribbon about ten or fifteen inches long with a small weight tied to one end will serve our purpose for this experiment. Many magicians and pseudo-mystics have very

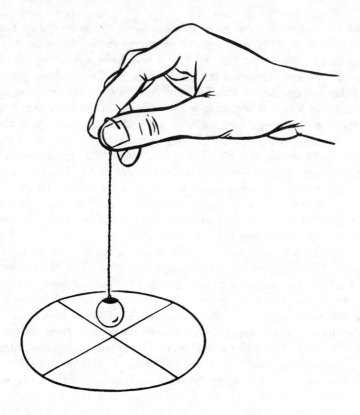

Figure 5.   Pendulum experiment.

intriguing pendulums of crystal, onyx, glass, plastic, etc., mounted in all sorts of settings and with "magic" potions, seeds, hairs and so on embedded within the sphere. Various types of such pendulums are advertised in low-grade magazines and are offered for sale in novelty stores. All sorts of unfounded claims are made for the "magic power" of these items. Any shoelace, piece of string or ribbon with a weight attached works on exactly the same principle as the most elaborate and expensive pendulum you can buy.

Back in the 'twenties a great deal of interest was generated in a device called a "Ouija Board". This device consisted of a flatiron-shaped object that would slide over a card on which the letters of the alphabet were imprinted. The fingers of the operator, or operators, were supposed to be placed lightly upon the surface of the movable piece in such a manner as to cause it to act as a pointer. A question would be thought of, whereupon the piece would point out, one by one, the letters forming a message or an answer to the question.

Exactly the same thing can be done with a pendulum which can be made to swing back and forth, slowly changing direction as it swings toward letters imprinted on a surface below, spelling out "answers" to any question in the mind of the operator. Both devices are actually motivated in the same way, through ideomotor activity. There is no mysterious "compelling force" involved.

It is easy to see how devices such as these can be demonstrated and described, to those who do not understand the principles involved, in such a way as to make it appear that some supernatural power is guiding the device or the hand that is holding it. Doubt and skepticism that are actually valid can be removed and replaced by belief in something that is really not true. Developing belief in anything that is not true is not a good basis upon which to build any form of procedure, and it is unfortunate that some systems of self-improvement attempt to do just that.

Many hypnotic techniques, either directly or by inference, depend on leading the subject to believe that there is a power or force at work in the process, the gadgets used or the hypnotist himself. This is not what we wish to do here. We do not wish to develop any false beliefs. Instead, we hope to remove even the smallest shred of implication that may connect this technique, in the mind of the reader, to any mysterious, supernatural power or force, and thus to establish a firm belief in its scientific base. What is more important, we seek to secure an understanding and belief of the reader in himself.

In these experiments the responses are evoked by ideas or images in the mind of the subject that generate impulses in the nervous system. These impulses bring about muscular activity appropriate to any idea of action involved in the thought processes of the subject during the experiment.

This muscular activity is often only a small fraction of the activity that would occur if the subject were actually to perform the full movement instead of simply imagining he is doing so. To observe this muscular activity with the naked eye is, therefore, usually difficult, but it exists just the same. If delicate measuring instruments are attached to the appropriate areas of the body while the subject is thinking about activity of any kind, these instruments will record changes in the electrical potential as well as evidence of movement in the muscles that would be used in the actual performance. A person thinking of playing a violin will have muscular activity going on in his fingers. The thought of throwing a baseball will generate muscular activity in the arm.

This is the same principle utilized in polygraphic (lie-detecting) equipment. The questions asked during a lie-detecting test are designed to evoke, in the mind of the subject, thoughts related to the circumstances being investigated. Regardless of the answers given, which may be wrong, the subject will respond to the questions with changes in rate of breathing, pulse-rate, and electrical resistance of the skin. Although these changes may not be directly observable to the naked eye, the equipment magnifies and converts them into mechanical movement that can be recorded and evaluated by an expert. Certain questions used during the test are called "control" questions. These are purposely not connected to the investigation. Such questions as "Was it raining today?" or "Is your name John?" are used to establish the "normal" reaction of the examinee. Interspersed with the "control" questions will be others regarding things connected with the episode under investigation. Let us say that the test is to determine what, if anything, the individual knows about the theft of some diamond rings from a house in "Concord". It is known that a black dog had chased the thief, and that the rings had been hidden in a shoe box. Questions such as "Were you in Concord Tuesday night?", "Do you like black dogs?", "Do you have any diamond rings?" will evoke responses that can be compared to the control questions. The guilty person, or one knowing the details of the crime, would be expected to respond with a greater degree of difference between the two types of questions than would one who had no knowledge at all of the crime.

Let us now proceed with the description of the pendulum experiment and we will then discuss further the relationship of the resultant responses to those mentioned above.

■ While standing or sitting near a table or desk, hold your pendulum between thumb and first finger and in such a position that the weighted end is about one-half inch or so above the surface. Use your other hand to steady the weight until the pendulum remains reasonably immobile over one spot. (See figure 5.) Now imagine a line drawn on the surface of the table directly under the pendulum and running from left to right. As you imagine the line, the pendulum will swing, slightly at first, back and forth along the imaginary line. Once it starts to swing, it will increase its motion even if you think intermittently of something else, as long as your thoughts do not involve a different motion. You will notice how each time you form a good image in your mind, the pendulum reacts accordingly and with increased amplitude.

After you have done this for a minute or two and, if you wish, while the pendulum is still swinging, change your image to one of a line going toward and away from you. As you form this image, the pendulum will slow down and then begin to swing with increasing amplitude along the new line. You can then cause it to swing in a circle by thinking of a clock or anything circular in shape. Once you get it going well in one direction, you can even cause it to stop and then to revolve the opposite way by thinking of a circular arrow pointing in that direction or by thinking of a merry-go-round or some similar device.

☐ Most people will react very readily as described. If you get only a slight motion or a lazy response from the pendulum, it would be a good idea to stop for a moment and prepare a white paper (as shown in figure 5) by drawing a large circle with a cross inside that touches the circle at four points.

■ Place this paper on the table and begin again. This time, start with the pendulum over the intersection of the straight lines and imagine only one line at a time. This should help you to get the desired reaction. If you still have difficulty, draw only one line on the paper and work on getting the pendulum to swing in one direction. After that you can change the paper so the line runs the other way. When you have mastered this, you can then work with a circle.

When you have a definite response in all three motions—back and forth, to and fro, and circular—you can then, if you wish, use the pendulum to "answer" some questions. You can either have someone ask you the questions or think of them yourself. You then should designate "no" as being from side to side and "yes" as to and fro. These motions most closely resemble those of nodding or shaking the head. As you think about the question, the pendulum will swing one way or the other to indicate your answer.

If your question cannot be answered by a "yes" or "no", you must prepare a more elaborate answering service. In this event you should draw a circle at least four or five inches in diameter and place the letters of the alphabet around *half* of the circumference. Then, as you hold the pendulum over the center of the circle and think of the question, the pendulum will gradually spell out your answer.

☐ The answering of questions is not necessary for you to do if you are not interested. It is described only as an incidental matter of possible interest.

The motion of the pendulum in response to your thinking is the essential part of this experiment, and the ease with which it occurs will be some indication (although not conclusive) of the facility you will have in developing self-hypnosis. As is also true of the reaction of your arms in the semaphore experiment, the responses of the pendulum can be correlated to some degree to your ability to understand and follow instructions, to imagine specific symbols and to adhere to systematic procedures.

You will notice, regarding the use of the pendulum for obtaining answers to questions, that I referred to the result as indicative of "your answer". This is exactly what it is. Not "the answer", but "your answer". The direction of the pendulum is governed solely by impulses generated by your thinking and is a reflection of your deeper motives and desires. The greater the emotional significance the question contains for you, the greater the difficulty in evaluating your response as indicated by the motion of the pendulum. If you attach considerable importance to the question, your response could easily be affected by anyone observing you, especially if they were in any way involved in your answer. We will go into emotional responses in more detail later. Realization that the described responses are the result of processes operating only within yourself and are not due to any unknown power or force will be adequate for our present purposes.

Experiment with the pendulum phenomena until you are thoroughly familiar with them and with your responses to them. If the question and answer part intrigues you, then work with it for a while until your curiosity is satisfied. If not, make certain that the responses to the lines and circles have been experienced and are understood; then go on with the next experiment.

THE PHANTOM WEIGHT

This experiment involves no new factors or principles, but it is another step toward psychical control of our physiological responses and will facilitate development of the self-hypnosis pattern when we get to that point in our training.

■ Read the instructions until you completely understand what you are to do; then choose an appropriate time for following them. Although you may not need it, you should plan to have at least one hour of uninterrupted time for your first session. It is important that you have no feeling of urgency.

If you feel it helps your mental perception to see an actual object before attempting to imagine it, then it might be a good idea to locate the appropriate articles and to observe them. If you can form a good

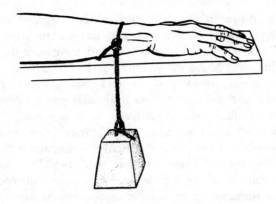

Figure 6.   Phantom weight experiment.

image of a strong rope and a heavy weight, fine. If not, you should take time to find and look at the actual objects.

When ready, sit in a comfortable chair or lie on a sofa or bed with one arm resting comfortably on the arm of the chair or near the edge of the bed, as the case may be. Your arm should be in such a position that a short movement away from your body will allow it to drop toward the floor.

Close your eyes. Then imagine a strong rope tied to your wrist and a heavy weight suspended halfway off the floor. Imagine that the weight is pulling at your wrist, causing it to slide toward the edge and off toward the floor. Also imagine that after your arm drops toward the floor the weight holds it there, making it difficult for you to lift your arm. Imagine, or think through, the entire sequence. Let yourself believe there is actually a rope tied to your wrist and a heavy weight attached to the other end that is causing your arm to slide off and drop toward the floor. Then think the following words: "Your arm is heavy, very heavy. Each time you think the word 'heavy' your arm is heavier and slides toward the edge and will drop toward the floor."

Next, develop an image of yourself writing the word "heavy" on a blackboard, or any way you choose. Then suggest to yourself: "Each time you write the word 'heavy' your arm becomes heavier and slides off toward the floor."

That completes the instructions, but before you start let's go over them again to make certain you understand everything perfectly. This is important. Once you are in the position described, you are to picture the rope weight and movement of your arm. You then think in words, using the second person, the description of the imagined sequence. You imagine writing the word "heavy" and suggest to yourself that the "thought" of the word itself, writing it and imagining the action, will cause it to happen. Make up your mind that once you start you will think as concentratedly as possible about these ideas. If any other thoughts occur, you will force them aside and get back to the idea of heaviness. If you find yourself analyzing what is actually happening to your arm, this will be the signal to get your mind back on the sequence.

In using words to form the suggestion, it is important that you think in terms of the "second" person. Think "you", not "I". Think of this as if your "conscious mind" were giving orders to your "subconscious". This is true of any suggestion you make from now on. It keeps the identical terminology whether you are thinking, reading or listening to the suggestion. Again, all through this process think of yourself as "you", rather than as "I".

☐ It is easier for some people to retain itemized instructions. For that reason I shall list each item again:

■ 1. Imagine the rope, the weight, and your arm moving as described.
2. Form the imagery of writing "heavy" and accept it as a symbol that will cause the response to occur.
3. Think, or say, the word "heavy" and accept this also as a symbol. Alternate between thinking of the symbols and the imagery of the response.
4. Avoid analyzing, or thinking of anything else, once you start.

Work on this until the response is satisfactory; that is, until your arm actually slides off and feels noticeably heavy. This heaviness will disappear once you resume your normal activities.

☐ Do not be discouraged if you do not get immediate or complete results. Although many will be able to do this the first time, others may require several practice sessions.

After your arm responds satisfactorily, keep thinking for a little while about the weight holding it down. While picturing the weight, try to lift your arm, and notice how heavy it feels. Try to adopt the concept that each time you try to lift your arm it will respond only by feeling heavier.

Your attitude as you go further is a major factor in achieving good results. Each time something happens in a satisfactory way, you should let the success build your confidence and belief in your ability and in the technique you are using. Magnify this in your mind as much as you can. Try to minimize any lack of response and simply think, "It will happen soon and will then be a better response than if it had happened too quickly."

The proper degree of cooperation is important. Now, this does not mean that you should just go ahead and perform the response consciously. It means, rather, that you should eliminate any doubt in your mind that the response will occur. You should act "as if" the imagined situation were actually in existence and as if the response were actually occurring because of existing circumstances.

Suppose you were an actor (or actress) trying out for a part in a play, and the director asked you to act the part of a person so tired he cannot raise his arm. You might read the script provided for this scene and then go through the act believing, as completely as possible, that you are the character you are depicting. In doing this (that is, pretending that your arm is heavy), there would actually be some feeling of heaviness in your arm. This is the type of cooperation we are talking about. Act "as if" the imagined circumstances are true.

■ Should you still have difficulty in developing satisfactory responses, there is another procedure you can follow that will help to bring about good results. If you can avoid resorting to this, it would be better. So follow these instructions only as a last resort.

Just prior to a regular practice session, place your arm outside the arm of the chair or along the edge of the bed or sofa. Now press hard toward your body, and keep pressing until you can do it no longer. Then, immediately place your arm on the arm of the chair (or edge of the bed, as the case may be) and proceed with the original instructions.

This procedure not only brings about an actual feeling of tiredness and heaviness of the arm, but also predisposes the muscles to respond as desired.

If you understand and follow these instructions properly, it will be literally impossible for you not to succeed. Keep at it until you do, before going on to the next experiment.

□ The question may arise as to whether or not your assistant, if you have one, should be helping you now. The answer is no, not directly. He can help you in obtaining a clearer understanding of the instructions by reading them to you and discussing them with you. And he can help to evaluate your responses as you practice. He should not, however, take an active part during the experiments listed in this chapter. In subsequent chapters there will be definite instructions pertaining to the assistant and how he can best help you.

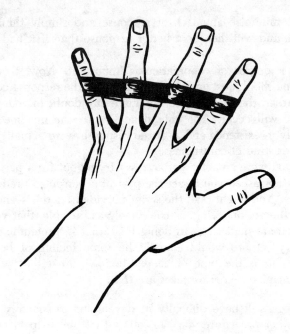

Figure 7.   Rubber band experiment.

THE RUBBER BAND EXPERIMENT

■ While sitting or lying down in a comfortable place, put one arm in such a position that by bending your wrist you can easily keep your eyes focused on the fingers and back of your hand. (See figure 7 above.) Keep your eyes fixed on your hand as you spread your fingers apart, and strain to force your fingers just as far apart as you possibly can. Now imagine there is a strong, thick rubber band stretched around your fingers. Think of this rubber band as having been small in diameter yet very thick, that you have inserted your fingers through it, and have stretched it out as far as possible. You can now feel it pulling your fingers together. Think to yourself: "The harder you try to keep your fingers from drawing together, the more they tend to do so." See this happening in your mind. From this point on you can close your eyes. But keep building the image of the rubber band drawing your fingers together. Imagine that you are trying very hard, but to no avail, to keep your fingers from finally touching each other. Think: "Once your fingers touch, you will not be able to take them apart!" Alternate with the series of images of the rubber band drawing your fingers together, the words suggesting: (1) that the harder you try to keep your fingers apart, the more tired they feel and the more they will draw together and (2) that once they touch you will *not* be able to take them apart.

Work on this until the response is good. After your fingers touch, retain the image of the rubber band as if it were squeezing your fingers very, very tightly together. Then imagine that the rubber band is gone, and your fingers are relaxing back to normal.

Continue to observe the rules previously mentioned and maintain a strong, positive attitude. If you have any difficulty it will help actually to perform this experiment once or twice with a real rubber band in order to feel the sensation of real pressure.

THE MAGNETIZED FINGERS

While sitting in a comfortable place, clasp your hands together, and, with your elbows resting against your body, hold your hands about ten inches away from your face. Stare at your first fingers (see figure 8) for a little while and then close your eyes.

Figure 8. Magnetized fingers experiment.

Imagine that your first fingers are made of metal and that they are strongly magnetized so they will draw together after being forced apart. Once this idea is developed clearly, keeping your other fingers tightly clasped, slowly straighten your first fingers and hold them as far apart from each other as you possibly can. Try hard to keep them apart but think also of the idea that they are magnetized so strongly they are being drawn together anyway. Imagine that as they draw together the force becomes even stronger and that once they touch you cannot take them apart. Think, too, that the harder you try to separate them the more they will stick together.

You should find it very easy to develop this effect to the point where you actually cannot take your fingers apart for a few seconds or longer.

Although it probably will not be necessary, you could if you wish get two small magnets and experiment with them to familiarize yourself with the forces involved. Once again, complete this experiment satisfactorily before going on to the following two experiments, which will wind up this sequence.

THE HAND-CLASP EXPERIMENT

Clasp your hands as before, then slowly rotate them and extend your arms out in front of yourself with your elbows straight and so you can see your fingers and the backs of your hands. (See figure 9.) This is called the "Chinese handclasp". Your thumbs may have a tendency to separate. Try to keep them locked along with the rest of your fingers if at all possible.

Now close your eyes and imagine a strong rope being looped around your arms at the elbows in such a manner that it draws your elbows toward each other. Imagine also that there is a strong liquid glue being poured over your hands and that it is drying hard and sticking your hands together into one solid mass. Think again about the rope around your arms being drawn even tighter. Develop this to the point where your arms are strained and stiff. Think again of the glue as now being hard and solid around your hands. Keep this in mind as you go back once more to the rope. When you are imagining the rope vividly as getting even tighter, you can try hard to take your hands apart, but you will be unable to do so. Let the thought go through your mind that the harder you try, the more firmly your hands are stuck together. You will find this is so!

Don't keep trying to separate your hands for more than a few seconds. Although it is important for you to experience this difficulty, remember

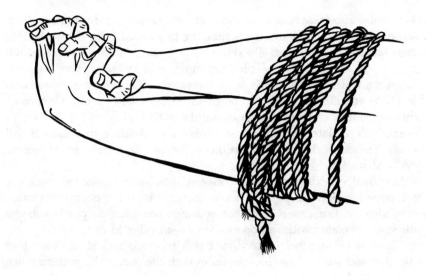

Figure 9.   Hand-clasp experiment.

it is not being caused by some external force but by responses developed as a result of your own mental processes. This is what you *want* to have happen as a step toward more important accomplishments. Accept the response of your hands feeling stuck together for a few seconds as evidence of your effective use of imagery in bringing about a physiological reaction.

☐ You are learning that you must separate the *conditioning* of a response from the *testing* of the response. If during the conditioning or suggesting procedure you are thinking about whether or not it is going to work, this will lessen the effectiveness of the conditioning. If, on the other hand, you "know" it is going to be successful, this will help to make it so. The systematic compounding of one belief, held even temporarily, upon another leads to conviction. And it is conviction that we are seeking here.

You may at some time, as you go through these experiments, have some negative thought crop up such as, "This procedure is really only talking to one's self."

Don't make this mistake! Remember that any systematic procedure that will enable you to develop symbolic control over physiological functions must *of necessity* involve your own mental processes. It is *you* who must experience, understand and instigate these responses. In a sense it *is* "talking to yourself" or thinking to yourself. But this technique goes far deeper than that. By systematically going step by step through a series of increasingly complex psychosomatic episodes, you are conditioning yourself to respond with increasing efficiency at *subconscious* levels to stimuli that can only originate at *conscious* levels. Once conditioned, many of these responses will be autonomic.

You will see later on how the symbols we establish in this manner will evoke responses that are impossible to inhibit or reverse by conscious effort alone.

Our final experiment in this series is intimately associated with the self-hypnosis pattern, perhaps more so than any of the previous ones. It is also the first experiment that you may recognize as possibly being directly associated with responses of practical value to you.

There is one symbol utilized that will be explained later. Use it as directed and you will see how it ties in with the rest of the pattern when you get to that point.

You should plan on at least one hour of uninterrupted time for this one; do not start it until you are assured of this.

Read through the entire set of instructions and go over them until you have the ideas clearly and completely in mind, to the extent that you do not need to refer to the text again. These instructions are not complicated, but they are vital to the patterns that follow. So be sure to follow them implicitly and, if anything, spend more time on each step rather than what you may feel is sufficient. Any attempt to hurry through may interfere with your success. In fact, over-anxiety in any form is apt to be inhibitive. You will find that working on the desired effect rather than concerning yourself with the time it takes to achieve the effect will always bring better results. Be encouraged by the fact that hypnotic phenomena seem to have a way of speeding up "by themselves". Consistent practice with emphasis upon the desired effect will cut down on the time interval required to achieve that effect.

We have all experienced how "contrary" our mental processes can be as we try to remember a forgotten name. Familiar as is the name, it often appears that the harder we try to recall it, the more stubbornly the mind refuses to relinquish it. Yet once we stop trying, the name appears "out of nowhere", and many times we have even forgotten by that time that it was something we were attempting to recall. This is what frequently occurs with hypnosis.

Regular, systematic practice with an attitude, ambiguous as it may seem, of not caring whether or not you get results is much more effective than intensive effort and feelings of urgency.

FRACTIONAL RELAXATION

This experiment should be performed while you are lying flat on your back. There should be a small pillow or rolled-up towel under your neck, and your head should be on the same level as the rest of your body; that is, with no pillow under it. A pillow should be under your knees, however, and your entire body should be supported as evenly and comfortably as possible.

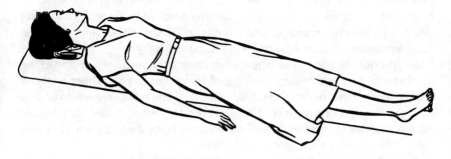

Figure 10.   Fractional relaxation.

There should be a comfortable temperature in the room, with no likelihood of change or of draft.

You should have eaten recently enough so that you will not be hungry, and there should be no immediate need to interrupt the experiment by such contingencies as going to the bathroom.

Reasonable quiet should prevail, with no possibility of sudden, sharp noises. Complete silence, however, is neither advisable nor essential.

Environmental odors such as of food or smoking should be eliminated and, if pleasing to you, an odor of a mild nature may be sprayed or otherwise introduced into the room.

Your body should be either nude or loosely clothed in garments that will allow easy movement of your limbs without binding or restricting circulation or respiration. Dresses or robes are not as preferable as pajamas or slacks. Belts, ties, collars, etc., should be removed or loosened.

Dim illumination is best, or complete darkness, rather than bright lights or reflections.

If it does not interfere with any medical regime advised by your doctor, you should not be under the influence of any drugs, tranquilizing or otherwise. The responses we wish to evoke will be more truly evaluated when attributable only to the procedures you are using.

■ When you are in the position described and have fulfilled reasonably the suggested environmental atmosphere, you should close your eyes and imagine your body as being made of fabric, for example like that of a soft, rag doll. Think of your muscles as cords of rubber which had been stretched tight and are now relaxing and going back to a limp, heavy state. The symbol this time is the number "1000-3" or "one thousand-three". This is the first time we are using an abstract symbol and the significance of it will be explained later. You are to tighten up certain small muscle groups and then, as you let them relax, you are to think repeatedly of the symbol "1000-3". It doesn't matter how you think of this symbol. It can be simply saying the words to yourself, imagining you are writing the words or the number, or seeing either illuminated in an electric sign. Do it any way that is easiest for you.

As you tighten each muscle group starting with your toes and working up through your body, keep thinking of these muscles as rubber ropes or bands being stretched tightly. As you let them relax, repeat over and over the thought or image of "1000-3". Also try to adopt the attitude that all the muscles of your body will continue to relax deeper even after you can no longer feel them doing so.

The entire procedure will now be described in detail, and you should know it by heart before you actually go through it in practice.

Starting with your toes, curl them under and squeeze hard as you think of these muscles as rubber strands being stretched tight. Then . . . let them relax as you think, "1000-3", "1000-3", "1000-3". Picture those muscles now as being like pieces of limp string with no tension...no energy . . . limp and relaxed. Next, bend your ankles so your feet are pointing up toward your body; then repeat the same procedure. First, tighten so you are aware of the muscles and the area involved, and then relax while thinking over and over, "one thousand-three", etc. Your legs are next; you should push them out straight, with your toes pointed away from your body. Tighten the calf muscles and those in the thighs— as tightly as you can. Then...let them go limp. Limp and relaxed while thinking of the symbol "1000-3". Take at least ten seconds or more on each group of muscles. Work up through your buttocks in the same way. Then take a deep breath; slightly arch your back while holding your breath, and go through the same procedure, relaxing as you exhale. Repeat this, without arching your back. Hunch your shoulders forward, tightening the back muscles and with, again, the same thoughts of 1000-3 and imagery of your muscles. Your arms are next. Push them right up straight toward the ceiling with your fingers extended. Push hard; then slowly curl your fingers into tight fists and slowly bend your elbows, bringing your fists down to your shoulders, keeping the muscles in your hands and arms tight. Then let your arms flop to your sides, limp and soft, thinking again, "1000-3, 1000-3".

Move your head forward until your chin touches your chest. Tighten the muscles in the back of your neck. These muscles are particularly important as they are close to the nerve-trunks descending from your brain. Now, slowly turn your head from side to side, keeping tension on all your neck muscles. Do this three or four times; then let your head fall back to a comfortable position, thinking continuously of the imagery of your muscles relaxing, and 1000-3. Next, squeeze your eyes tightly shut, etc. Then move your jaw from side to side, etc. Finally, press your lips together and fill your cheeks as if blowing up a balloon. This tightens your facial muscles. Then . . . let them relax and think of 1000-3.

This completes the routine as far as any movement goes. You should go through the process three or four times again, in imagery only, and imagine each muscle group becoming further relaxed.

Then you should go through the following imagery before ending the practice session:

Imagine that you are walking in a forest on a beautiful sunny day. There are light, fleecy clouds overhead. You feel wonderfully free. As you walk along you notice the flowers, the shrubs, the trees and the patterns of sunlight shining down through the branches. You hear the sound of water bubbling over the rocks in a nearby stream. As you follow a turn in the path, you come out into a clearing, and you are near a small beach on the shallow river. There is a small sailboat pulled up on the shore, and you decide to go for a ride in it. You step in and push off easily. The boat is lined with soft pillows. You lean back as the boat drifts along, and you notice the trees on the shore as you go slowly past them. You lean back further into the soft cushions and lazily look up at the soft white clouds. You notice a tiny airplane off in the distance, and as you watch the plane emits white smoke and slowly spells out "one thousand three" in giant letters across the sky. You drift along for a while, letting your imagination develop several more instances in which the symbol "1000-3" occurs in different ways.

This completes the instructions. Read them through several times until you are sure you understand and remember everything clearly.

☐ The entire procedure should be practiced several times until very definite feelings of deep relaxation are experienced.

The scene described is designed to lead your imagery into progressively increasing, subjective responses of dissociation. When you conjure up phantasies of another person, this is a kind of "objective imagery". The physiologic responses resulting from it are not as satisfactory as those resulting from the "subjective" type in which you think of yourself as being "there", seeing, doing and feeling as you would in your normal activities.

Unless this point is examined critically, the differences in types of imagery and the relative value of each are likely to be overlooked. After any episode involving imagery, it has been my experience that the individual is apt to report having confused one type with another. When subjective type imagery is reported it is correlated with better results in the responses evoked. When a person reports imagery of the objective type, we usually suggest scenes that have a tendency to convert gradually the imagery to the subjective type.

If you were asked to imagine yourself in a large room with a blackboard along one wall and a big window on the opposite wall, there would be little to influence your type of imagery at this point. If it were further suggested that you were standing near the blackboard with a piece of chalk in your hand, the chances are you would see yourself in an objective way; that is, as if you were looking at another person, or a mirror image of yourself. If, still further, it were suggested that you write something specific on the blackboard, then put down the chalk and walk over to the window, your imagery might change to "subjective" while you were writing, and then change back to "objective" while you were on your way to the window.

This is important. Imagery is an integral part of anything you may wish to accomplish with self-hypnosis. The term "imagery" includes responses in all sensory classifications. Many people are prone to think of imagery as being exclusively "visual". This is far from true. We can imagine, in varying degree, all categories of auditory, gustatory, olfactory and tactile as well as visual imagery. We can even imagine the emotional feelings that are difficult to categorize, such as fear, happiness, inferiority, confidence, depression, elation, etc.

Most of us do, it is true, seem to imagine best in a visual sense. However, it is far from uncommon to find individuals who can imagine other kinds of sensory impressions better than the visual ones. Occasionally there is one who reports that he can "see" only poorly, or not at all, yet he can imagine sound, odor, taste and feelings of touch and motion without difficulty.

This is seemingly disrupting, because most techniques have been based on visual symbols. Some hypnotists feel it is difficult or impossible to hypnotize a person who cannot imagine in a visual sense. My experience has indicated that it is definitely possible.

I was once asked by a physician to cooperate in evaluating the hypnotic susceptibility of a patient with a severe skin problem. Although this patient easily achieved a deep trance in the first and subsequent sessions (and, incidentally, remarkable relief from his symptoms), he reported that he did not once "see" the suggested imagery. Even after extensive questioning, it was impossible to arrive at any understanding of how the patient "thought". He said merely that he was able to "think" very clearly of anything suggested, and he could retain numbers of seven digits or more to the extent that he could repeat them in reverse order, after hearing them spoken once. Three years later, I talked to this man and he said he could still put himself into a deep trance easily. He had suffered no relapse to his previous symptoms, but he still could not explain what went on in his mind during the trance. There was no amnesia factor involved, as he could recall trance phenomena in detail.

Not long ago I had occasion to work with a physician on a minor problem of his own. He proved to be an excellent subject for hetero- and self-hypnosis, and we were easily able to accomplish the desired result. We discovered very quickly, however, that his imagery was unusually clear and vivid in auditory, olfactory and tactile experiences, but very poor in the visual sense. In one particular scene, in which he imagined descending in an elevator, he reported that the feeling of descending, the subtle sounds of the elevator and even the odors were as vivid as an actual experience, but the visual imagery was intermittent and dim. We were both interested in this and spent several hours attempting, with little success, to improve his visual imagery. Yet he did achieve the results that he felt were most important to him.

There have been many cases in my experience in which the subject reported little ability to imagine visually. With few exceptions this did not inhibit successful induction of the trance upon instructing the person to think in any way he could of the things suggested to him.

As we proceed through the various stages of development of your individual self-hypnosis pattern, there will be many requests for you to imagine various symbols and scenes. If you are one of the rare persons who cannot visualize well, do not despair. You may or may not find visual improvement as you go along, but you will still, quite probably, be able to achieve your goals by thinking in your own special way.

■ Whenever you, yourself, plan a sequence of imagery, remember to proceed toward situations in which you tend to think, or imagine, subjectively rather than objectively. "See" the things and scenes themselves, rather than "See yourself seeing them."

☐ If at all possible, you should have an assistant. So doing may save considerable time and effort and assure you of a much higher degree of success. Your assistant should read the entire book and then study the chapter on "Instructions for an Assistant" until thoroughly familiar with the principles involved.

CHAPTER 3

PERCEPTION AND ADAPTATION

THINGS ARE NOT as they seem, is an observation attributed to some ancient sage whose name has long been forgotten. As with many wise sayings, this can be regarded as true, but at the same time it can also be considered as false. Its truth or falsity depends upon the specific connotation intended or the manner in which the term is applied. A "frame of reference" must be constructed within which "trueness" and "falseness" can be evaluated. Only then will this, or any other statement, be worthy of consideration.

Some things can be shown to be different than they seem, but, upon learning that this is so, the observer alters his perception to conform to his new knowledge, and then, to him at least, the entity under consideration would be as it seemed to be.

If a frame of reference is established, delimiting consideration of the phrase to the perception of a specific individual, its "trueness" or "falseness" can be considered as highly correlated to the extent of the individual's knowledge. The question of "completeness" then logically arises. In other words: Should the phrase be held to be true if the chosen individual has no knowledge of the underlying factors contributing to his perception?

Should the connotation be placed upon the phrase, that if one thing can be shown to be different than it seems, that the phrase is true? Or should it be that if one thing can be shown to be the same as it seems the phrase is false?

Are crows "black" if one white one can be found? One way of looking at it would be to say: "Most crows are black, but there are some white ones." This, of course, is a compromise of a pragmatic nature. The theoretical or philosophical aspects of such questions can be argued *ad infinitum* with little chance of arriving at a practical conclusion. Compromise seems the most likely course to follow if practical value is to be derived from the consideration of perceptions.

In the preceding chapter several experiments were described to demonstrate the fact that perceptions can be altered. Whether or not the new perceptions, if such were developed, are the "true" ones is not so important as the realization that they can be developed. To be sure, this is a compromise as far as theory goes, but we are more interested in the practical aspects of the situation. If "negative" perceptions, such as those evoking responses of pain and anxiety, can be altered so as to diminish the frequency and/or intensity of those responses, our end will have been achieved. The "trueness" or "falseness" of the altered perceptions will then be of little concern.

There are a number of ways in which perceptions can be altered, but first let us briefly consider the manner in which they are formed.

When we see someone walking toward us it seems obvious that our perception is owing to the movement of the image across the retina of the eye. Upon further consideration, however, we find that images also move across the retina when *we* are moving, even though the object we are observing may be *standing still.*

The movement of the retinal image is not sufficient evidence upon which to base the conclusions that an object is in motion and we are standing still, that we are moving and the object is standing still, or that both we and the object are in motion and other objects are standing still.

Obviously there must be other factors involved. To discuss each of these factors even in a cursory manner would be a tremendous undertaking and not of practical value to us here. Some mention of their collective functioning will, however, add to our understanding of the discussions that follow.

All sensory organs, upon stimulation, convey information to the brain which in some way "interprets" this information. The manner in which the brain interprets this information is dependent upon still other factors. The type, frequency and intensity of the stimuli affecting the sensory organs adds still other factors. The sum total of all these factors, at any given moment, could be considered (in an elementary way) as the stimulus-pattern evoking the perception of that *particular* moment. It would seem logical that if any of these factors are changed, the stimulus-pattern would be altered, and if this occurs, the perception would also be changed.

Now we already know that many of our responses are autonomic—that is, they are evoked with no help from our higher mental processes. We also know that many of our responses are evoked through sensory stimulation that is first conveyed to the brain for "interpretation", and the nature of the response is dependent upon the result of the interpretation. Here again it would seem logical that if the interpretation is altered the response too would be altered. This brings us to the consideration of practical means of altering our perceptions.

There is rather substantial evidence that the brain "adapts" to certain types of stimulation. For example, the retinal image is known to be "upside-down", yet the brain reverses this in order for us to perceive the objects around us as "right-side-up". When watching television it is not uncommon for many viewers to recline or assume positions in which the retinal image would be at an angle to that of the screen. This usually causes no problem at all for the viewer; in fact, he is rarely aware of it. The brain has immediately adapted to the situation and the viewer's perception of the image is "normal".

This is only one example of the infinite number of ways in which adaptation, in this case of a helpful nature, takes place. As a result, confusion is lessened, and, although some may debate the point, more pleasurable responses ensue.

There are, on the other hand, many instances in which the brain adapts to stimuli in such a manner that undesirable responses are evoked. Let us consider an actual incident which is an excellent example of this. A friend of mine once told me that he became genuinely seasick, to the point of feeling nauseated, while watching a *movie scene* in which a boat was trapped in a violent sea. Ordinarily such feelings are evoked through actual stimulation of the semicircular canals. In this instance there was no real motion involved, yet the undesirable response was evoked. The brain was "adapting" to the visual stimuli in the manner to which it had been conditioned to respond to *motion*.

Probably the major way in which our adaptation patterns are formed is through processes of conditioning. The brain is conditioned to adapt to specific stimuli in a specific way, but it will also adapt, as shown above, in a *similar way* to *similar stimuli*. Much of this conditioning occurs through trial-and-error types of stimulation in which the frequency with which "correct" responses occur, in ratio to the frequency with which "incorrect" responses occur, tends to establish the response which occurs most frequently, whether it is correct or not.

A variation of this is when a stimulus-response sequence is repeated with great frequency. The response may not be the "correct" one, but it can become so firmly established that it may be perceived as "correct" or possibly as having no alternative.

We may be aware of such conditioning as it takes place, in which case factors involving attention are at work: movement, contrast, size and frequency, to name some *external* ones. Interest, motivation, need, expectancy and mental ability would be considered *internal* ones.

However, perceptions and adaptation-patterns can also be conditioned without our being aware of it. This could be owing to lack of knowledge or understanding of the relationship between the stimulus and the response as in the case of a person with a fear of electricity who avoids *all* electric devices because he once suffered a shock while changing a fuse. The latter incident may have occurred so many years previously that it is now forgotten, but the avoidance response still remains to stimuli of the same or similar nature.

Our perceptions may be "true" or "false", but in either case they contribute greatly toward conditioning the brain to adapt as it does.

Many "false" adaptations or interpretations are of little consequence, as they evoke harmless, or even beneficial responses. An example is the adaptation that allows us to perceive the sequences of still pictures as "moving" pictures. Some, however, may deter us from progress toward knowledge, as when we accept our perceptions as true and do not recognize the possibility of their being otherwise. Again, and more unfortunately, we may recognize the possibility but not take the trouble to investigate. There is, for example, the perception with which most of us are familiar of a stick, partly submerged in water, appearing bent at the water line. If no one had ever taken the trouble to investigate this phenomenon we might have been conditioned to believe that all objects bend upon being partially submerged in water. But the principles of refraction having been established, we understand now that many perceptions involving optical phenomena are erroneous. Some we can change, and some persist even though we know they are wrong, but we would never have known if we had simply accepted all our perceptions as being truly representative of the facts.

Still other "false" perceptions condition adaptation patterns that are harmful and destructive. These are often involved in our anxiety and guilt responses. If, for example, we perceive a certain form of behavior as "sinful" yet find ourselves strongly motivated to express or experience it, we would quite likely have guilt feelings as a result even though our perception of such behavior as sinful may be erroneous. We may suffer untold agonies over circumstances we perceive as dangerous to us, and yet these anxiety-responses may be completely unfounded or unrealistic.

Children are often told that certain forms of behavior are "bad", "dirty", "sinful" or "harmful" without explanation as to why this is so. This often results in adverse responses that may be so thoroughly conditioned they remain evocable as long as the child lives. Consider the case of an overprotective mother who wishes to confine her child to certain limitations of behavior. She may teach him it is "bad" to leave the yard, that it is "dirty" to show interest in bodily functions, that it is "sinful" to express strong desire and that it is "harmful" to drink coffee. If such conditioning is intense it could result in the child experiencing, even in later life, feelings of anxiety and guilt each time he is exposed to *similar* stimuli. As an adult he may have feelings of guilt each time he takes a trip away from his home, he may feel squeamish in situations involving his toilet, he may feel guilty whenever purchasing a luxurious item, and he may feel insomnic after drinking a cup of coffee.

Our perceptions are influenced by what we are taught and by our experiences as we go through life. Our perceptions, in turn, affect the manner in which our mental processes adapt to our environment.

When our environmental situations evoke more negative than positive responses we become dissatisfied with life. This dissatisfaction may be manifested in physical or emotional ways or in varying proportions of both. Our "adaptability" is low. We must seek means for increasing the frequency and intensity of our satisfactions—our positive responses. There are three possible ways in which we can bring this about. We can change our environment, a course of action which may or may not be possible or practical, or, if it is, may not be the answer. We can attempt to increase our adaptability. We can attempt to alter our perceptions.

ENVIRONMENTAL CHANGES

Environment, in the broadest sense, is not limited to external stimuli. Internal stimuli that contribute to our development of needs, desires and feelings of satisfaction or dissatisfaction are also included.

Environmental changes may be brought about by changing geographical location but may also be affected in other ways. As mentioned previously, *similar stimuli* can evoke *similar responses*. In fact, many times the use of substituted stimulus-situations are more desirable than the actual situations would be. A person who likes to travel can obtain a great deal of satisfaction from imagery of taking a trip, without suffering some of the disadvantages such as expense, tiredness, loss of time, etc. Then too, we all tend to think of the best features we expect to encounter during trips we are planning. When we actually experience them they are not generally so ideal. Expectation is often more satisfying than realization. This does not mean that imagery alone is the answer to every problem; there are disadvantages too. Imagery, in order to be as effective as actual experience, usually must be repeated many times, and there may be feelings that the imagery is not "substantial" enough to be completely satisfying. The artificiality of imagery may become so apparent that a desire is developed for the "real thing".

When a person recalls the pleasant episodes of past experiences there are generally very satisfying responses evoked, but if the tendency is to dwell on the unfortunate episodes the resulting responses are just the reverse.

We hear of many cases in which improvement or complete recovery from debilitating symptoms has been accomplished through a change in geographical location. There are as many more, though, in which this has been attempted with little or no relief and other cases in which varying degrees of relief were obtained only to have a relapse occur at some later date. This would seem to indicate that the symptoms were not fully understood or at least that their underlying causes had not been determined. Diagnosis and analysis of these things is extremely difficult, and it is doubtful if they can ever be completely and accurately accomplished.

A great deal of critical comment has been made against "direct symptom removal" by hypnotic suggestion, and there have been charges that these procedures only result in "symptom transfer". Although there may be some justification for such criticism, it is just as much, if not more, of a mistake to make so sweeping an indictment. Although in some cases direct symptom removal may be unwise, it may in other cases be an ideal approach to the problem. After all, what is most drug therapy if not direct symptom removal? Are the underlying causes always known when medication is prescribed for a headache or an anxiety reaction?

The cases in which symptom transfer is said to have occurred are really impossible to evaluate intelligently. How can anyone know that the "new" symptom would not have been manifested whether direct suggestion was used or not? Such a criticism of direct suggestion is really ridiculous when viewed from another light. Usually the implication in such criticism is that the person to whom the suggestion has been made desires to retain the symptom in order to obtain some secondary gain and that if he cannot obtain this gain he will, after removal of his particular symptom, develop another symptom to take its place. This might be a reasonable conclusion if it were not for the fact that the patient comes to the physician for help. Evidently, therefore, the patient considers removal of the symptom to be of more importance than any benefit he may be deriving from secondary gain and retention of the symptom. Of course, this statement might be countered by saying that the patient does not consciously know why his symptom occurs and that there is some sort of "subconscious reasoning" going on. Whether or not reasoning can occur on a subconscious level is a moot point, but there is considerable substantiation for the view that conditioning can and does occur at these levels. This being so, we might speculate that any symptom that occurs subsequent to removal of a different symptom by direct suggestion, or by any other means, would be attributable to stimulus-patterns developed by conditioning rather than to a desire on the part of the patient to obtain some kind of secondary gain.

It may seem that we have drifted away from the main point of our discussion on environmental changes. However, the subject of symptom removal is very pertinent. If a person is advised that a change in climate may be desirable as a means of alleviating his symptom—attacks of asthma, for instance—this really is an attempt at direct symptom removal, and the criticism of this approach is no more valid than if the removal were attempted through hypnotic or any other type of suggestion or treatment.

As we are mainly concerned here with relating these discussions to hypnosis and self-hypnosis, we should point out that the use of imagery can be greatly facilitated and brought under excellent control with the use of hypnotic techniques. Several cases will be mentioned later in the book in which environmental changes were brought about through the use of these media.

INCREASING ADAPTABILITY

Although it is considered advisable to separate material such as this into different classifications, it should be understood that no one classification can be considered independently of any other. The chapter on conditioning of responses is intimately related to all the other chapters, as is true of each of those. Our subject or any subject dealing with human behavior is so complex that volumes could be written on each tiny segment of it. It is hoped, therefore, that the reader will appreciate this and try to incorporate into his total concepts the relationship of the material in one chapter with that in another and, what is equally important, the relationship of the total material as it applies to him.

Having said this, we will refrain from theoretical discussions during the balance of this chapter, and more emphasis will be given to the practical application of these principles.

When a person feels excessively anxious, guilty, frustrated, or suffers any other negative reaction, he manifests either an inability to adapt to the situations involved or an erroneous adaptation of his mental processes. Let us consider a typical case of this type of reaction and examine it from various viewpoints.

Our subject could be a young married man who is having problems in his marital relationship. Perhaps he has reported that he feels guilty after sexual intercourse with his wife yet can think of no reason for this reaction. He may be perfectly well-adjusted in most other ways, have an excellent understanding of sexual matters and still be unable to cope with his guilt feelings. Upon further questioning it may be found that he once had erroneous ideas about sex. As a boy he may have been taught that self-gratification would cause "brain damage" or bodily harm or that such behavior was sinful. As he grew older he may have learned the truth of the matter, but the feelings of guilt remain and are evidenced each time he participates in any sexual activity.

Now, we have mentioned that one way to extinguish a negative response is to repeatedly apply the stimulus that evokes the response, or a stimulus that is similar to it, under conditions that do not allow the negative response to occur. According to this, once our subject realized no harmful results followed upon the self gratification he perceived as sinful, his guilt feelings would be desensitized. The difficulty here lies in his perception of what the word "sinful" implies. If, as is often the case, he has been led to believe that he will be punished for his sins at some later time, as by not being allowed to go to heaven, he will not be able to resolve his question, for there will remain his great concern for the future possibility. The same is true of "bodily harm" and "brain damage". If when he was a youngster he believed these negative results would ensue from acts of self-gratification, but his needs became so pressing that he frequently performed the act anyway, his fear of future retribution would serve to condition his negative responses even though he hadn't experienced harmful results at the time.

In order for our subject to adapt to this situation as an adult, he must find a way to evoke a positive response that will dominate the negative one; it must, of course, be evoked by the same or a similar stimulus. The thought may occur that the climax itself would serve as a most intense response but this, actually, is not the part of this syndrome we are concerned with. Instead, it is the response evoked immediately after experiencing the climax. The climax is certainly a powerful entity in this sequence of events, but up to this point it is really a response to previous stimulation. If, however, it can be utilized as a stimulus-response entity and be conditioned to evoke positive responses immediately after it occurs, then the negative responses can be desensitized. Direct suggestions made during the self-hypnotic procedure can often condition this type of response, thus increasing the subject's adaptability to life situations.

Another example could be the case of a person with acrophobia, or a fear of being in high places. There are many variations of this, in which the individual symptoms may involve a fear of being unable to refrain from jumping when in high places, undesirable imagery of falling, thoughts of being unable to climb down, etc. Now, part of such anxiety it always adaptable—it serves a useful purpose. Anyone who considers going up to a high place should, for the sake of safety, think also of the dangers involved. If, having done this, the subject still feels excessively anxious, or if anxiety is evoked even though he does not expect to be exposed to dangers, then his anxiety is unadaptive and should, if possible, be diminished.

Here again imagery can be utilized to increase the person's adaptability to life situations. If a pleasurable response, such as one evoked by the thought of some highly desirable object, can be made to occur simultaneously with the negative response to stimuli involving height, the negative response may be weakened or extinguished. As a simple and brief example, we could use the idea of owning a new car as the pleasurable response and, while the subject is under hypnotic trance, suggest that he must "climb a hill" in order to inspect the car of his choice. Or he could imagine driving the car over increasingly higher roads. In such a procedure the imagery should first involve the positive and pleasurable stimulus-response entities, with the negative imagery that is to be desensitized brought in carefully and gradually. The subject might imagine walking up a few steps, for instance, and then an increasingly greater number of steps until he experiences no anxiety from the imagery. The responses to life situations closely parallel those of the imagery and should carefully be evaluated during such procedures.

ALTERING PERCEPTIONS

Many anxieties are developed and perpetuated owing to erroneous perceptions of circumstances that, if viewed from a different perspective, may not be dangerous or undesirable at all. Quite often the individual suffering from such anxiety is unable to understand his true position in the constellation of relatives and friends, and no amount of reasoning seems to help.

A mother who has "given her children everything" may feel ignored when the children begin to develop interests outside the home. The husband who lavishes all sorts of luxuries upon his wife may not understand that she would prefer the attentions he bestows upon his secretary. There are innumerable instances of people who, feeling the need of bolstering confidence in themselves, will attempt to do so through minimizing the attributes or efforts of others.

There are many situations in which men with beautiful and intelligent wives are actually rude and inconsiderate toward them and yet will show every courtesy to other women. Many of these husbands admit to being afraid of losing the respect of other men if they show too much concern for their wives. This sometimes is a form of testing in which the person (it can be the woman as well as the man), feeling inferior to the spouse, attempts to see how much the other will take, thus assuring themselves of their loyalty. The trouble is that this testing may go on indefinitely. The person simply cannot believe that the other "really" loves him and he may increase the frequency and intensity of the tests.

Still acting upon his original erroneous perception, the person doing the testing may further conclude that the spouse is really inferior. Perhaps he thinks, "If she (or he) is willing to put up with all the indignities I have imposed upon her, she must be trying to hang onto me. Maybe I deserve something better than this."

An amazing peculiarity that often accompanies such situations is the fact that many of these people can recognize that the same thing is going on *in other relationships* and yet cannot accept the truth as applied to themselves. There are also those who *can* see the fallacy of their own behavior, but cannot seem to alter it.

The technical term for this is "logic-tight compartments", which aptly describes the thinking of an individual who recognizes the logical implications of a particular set of circumstances yet applies different "logic" to his own behavior.

I recently met a woman who considered herself a financial genius and her husband dull and stupid. She explained that her money had subsidized his business and that if it were not for her, neither would have anything. Upon further discussion it turned out that her husband had accepted a few thousand dollars from her upon their marriage and through shrewd investments had made it possible for them to live very comfortably, acquire several valuable pieces of property, raise and educate two children and accumulate a substantial fortune. Whatever she knew about finances she had gleaned from him, yet each time an investment had turned out poorly she had berated him for it, and when it turned out well she had complained that it should have been better. Without being aware of it she had been, over the years, simply "feeding back" his own information. She had never been willing to put forth a positive proposal, avoiding such a commitment on the grounds that he "would never listen". The poor man could not win! Yet the objective observer would draw the obvious conclusion that her husband must love her very much or be a most patient person—probably both.

It is easy, as we have said, to evaluate these situations with great wisdom—when they involve the other person; but we rarely use such sage and penetrating reasoning when it comes to ourselves. And you, dear reader, and I are no exceptions. This is why, if we really wish to achieve insight into our own behavioral characteristics, it is always advisable to seek the advice of a qualified practitioner. We are generally much more easily convinced of the unreability of our perceptions of physical phenomena than we are of any weaknesses in our observations of ourselves. An interesting experiment is to notice the criticisms we make or would like to make of others and then see to what extent they may be applied to ourselves.

A more extreme example of "logic-tight compartments" is one involving a professional man who is continuously doing wonderful things for practically everyone he meets. His family and acquaintances appear to idolize him. Yet, one by one, the recipients of this man's benevolence turn out to be unappreciative. Many are awkward and uncomfortable whenever he is present. The conversation becomes stilted, guarded, and those present appear embarrassed and ill at ease. The observer of all this begins to wonder what makes people so ungrateful. It almost makes one lose faith in humanity. But . . . the whole picture has not yet been revealed. When it is, the reactions do not seem so strange. Upon more detailed study one finds a certain similarity about this man's kind deeds. They appear genuine enough and are, perhaps, performed with no thought of return—at least of a tangible nature. Sooner or later, however, an occasion arises in which our giver of gifts makes specific suggestions as to how the lucky recipient, and sometimes his family too, should conduct some activity of his. This often starts with a suggestion or two regarding some little thing such as the placement of a piece of furniture or the kind of bread that is best to eat, but the suggestions then occur with more frequency and develop to a point of insistence regarding most everything that is done or contemplated.

On one such occasion the purchase of a piece of property was made even though everyone else preferred another location. In another instance, a major issue arose because these folks had the stupidity to purchase a particular electrical appliance after having been advised that another type was the "only one to buy". This invasion of privacy began to irritate everyone concerned, but because of feelings of gratitude they tried to do things his way. This led to further annoyance because often their efforts to please him were futile. It appeared that no one could do anything exactly the way he felt it should be done. Finally these and other families to whom the same things had occurred began to avoid this man. They began to realize that they were not actually as stupid as he made them feel and that, even if they were, they preferred to make a few mistakes as long as they could make them in their own way.

This man probably never realized the extent to which he carried this behavior. He seemed to recognize the need in others of developing a sense of responsibility, for he often advised others to allow those around them to make decisions on their own. Those around *him*, however, were rarely allowed the same opportunity. He was in every other way a fine and understanding person. It was unfortunate that all he could receive in return for his many good works was avoidance by those he had befriended. But the love he sought was only to be won if he could recognize that under the guise of helpfulness he was actually bolstering his feelings of self-superiority.

In discussing illustrative cases such as these, the writer does not intend to stand in judgment. The question here is not so much one of rightness or wrongness as it is of whether or not a change in perception on the part of one or more of the individuals concerned would improve their adaptability to life situations. The reader may, for instance, feel that the man who attempted to impose his ideas on others was at fault and should have altered his perceptions. Perhaps so. If he had, he might have obtained more satisfactions from life. Then again, he might not have— unless he found some other way to maintain his self-image. It is possible that he would have made more friends had a change in perception brought diminished concern with other people's affairs. But it is also possible that in the acquisition of these friends his need to perform "good deeds" would lessen. Then again, even though he recognized his interference as a fault, the effort to contain himself upon seeing someone about to make a "mistake" might be more than he could expend without disrupting some other function of his adaptability.

We should also consider the possible effects of changes of perception of the other people involved. To accept the kindnesses and attempt to avoid the consequences can, of course, be construed as receiving without giving. And to shun the giver later may not be indicative of fairness on the recipient's part. The tendency to feel inferior and embarrassed upon the intrusions of privacy may indicate weaknesses, from one point of view, or simply a desire to avoid argument, from another. Each individual must evaluate such things himself in order to achieve maximum ability to adapt to the problems that arise in his environment. Others can point out factors that he may overlook regarding his behavior and his relationships with other people, but it is he himself who must make the ultimate decision. The adviser in such matters should attempt as far as possible to open the eyes of the one seeking help, but he should not tell him where to cast his gaze to find "right" or "wrong". This we must each see for ourselves. Nor is the person seeking help always the one who needs it most.

We can see reflections of ourselves in the criticisms we make of others, but we can also become unduly intolerant of ourselves if we carry this too far. Here, as in the philosophical consideration of such questions, the practical conclusion seems to be one of compromise. We should attempt to see ourselves as others perceive us, but we do not have to accept their perceptions as factual.

OUTLINE OF THE TECHNIQUE

L ISTED BELOW are the nine major elements of this technique. This list is separated into three sections to make it easier to distinguish and remember the significance of each element. Following the list and numbered to correspond with it are detailed descriptions of each of the elements.

This material may seem voluminous, but it will appear less so as it is absorbed and understood. You should learn the meaning and significance of the symbols, but since they will be repeated frequently throughout the text and during your practice sessions, this will not be too difficult.

PRE-TRANCE INSTRUCTIONS

■ While in a comfortable place and with eyes fixed straight ahead:
1. Think of the time you wish to "wake up".
2. Formulate your suggestion.

TRANCE-INDUCTION PROCEDURE

3. Imagine "1000-1", the symbol for evoking tiredness of the eyelids.
4. Imagine "1000-2", the symbol for evoking eye-closure.
5. Imagine "1000-3", the symbol for relaxation.
6. Imagine "1000-4", the symbol for emotional tranquillity.
7. Imagine "1000-5", the symbol denoting "hyper-suggestibility".
8. Imagine a circle enclosing an "X", then carefully erase the "X".

DEEPENING PROCEDURE

9. Imagine, one by one, the letters of the alphabet, as if writing "A" in the circle, then erasing it, etc.

☐ The conditioning of proper responses to these symbols is accomplished through practice sessions of from ten to fifteen minutes duration, at intervals of at least once each day, or, if possible, two or three times daily. You should be sitting or lying down in a comfortable place, reasonably free from noise or interruptions. You should then choose a spot, preferably a little above eye-level, and stare at it with as little blinking as possible. Or stare off into space, keeping your eyes fixed in one position. After assuming this position, you practice according to the following instructions. Read them carefully, to the point of complete familiarity, before beginning your practice sessions.

■ I. THINK OF THE TIME YOU WISH TO "WAKE UP".

Form an image in your mind of the face of a clock with the hands set at the time you wish to emerge from the trance-state. Also think, "You will be awake at —— o'clock."

2. FORMULATE YOUR SUGGESTION.

Develop imagery of your suggestion. "See" yourself performing or experiencing the desired effect. In addition to this, use words in the "second person" describing your suggestion.

3. IMAGINE "1000-1".

This is the symbol for evoking tiredness of your eyes. As you have already been staring (during items 1. and 2. above), your eyes should be somewhat fatigued by this time. Thinking over and over of "1000-1", while staring straight ahead, will soon condition this response. Continue until your eyes are nearly closed.

4. IMAGINE "1000-2".

This is the symbol for causing your eyes to close. Upon experiencing the tiredness and heaviness of your eyelids, as a response to "1000-1", you should then develop imagery of "closed eyes" and think, "When you think of '1000-2', your eyes close, and it is impossible to open them until the time you have set has elapsed." Repeat until your eyes are firmly closed.

5. IMAGINE "1000-3".

This is the symbol for physical relaxation. It is conditioned by imagining relaxing scenes which include "1000-3" or "one thousand three" somewhere in the scenes, and by going through the process of "fractional relaxation" as will be described later.

6. IMAGINE "1000-4".

This is the symbol for emotional tranquility. It is conditioned by imagery of tranquil scenes occurring simultaneously with imagery of the symbol. The "dissociation" resulting from the systematic procedure is also a contributing factor.

7. IMAGINE "1000-5".

This is simply a symbol representing a highly suggestible state. You think of it once only.

8. IMAGINE "⊗".

This is the symbol for evoking a deeper trance. It is conditioned in a number of ways which will be described in detail later. Care should be taken to imagine the symbol as clearly as possible and then to erase the X without "touching" the circle.

9. DEEPENING THE TRANCE.

It is at this point that your subconscious becomes conditioned to accept suggestions. There are a number of means for accomplishing this which will be described later.

It is important that you try to adopt and maintain positive attitudes regarding the technique you are learning as well as confidence in your ability to achieve the results you desire.

☐ Immediate or dramatic results should not be expected, although they sometimes occur. It is much better to expect that at some future time you will have accomplished your objectives. Over-anxiety can be inhibiting to your progress. After all, what you wish to accomplish is probably very important to you and should be worth whatever time is necessary for you to achieve it.

As has been explained, there is no "outside force" that causes you to respond. No "power" can bring the desired responses if you resist. It is *you*, through the use of *your* systematic imagery, who has the power to condition yourself to respond with increasing efficiency to subconscious reactions under the direction of your conscious mind.

In developing any technique of self-hypnosis there is always a major obstacle to surmount. This has to do with the manner in which a desired suggestion is conveyed from the conscious to the subconscious areas of the mind. Most of the difficulty lies in the paradoxical situation that conscious activities recede as the hypnotic state is approached, with the result that the ability to formulate or manipulate suggestions decreases. The question arises then as to how to expedite implantation of suggestions into the subconscious.

In the opinion of the author it is a mistake to think of a suggestion as an entity in itself, as a sort of pill that can be implanted. Nor is it feasible that the conscious can talk to the subconscious and instruct it in any way. Any suggestion that can reasonably be expected to work must of necessity be a response to a stimulus evoked by the subject himself. By establishing symbols that represent desired responses, it is conceivable that less conscious activity need be involved in retaining the symbol at a low level of awareness so that responses conditioned to the stimuli of the symbols can be evoked with a minimum of conscious effort. Any resist-ance or skepticism on a conscious level would be minimized by converting the resistance-evoking idea into a symbol of a neutral nature. Imagery is possible at a subconscious level, and such imagery can be helpful in many ways. To initiate or direct this imagery while it is occurring, however, requires that instructions be given at that time. The subject would naturally be unable to give such instructions, and if someone else does so it is of course hetero- rather than self-hypnosis.

A systematic series of responses can occur in an automatic or semi-automatic fashion when evoked by the stimuli to which they have been conditioned. These stimuli are in the form of a progression of neutral symbols that the subject can keep in his mind even as other conscious activities decrease. The associated responses are evocable, automatically, in subsequent hypnotic states.

It is not really necessary for the purposes of this book to delve into the theory for this phenomenon. We are not attempting so much to substantiate "why" this technique works as to develop and utilize it as a technique that has proven successful in many hundreds of cases. Accept the fact that there is a very good reason for using symbols as we describe.

When during your practice something of a positive nature occurs, accept it as a good sign of progress and let it increase your confidence in your ability to execute the next steps. If something suggested does not occur, try to minimize this and expect that it will happen later. Develop, then, a neutral attitude about anything negative and a feeling of elation at positive results.

When you make a suggestion you should not just "do" it, without conviction. You should not, on the other hand, resist it either. Avoid the idea that something is going to occur in spite of your resistance. These responses are going to occur *because you want them to occur*—because you are allowing them to occur—because you are conditioning them to occur.

In many ways this procedure will seem like "acting a part" in a play. In a way that is what it is—but it also goes much further than that.

Neural patterns will be changing. At some point you will find that you have practiced "acting" so well that you then have the actual characteristics you were portraying.

Remember, this is a systematic procedure. Each step is important, not only in itself but also in its sequential correlation to the step preceding and to the one subsequent. Do not think of hurrying. Work toward achieving the *effect* regardless of the time it takes. Once the effect is established, the process will accelerate itself.

You will know when you have established the pattern by a feeling that each time you practice or make a suggestion, everything is functioning better and stronger. You will notice feelings of going "deeper" each time, and you will have no problem at all remembering the symbols as they will then have become part of your personality structure.

Learn to separate the "suggesting" part from the "testing". While formulating a suggestion, the feeling of knowing and believing that it is going to happen will help to bring it to actuality.

This procedure is so designed that effects easy of development are suggested first. As you experience these effects, you establish a firmer belief in the steps that follow. We call these steps "convincers". Try to convince yourself, with little or no desire to test or question your progress.

THE TECHNIQUE ITEMIZED

When the pattern outlined above has been established and is functioning properly, a typical example of what occurs with a given person is:

The person is sitting or lying down in a comfortable place free from interference. He is staring straight ahead in a fixed manner. He thinks briefly of the time he wishes to wake up, knowing he will awaken at precisely that time. He does this by imagining a clock with the hands set at the suggested time or by thinking of the words "You will awake at — o'clock," or by thinking of both imagery and words.

He then thinks of his suggestion, using imagery, words, or both. Let us say, for example, that he wishes to develop "arm-rigidity". In this event he formulates his suggestion by imagining his arm moving out straight in front of himself. He "sees" it become stiff and rigid. He sees himself trying to bend it, but it only becomes more rigid with each attempt. He may also use words in formulating this suggestion; he thinks to himself, "Your right arm will move up until it is straight out in front of you, and it will become so rigid you cannot bend it, until you release it by touching it with your other hand."

He then thinks of "1000-1", and instantly his eyelids feel heavy. This heaviness increases until his eyes are nearly closed. He then thinks of "1000-2", and his eyes close firmly and stay closed until the time comes to wake up. He knows that if any emergency arises he will know of it, probably sooner than if he were awake, and that he would be able to wake up instantly in such an event. He thinks of "1000-3" several times, and his body relaxes and continues to relax more with each breath. If anyone lifted his wrist, at this point, and released it, it would drop limply to his side. There would be no evidence whatever of tension. As he thinks of "1000-4", he feels peaceful, tranquil, emotionally relaxed, and somewhat dissociated. Any sounds of environmental activities only serve to make him go deeper and to become more dissociated. After thinking of "1000-5" once or twice, he finds that he has just enough awareness to think, in a rather lethargic way. He then imagines a large circle as if it were drawn on a blackboard. In the circle he imagines an "X" which touches the circle at four points. He imagines erasing the "X" very slowly and carefully, without touching the circle, and, as he does so, he goes into a deep trance. He keeps going deeper until he reaches his maximum depth. As he drifts into the deeper trance, his arm actually moves up, as suggested, and becomes increasingly rigid. If included in the suggestion was the fact that he will at this point slowly wake up, he will do so. Although fully awake, he has no control over his arm. He cannot bend it; he cannot lower it. In fact, even the attempt to do so would cause it to become *more* rigid, sometimes to the point of discomfort. He has absolutely no conscious control over the arm. Yet the instant he touches it with his other hand, the arm relaxes quickly, and becomes perfectly normal.

It may seem that the ability to make one's arm rigid in such a way is not much of an accomplishment, from any practical point of view. The value, however, lies in the fact that it serves as an immediate means of evaluating one's ability to make suggestions properly. It also serves as a "convincer" to the subject. Presumably, if he can cause his arm to react in such a manner, other, more important suggestions beyond conscious control can be effected.

It will be noted that item 9 in the above list was not involved in this description. This is because we were describing an example of a well-developed pattern. This subject had gone past the point where he needed to use the alphabet any longer. The reasons for this will be set forth in more detail later; here it is enough to say that this type of subject has advanced to the point where thinking of the circle and erasing the "X" puts him immediately into a deep trance. With practice you will reach the same point.

Although you may have an assistant, these instructions are for your daily sessions when you practice alone.* In working without an assistant you must expect that more memorizing of instructions and symbols will be required and that the whole procedure will take longer than with someone helping you.

Your ultimate goal will be to perfect your responses to at least one physiological suggestion and one psychological suggestion. Each of these will be a criterion for evaluating the degree to which you have established the pattern of self-hypnosis.

You should practice several times daily, if convenient; and if not, at least once daily. To skip even one day, especially at the start, may be inhibitive to your progress.

■ While sitting or lying in a quiet, comfortable place, do the following:

Move about and adjust yourself into a comfortable position. Loosen your tie, belt etc. Do not have your legs or arms crossed or folded. Settle down. Fix your eyes on some object or spot a little above eye-level and keep staring in a fixed and continuous manner, *without wavering*. Think of the time you wish to awaken. It does not matter whether you set a time of minutes or hours. You will soon find that you will awaken at almost precisely the time you have set. If you have something important to do, it would be a good idea to set an alarm clock or arrange for someone to awaken you, until you prove to yourself you can do it. This will allow you to relax and not be too concerned about awakening.

It is unnecessary to establish any elaborate symbol for awakening. Simply knowing the time you wish to wake up is enough. Some people use imagery of the face of a clock set at the desired time. Some think simply in terms of words designating the time. Some use both. Whatever your method, it will suffice.

After thinking of the awakening time, you should next think of your causal suggestion. We will discuss the more important suggestions later. Since at first you wish to improve your procedure, your suggestions should be limited to "going deeper each time", "you will be more relaxed", "you will awaken feeling fine", etc.

Your eyes should be fixed and staring during this period of thinking. This will add to the fatigue of your eyes, which we wish to condition to the symbol of "1000-1". Your suggestion can be made in imagery, in words, or in both. Whatever words you use should be, as previously

---

* Instructions for an assistant are given in chapter 5.

stated, in the form of the second person—as if your conscious were talking to your subconscious. If your suggestion involves feelings of happiness or confidence, use imagery of yourself smiling and acting in a confident manner. There will be more regarding this later.

When your suggestion is clearly in your mind, start imagining the symbol for eye-heaviness: "1000-1". You have already been staring for some time, and your eyes (or rather your eye-lids) should be feeling tired and heavy. As you think of 1000-1, over and over, imagine that there are heavy lead weights on your eyelids, or tiny threads tied to your eyelashes, pulling your eyes closed. Now, there is no actual force that is going to make your eyes close against your will at this point. But if you act with enough conviction, the result will be the same as though there were such a force in action. Without question, your eyelids will get heavy. No one can stare for any great length of time without this happening. What we want to do is condition this heaviness as a response to the stimulus-symbol, 1000-1, so that the symbol evokes a rapid response whenever it is applied in the proper manner. You should consistently incorporate this into all your imagery patterns: that you will not go into a trance nor will your eyes close or get heavy unless you are in a proper and safe place. The response of heaviness of your eyelids is impossible to avoid if you follow instructions.

☐ Once in a while a person will tell me: "I tried this method and it didn't work." I have pointed out as patiently as possible that such a negative result is impossible. It is not that "it" didn't work, but that "they" didn't work! It is true that some people can stare longer than others, but I have never seen anyone who can stare for more than a few minutes without his eyes becoming tired. If he forces himself to contest the technique by seeing how long he can keep his eyes open, he might extend this to another few minutes. Such a peformance requires extreme effort and is evidence of a contest. The idea of a contest is contrary to this concept; it indicates a misunderstanding of the technique and a false challenge. The effort involved in such an attempt should be applied in the opposite direction.

When you understand that you are to experience a tiredness in your eyes that is physiologically impossible to avoid and when you assist this with imagery that to you represents tiredness, the overwhelming odds are in the favor of your eyes closing. When this effect is simultaneously evoked with *symbolic* imagery, the symbol becomes the stimulus for evoking the heaviness response.

With this accomplished you can never truthfully say "it" didn't work. If the response is not yet established you must practice some more until *you* are "working" properly. Most persons will react quite readily. Those who do not must practice for whatever time is required. There will be some consolation in knowing that once a response is established, the next one will be much easier and quicker.

■ When your eyes are nearly closed because of thinking "1000-1", you should change to the symbol "1000-2" and make a special effort, at this point, to alternate this with imagery of your eyes being closed tight, excluding any other thoughts if possible. Your eyes will close with increasing ease upon practice, especially if you keep suggesting that they do so. You should soon experience the heaviness and closing of the eyelids by these two symbols within a few seconds after you start to practice. Make up your mind that once your eyes are closed it will be impossible for you to open them (except in an emergency) until the time has elapsed that you have set for yourself to awaken. You should "act this out" several times by making believe that it is true and going through the motions of trying to open your eyes and not being able to. This will develop an image in your mind of what you hope to establish, and at some point you will find that you are no longer "making believe". It will be absolutely true, as you will see.

Try not to be too anxious to make these tests right away. Rather, you should divert your anxiety into working on the firming of your beliefs and the developing of proper attitudes. Work on your imagery for evoking the response; then, when you feel you have done a good job, you can test all you wish to and the response will hold.

Once your eyes are closed you can repeat "1000-2" several times and then think, "As you count from one to ten you can try to open your eyes, but you will be unable to until you reach ten." Then act it out. Actually count, to yourself, from six to nine, and while doing so, "try" with each number "as if" it were impossible to get your eyes open. When you get to ten, let your eyes pop open and think, "That works just fine. You cannot get your eyes open until you get to ten."

Practice this eye-closure several times each session and as often as you can for a few days until you feel an increase in the response to the symbols rather than to the staring or the acting. This feeling is difficult to describe, but you will recognize it when it happens. If you are in doubt about it, practice longer until the doubt is gone. Only when this occurs should you make the following test:

With your eyes closed through the above procedures, imagine the figure "6" as if it were drawn in ink on the middle of your forehead. Roll your eyes upward and focus them as if you were looking right through your forehead at this number "6". Keeping your eyes on the number, you can try as hard as you like, but you will be *unable to open your eyes!* In fact, when you try to open them, your eyes will only become more firmly closed.

Stop trying, and imagine the number "7" in the same manner. Once you can imagine it clearly, keep your eyes focused on it and try again. You will find it is impossible. Continue with each number until you get to ten, at which time your eyes will open easily.

During the period of your development of "eye-closure", you will find a number of one or two-minute sessions, after your eyes are closed, preferable to longer sessions. It is perfectly all right to practice before going to sleep each night and to drift into a natural sleep after your eyes are closed. In addition, however, several short sessions will prove most beneficial to your progress.

You may find that you have already begun to think of 1000-3 in each session, after your eyes are closed. If not, you should start doing so after you have made the above test. You should have no difficulty at all in becoming deeply relaxed simply by thinking several times of 1000-3. If you wish to deepen this relaxation even further, you can practice again the imagery of fractional relaxation as described in the previous chapter. You might even wish actually to go through the fractional relaxation routine. It will certainly do no harm and may help to condition the responses more firmly.

☐ It will only be necessary to do either of these a sufficient number of times to adequately condition the relaxation responses to the symbol. After that the symbol alone will evoke the responses. At some point you can proceed from one symbol to the next with neither thought nor imagery in between, and the responses will be evoked automatically.

"1000-4" is the symbol for emotional tranquility. It is best conditioned by imagery that tends to dissociate you from your environment. The following scenes are described, not as instructions to follow in detail, but to give you ideas to adapt to other scenes of your own choosing, to best bring out these feelings for you. Most of us, as individuals, have certain ideas that please us and cause us to react differently than others to the same ideas or situations. After reading these three scenes you can tell very quickly which one suits you best, and then adapt it for your own use or develop a new one on your own that includes the same progression of imagery and symbols.

It should be understood that the purpose of the imagery in this particular instance is to condition responses of feelings of dissociation to the symbol "1000-4". Once these responses become firmly conditioned, the symbol by itself will evoke the response as part of a progression in a series of responses.

The major value in this technique does not lie in the single conditioning of one response to one symbol. It is in the autonomic progression from simple to complex responses evoked by the progression of symbols to which they have been conditioned that a self-reenforcing pattern, difficult to achieve by other means, becomes established.

Neither words, numbers nor any other symbols have the power to evoke responses until a meaning is attached to them. Take, for instance, a hypothetical word such as "nomel", which evokes no significant response. Notice that it is made up, in reverse order, of the letters in the word "lemon". It is only after the symbols are put in proper order that a significant response is evoked. This indicates that a group of symbols, such as individual letters, can be altered in their ability to evoke responses by changing the order of their grouping. "Lemon" not only evokes imagery of a particular object, but other responses as well: those associated with the stimulus pattern contained in the individual's imagery of the object, such as an increase in the flow of saliva. In this example meaning has been given to the word as the symbol of an object that, when eaten, acts as an unconditioned stimulus that evokes an increase in our flow of saliva. Although we may have learned the word "lemon" and the meaning of it years ago and, perhaps, have had no occasion to read or think of it for weeks or longer, the reading and thinking of it now immediately evokes the responses to which we were originally conditioned.

The symbols 1000-1, 1000-2, 1000-3 and 1000-4 are taking on meaning and response-evoking ability because of imagining and thinking of them while we simultaneously respond to other imagery and conditioning through environmental stimuli.

It is, therefore, important that any scenes we use not only tend to bring about the desired response but also include imagery of the symbols to which we wish to condition the responses.

If you like to take automobile trips, the symbol of 1000-4 could be included in the imagery as the number on the license tags of the car, as signs observed along the imagined highway and as the number of a house that evokes pleasant memories. The imagined trip could be one you have taken in the past or one you would like to take in the future—it does not matter which, as long as it will evoke pleasant feelings or will lead to some imagined activity that will arouse feelings of dissociation. Many people like to think of shopping trips, working in a garden, building a house or a cabin. Others prefer a more passive and relaxing image of themselves gently swaying in a hammock, watching the clouds roll by.

The imagery should be pretty well planned out before you start the practice session, and when noticeable responses occur you should proceed to the next symbol. From then on just a fleeting image of the original scene is all that is required. In other words, you use the imagery only to condition the tranquil response and from then on you think of 1000-4; when you come to it, think of the predominant image in the "tranquil" series and go on to 1000-5.

The self-hypnotic technique can be used to strengthen itself, whenever you notice responses that seem unsatisfactory or weak, simply by your suggesting so, once the pattern is reasonably well established. You will also find that you can develop the responses to 1000-4 to the point where you can exclude all distractions except those that might mean danger to you or that you feel would be important not to miss. The surrounding stimuli can be minimized to an amazing degree, yet you will retain sensitivity to specific, weak stimuli. The cry of a child, the ring of the telephone, the sound of a step, or even a specific type of characteristic can be retained or excluded with adequate conditioning and suggestion.

■ 1000-5 is considered the point of hyper-suggestibility. After thinking once or twice of this symbol there should be a state of diminished awareness established in which there is just barely enough conscious ability to think of the next symbol.

Once you complete the conditioning to 1000-4 you should include 1000-5 and the next symbols, to be described, in every practice session from then on.

As soon as you reach 1000-5 and think of it once or twice, you go into a deeper trance (you are, whether you realize it or not, in a light trance at that moment) by imagining a large circle, as if drawn on a blackboard, and in the circle is a large letter "X" which touches the circle at four points. As you slowly erase the X, being careful not to touch the circle, you go into a deeper trance—deeper each time you practice.

At this point there are individual differences in the degree to which conscious activity has diminished. As this faculty is closely related to depth of trance there is an additional series of symbols we use, not only to induce further depth, but also as a means for evaluating the depth simultaneously. This series of symbols is simply the alphabet and the word "deeper". After erasing the "X" as described above, you should imagine writing the letter "A" in the center of the circle, erasing it carefully and then writing the word "deeper" off to one side without erasing it, then the letter "B" and so on, as far as you can go. Write in successive letters of the alphabet, erase and alternate with the word "deeper". Develop the concept that each imaginary act will cause you to go deeper into the trance.

As you practice this you will find yourself skipping letters, repeating them, and having difficulty thinking of the next one. This is fine; it is an indication that your conscious ability is decreasing and that you are going deeper. Do not try too hard to continue with the alphabet at this point. Just let yourself go. Each time this occurs it will be at an earlier point in the alphabet and soon you will go into a deep trance before you can get to the alphabet at all. You will be going into the trance, as suggested, simply by erasing the "X", after, of course, utilizing the symbols from 1000-1 to 1000-5.

Your suggestions, so far, should all have to do with relaxing further and going deeper. When you no longer can start the alphabet you can begin to develop the ability to use other suggestions—those that will lead toward accomplishment of your major objectives. The use of suggestion will be explained in detail in the following chapters.

When you put yourself into a trance before going to sleep at night, the trance will usually last only from one-half to two hours and will change into a natural sleep from that point on. You will have no way of knowing the point at which one has passed into the other unless you have someone to test your state with suggestions. If you respond you are in a trance; if not, in a natural sleep. Your suggested time of awakening will, however, still work out as a post-hypnotic response.

Although hypnotic relaxation is very beneficial and in many ways superior to natural sleep, it is still advisable to obtain several hours of natural sleep each night because of the physical activity of moving now and then, which does not occur under hypnotic trance. The complete immobility you maintain in the trance is excellent for a limited time, but not so good for prolonged periods.

☐ Until a number of successful suggestions have been experienced, it is difficult for most people to tell when they have achieved the trance state. The transition from the conscious to the hypnotic state is so gradual, and the psychological and physiological evidences of change so subtle, it is practically impossible, especially for the individual alone, to determine which state exists at any given moment. And too, there is always some consciousness, even in the deepest trance.

One very obvious reason for this difficulty is the decrease in conscious activity as the trance is approached. It is with conscious activity that we discriminate and evaluate; if these faculties are lessened we naturally cannot make judgments of any significant value, including, of course, evaluations of our own condition or state.

Some people have an automatic or spontaneous amnesia during trance events and may drift into a natural sleep, especially if they go into a trance just before their usual sleeping period. These persons will awaken later and have no idea of what occurred. The great majority of people do remember what occurred, unless a contrary suggestion has been made, but they still cannot tell whether they were in trance or not.

Although conscious functioning decreases considerably, it seems that it is never completely absent during even the most profound trance. It is the abilities to select, reason, discriminate and evaluate that are most drastically affected rather than a complete loss of conscious awareness. All the sensory receptors are still in operation and often seem, if anything, more sensitive than usual; that is, we can hear, feel, taste, smell and, usually with some practice, see and talk while in trance and do so much better than normally upon suggestions to that effect. After all, in hetero-hypnosis (hypnosis induced by another person) we must hear the voice of the hypnotist in order to follow his suggestions.

It is entirely possible for a person to go into trance with his eyes wide open and for his eyes to remain open all during the trance. It seems to be a matter of what the person expects and as most people associate the trance with some kind of sleep they respond by closing their eyes as they approach the trance state. Most hypnotists believe that a deep trance is necessary for a person to be able to open his eyes and still remain in trance; extended training is often required to bring this about.

There is considerable controversy among the experts as to whether or not hypnosis is a "conscious" or "unconscious" state. In the author's opinion it can, to some degree, be either or both. If the conscious state is defined as one in which awareness of environmental stimuli exists, then hypnosis certainly can be considered a conscious state; but if the unconscious state is defined as one in which there is no awareness of environmental stimuli, then hypnosis can be considered an unconscious state as well. The fallacy lies in supposing that hypnosis must be either one or the other. The argument is presented that an individual cannot be simultaneously both conscious and unconscious. This is really not true; one can be both—to a degree. The five sensory classifications of sight, smell, taste, touch and hearing are the usual criteria for establishing conscious awareness, and it is entirely possible for each or all of these to be altered in either a general or a specific way and in either direction— that is, increased or decreased in sensitivity. The only proof of such change, however, must come from the hypnotized person himself, because we are dealing with subjective phenomena. His abilities to perceive, evaluate and discriminate, and also to express these abilities, are still under the influence of suggestion.

It is beyond the scope of this book to attempt to resolve these controversies, but the reader, if interested, can obtain many texts that will go into such questions in great detail.

That the evaluation of hypnotic trance depth is not always easy should be fairly obvious. Nevertheless, there are various means for making such an evaluation, and these will be discussed.

Whenever any of our sensory receptors are stimulated, as when sound waves enter our ear or something touches our skin, afferent impulses are evoked which travel along neural pathways of an extremely complex network—our nervous system. These impulses may go more or less directly to the motor areas and evoke responses appropriate to the particular type of stimulation. On the other hand, they may go to the various cortical centers in our brain where appropriate sensations are perceived and responses of a discriminatory nature evoked. To the first type of stimulation the responses are apt to be of a reflex or autonomic nature, as when the leg moves in response to a sharp blow on the tendon just below the kneecap (the patellar reflex). The impulses which go to the higher centers, however, may be subjected to various discriminatory and evaluative processes before they evoke a perception or response of any kind. It is this type of impulse that is most affected by the hypnotic phenomena. Indeed, it may be that the reflex type of stimulation is not affected at all. It has been rather well established that the impulses from the receptors continue to travel to the cortical areas during the hypnotic trance and that inhibition of perception or motor response is quite likely a cortical function.

Hypnotic anesthesia then would not be restricted to specific areas as in chemical anesthesia, which must follow the neural pathways. This can easily be demonstrated. When a chemical such as novocain is injected into the mandibular nerve, for instance, the result is an inhibition of sensation only in the areas associated with this nerve and its branches: the alveolar and lingual nerves. This serves to paralyze the synaptic junctions, making it impossible for impulses to travel to the higher areas of perception; therefore, painful stimulation in the areas of teeth, gums, tongue and cheek does not result in perception of pain.

Hypnotic anesthesia, however, can be induced in any one of these areas without necessarily affecting the others. It is not confined to any specific area. A line can be drawn on any area of the body and anesthesia induced to, but not beyond, the line, if so suggested. There is nothing, then, that inhibits the afferent impulses until they reach the brain. It is at this point that they are made unperceivable or incapable of evoking painful response. The person acts "as if" he had not been painfully stimulated. This does not mean he has been "hurt" and is incapable of saying so. The ultimate effect is just as good and often better than with chemical anesthesia. It does mean that it is his perception that is altered by hypnosis and that an inhibition of efferent impulses has taken place. An appreciation of this statement and an understanding that this is also true of all sensory stimulation and perception will allow you better to understand and appreciate the problem of evaluating your own trance.

Outside of definite feelings of relaxation and dissociation, the only ways you can evaluate your own trance are through information provided by someone who has observed your responses to suggestions during the trance interval, or through evidence of the effectiveness of post-hypnotic suggestions. You may or may not be able to recall later exactly what occurred during the trance. If, however, you have made a suggestion that your fist will clench or your arm will become rigid and will remain in that state even after you "wake up", the evidence of successful response to such suggestions will be rather conclusive.

In the following list are some of the signs of hypnotic trance that will be evident to the observer. These phenomena, indicative of the point to which trance has deepened after appropriate suggestion, have been arranged in order of increasing depth:

The appearance of increasing relaxation and immobility.
Fluttering of the eyelids and deeper, more regular breathing, and sometimes an occasional sigh.
Increased swallowing and decreased responses to surrounding noises.
Inability to open eyes upon suggestion that you cannot do so.
Involuntary startle reaction upon waking up.
Lightness, heaviness, or catalepsy of the limbs.
Complete muscular inhibition by suggestion.
Partial amnesia for trance events.
Development, upon suggestion, of anesthesia in the extremities.
Sensory illusions such as taste, olfactory, or audible distortions.
Complete catalepsy upon suggestion.
Ability to open eyes and remain in trance.
Complete amnesia for trance events.
Complete control of anesthesia in any part of the body.
Positive and negative hallucinations.
Age regression, complex post-hypnotic behavior, and amnesia for specific periods or events.

The effectiveness of any suggestions, whether they are made to you by another or self-suggested as described, will depend greatly upon how the suggestions were made. This is explained in greater detail in the following chapters. For the time being, the evidence of relaxation, eye-closure to symbols, heaviness of the limbs and feelings of continued relaxation after the trance are sufficient indications of good progress.

CHAPTER 5

INSTRUCTIONS FOR AN ASSISTANT

As previously mentioned, many people find it helpful in developing their abilities in self-hypnosis to work with a professional assistant. If one is not available it may be found advisable to practice together with another non-professional person who, perhaps, is also working at self-hypnosis. In this way each individual may help the other deepen the trance and develop other abilities. It must be understood that neither non-professional person is acting as a therapist, since they are not qualified for this role. The purpose is purely for practice, much as two people may practice music together, or tennis or bridge.

Although this can be a reciprocal situation in which each person assumes alternately the role of subject and then assistant during each session, it is far better for one to continue in the same role over a period of time until the pattern has been firmly established. The assistant, meanwhile, can be practicing on his own. The seriousness or importance of the individual reasons for wishing to develop self-hypnosis should be taken into consideration along with an evaluation of apparent ability as evidenced through practice up to this point. If one or both persons are following the advice of a physician, the instructions for proceeding should be given by the physician in person to the one who is to be the assistant. Under no circumstances should any therapeutic procedure be attempted unless this advice is followed.

Everything else being equal, the person with the highest degree of ability should be the first to assume the role of assistant as it may slightly inhibit his ability as a subject later on. If both individuals feel they understand and have reacted favorably so far, then it will not matter who first assumes the role of subject, since sufficient practice will inevitably lead to satisfactory results. If it is decided that one person will continue in the role of assistant, then only that person need read the balance of this chapter at the present time.

Generally speaking, in a reciprocal situation it is best if both parties are reasonably well matched as to personality characteristics so that each will direct as well in the role of assistant as he will respond in the role of subject. There is always a certain amount of self-consciousness at the start of such a relationship, but this will soon disappear with practice and as familiarity with the procedures is attained. The prevailing attitude should be one of serious, down-to-earth interest, with a readiness to accept logical evidence as it is presented and explained.

The voice and manner of the assistant should be similar to that of a guide or instructor with no attempt at dominance or control. A thorough understanding and familiarity with what is to be said, why and when it is to be said, can only be achieved through reading the entire book at least once and the instruction material* several times.

Simply "reading" the passages to the subject is not nearly as good as "talking". In other words, feeling and expression are as important as what is being said, and as long as the same meaning is conveyed the identical words need not be used.

Watching the responses of the subject and timing the appropriate instructions to them can be done much more effectively when the assistant is not required to continually refer to the text. In many instances it is advisable to repeat a phrase many times and in different ways until the desired response is evoked. This requires judgment and observation and, of course, cannot be brought about by adhering strictly to the letter of the text.

An acceptance of hypnosis and self-hypnosis as scientific procedures with no connection or association with occult, mystic or parapsychological phenomena should be firmly established in the minds of both individuals.

It is very easy when two people are working on something together for critical attitudes to develop in one or both regarding the ability or efficiency of the other. The one acting as the subject must avoid this pitfall as much as possible; he must put aside any analytical or critical thoughts, at least during the practice sessions, with the idea that they can be discussed after the session is over.

During practice sessions there are many times when the subject is supposed to be thinking, as completely as possible, in a prescribed manner. Random thoughts may occur that seem difficult to put aside and it may seem also that attempts to put them aside only make it more difficult to do so. When this happens, it is best to stop trying to put

---

* Instruction material throughout the book is preceded by the ornament "■" and terminated by the ornament "□".

them aside and to think the random thoughts through—"If you can't fight 'em, join 'em." Usually you will find that when you decide to do this the random thoughts will occur less frequently and finally disappear altogether.

Once the arrangements have been made for two or more people to work together it is important that the entire text be read by each individual and any misunderstandings discussed and resolved. A schedule should be decided upon regarding when, where and for how long the sessions will be held and who is going to be the subject and who the instructor or assistant. In general, many of these questions are best resolved by the individuals concerned and mutual agreement between all parties arrived at to complete individual satisfaction.

Following are complete instructions, first for the subject, and then for the instructor. As we have mentioned before, in a mutual situation it is best to have half of each session devoted to one person as subject and the other half to the other person as subject. In this way a corresponding degree of understanding and progress can best be achieved.

AS A SUBJECT

Read or explain this section to the subject. *

■ Make up your mind to be as good a subject as you are an instructor, and put aside any critical thought or comment until the end of each session. You must be able to "let yourself go", confident that there will be no suggestion made, even in jest, that you will have any possible objection to, or the slightest reservation about following. If any such feelings occur you must get them straightened out to your complete satisfaction, even to the extent of changing the relationship or going about it on your own. If you do not have complete faith in the person working with you, it is better not to start at all.

You should understand that even when you are in a profound trance you will instantly wake up if anything occurs that is of any possible danger or that could be a source of embarrassment to you. Your instructor should include suggestions to this effect from the start, and if he is doing

---

* As this section consists entirely of personal instructions to the assistant, only instructions of particular concern to the subject are designated here by the symbol "■".

his job properly he will be doing so. You will know and recognize whether or not this is being done; if not, you should correct the situation to your entire satisfaction right at the beginning.

Do not expect to "feel" anything, except possibly relaxation, as you go into a trance. Let your instructor be the judge of how you have reacted, and put aside any inclination to evaluate or test until he asks you to do so. Remember, as you approach a trance state your awareness and ability to evaluate are diminished, and this is true to the extent that you cannot be aware of, and you cannot evaluate, your own degree of progress until you have achieved control of suggestion and can experience the effects of your own suggestions on yourself.

After reading this book through, as you will have done before assuming the role of a hypnotic subject, you will already have experienced some of the tests and effects that your instructor will ask you to go through again. Follow his instructions and realize that he is doing this in order to obtain information and induce responses for a slightly different purpose now than when you did these things before.

Whatever may be your purpose in developing self-hypnosis, you must put that purpose to one side temporarily and keep it separate from the development process itself! Think of self-hypnosis as a tool that you can use in various ways after you have developed it, but in order to use it you must first create it. You will find it far easier to develop this tool with suggestions that are "neutral" than with those that are more emotionally meaningful, because the very significance of your major purpose would be inhibitive to your progress. This cannot be overemphasized. Build and perfect the instrument. Learn how to use it properly. Then, and only then—use it! Properly!

To summarize:

1. Become thoroughly familiar with the principles outlined in this book.
2. Be certain your assistant is familiar with these principles and will adhere to them in working with you.
3. Separate the development of the technique from the use to which you intend to put it.
4. Follow instructions.

AS AN ASSISTANT

☐ The following instructions are intended for a professional person such as a physician who is working with a subject. However, as has been indicated earlier, practice sessions with another non-professional subject acting as "assistant" may be helpful in enabling both participants to expand their skills in self-hypnosis. The instructions may then be followed by the subject-assistant, bearing in mind that he is no therapist and that his function is purely to help his "subject" to perfect his skills. Think of your part in this procedure as being one in which you are assisting in the development of an ability to achieve rather than helping in the achievement itself.

If, after reading the entire text and participating in the experiments, you have doubts about yourself in the role of assistant, you should either try to dispel such feelings through further reading and discussion or give up the idea of attempting this role.

You must be familiar enough with the entire procedure to retain the over-all concept as you go along, with little or no reference to the text during any given session. The talking you do to the subject during induction procedures should sound smooth and sincere, and you must practice speaking out loud in order to do this.

Be sure you understand the previous statements. It is not necessary for you to memorize the entire text. It is necessary for you to memorize the concept, the symbols and their meanings, the sequence and enough of the speaking parts to do them smoothly and convincingly. You can use notes or keep the book open to the appropriate pages as long as you do not falter nor misstate the instructions. Identical wording is not so critical as is identical meaning. The reading out loud, several times, of the passages to be used just prior to the particular session to which they apply is an ideal way to improve your presentation.

The subject should be sitting in a comfortable chair so you can better observe the responses than if he (or she) were lying down. When the subject is practicing alone it does not matter.

The procedures leading from a waking state to one of hypnosis can be divided into six stages for easier understanding and evaluation of progress. These are "Mind-Set", "Attention", "Expectation", "Conditioning", "Hypnoidal State" and "Hypnotic State".

MIND-SET

Proper mind-set means that the subject has no apprehension about going into hypnotic trance and understands that there will be no loss of control or "will power". All questions have been resolved, and the subject knows that there will be no particular "feeling" of any kind other than one of deep relaxation. From the previous experience with the experiments, the subject has gained a good understanding of how imagery evokes physiological responses.

When your subject is seated and you are both ready to begin, you should instruct your subject:

■ "Move around and settle down to a comfortable position. Take your time. Keep your legs out straight (not crossed) with your feet flat on the floor. Let your arms rest comfortably on the arms of the chair or in your lap (hands should not be folded). Let yourself go as much as possible. Remember, it doesn't matter whether you hear the instructions or not. We will be going over and over them until they become part of your personality-structure. If you hear them, fine. If not, that is all right too. It isn't important for you to go into a trance at this time. As long as you think as much as you can about the things I ask you to think about, that is all that is necessary. Each time I work with you, you will go deeper. Each time you practice you will go deeper than before."

☐ Notice how your subject responds. If he quickly adjusts himself to the correct position it is not necessary to mention that part of your instructions. Emphasizing something that has already occurred may make him critical or impatient. It is important to mention the suggestions about going deeper each time, as they will have an increasing post-hypnotic effect on your work with him and on his own practice sessions.

If your subject has a tendency to nod or answer you in any way, you should gently mention that this is not necessary and talk a little longer to see that this is being accepted.

You should be seated to one side of your subject so you can observe his face and yet not be so close that your breathing may disturb him.

ATTENTION

You must obtain the attention of your subject to the point where, by his reactions, you know that he hears and follows your instructions to the exclusion of other sounds and thoughts. Your next step is to get him to look straight ahead, either off into space or at some object slightly above eye-level. It is all right for him to blink, but the eyes should not waver; if they do, you must talk gently, but persuasively, about it until your instructions are followed.

Typical instructions would be:

■ "Pick out something to look at, and keep your eyes fixed steadily in that position as you listen to my voice. As I continue to talk, you will think as often as you can of 'one thousand one'."

☐ Your subject, having already practiced to the point of physical relaxation (or "1000-3"), will be familiar with this symbol; you will assist by observing his eyes to make sure he is not wavering and by making certain that his attention is directed toward your voice.

EXPECTATION

It is now advisable for your subject to know what to expect. This will serve to alleviate any apprehension about what is going to happen and will also serve as a suggestion for him to follow.

■ "As I continue to talk you will think, over and over, '1000-1', and as you do your eyes get very heavy. When your eyes are nearly closed you will think '1000-2', and your eyes will close, firmly. As you think of '1000-3', your body will relax, and it will continue to relax deeper and deeper. When you reach '1000-3' you will go over the imagery of physical relaxation. You will think of each muscle group as if you were tightening the muscles and then thinking '1000-3' as you let them relax.

"I will go over the entire pattern of self-hypnosis as you are relaxing and I will include a suggestion of a simple nature and work with you on this suggestion as we get to the process of deepening."

☐ If your subject is responding well to "eye-closure" and to physical relaxation, you can proceed with the outlining of the entire technique. If not, you should work on each symbol that appears to need attention. For instance, you can talk about thoughts involving heaviness of the eyes in the following manner:

■ "Imagine there are heavy, lead weights on your eyelids. Your eyelids are so heavy, the harder you try to keep them from closing the more they feel tired and heavy. Imagine tiny threads attached to your eyelashes pulling your eyes closed."

☐ Watch your subject closely. If his eyes show signs of heaviness, you should suggest that he is beginning to blink, that his eyes are beginning to smart and burn, that the more he thinks about his eyes the more they want to close. If you notice a little moisture gathering along the lower lid it means his eyes are beginning to water. He will not feel this as quickly as you can notice it and if you mention that his eyes are beginning to water the suggestion will be very strong, since he will then feel it and be the more readily inclined to accept further suggestions.

Suggest that with each breath he is relaxing deeper. Suggest that he is breathing more deeply and more regularly and with each breath relaxing more and more.

You should occasionally make suggestions that each time you work with him he will go deeper and each time he practices by himself he will go deeper than before.

If after 15 minutes or so he has not closed his eyes, simply tell him to let them close. He is trying too hard to keep them open and evidently expects that "something" is supposed to force them closed. You should then explain that he should think more about the symbol of 1000-2 and imagery of heaviness of his eyes than about using eye-closure as a test. Point out that you will give him tests of this nature when you feel he is following suggestions properly.

If the subject has had trouble developing eye-closure on his own, you must help him with it by discussing the principles involved before you start the practice session, by describing the imagery to him as he practices and, if necessary, telling him simply to close his eyes as you go on through the pattern. You can then, while he has his eyes closed, tell him he is probably deeper than he realizes and that you are going to make a test before he wakes up. Tell him you are going to count from six to ten and that, as you do, you want him to do as instructed, and he will find he cannot open his eyes until you get to ten.

■ Gently touch his forehead and draw the figure "6" as you tell him to imagine the number being written in the center of his forehead. Tell him to roll his eyes upward and to focus on the figure six as if he were looking right through his forehead at it. Tell him that when his eyes are focused in this manner he can try as hard as he wishes to open his eyes but that he will find he cannot! As he tries and fails, go on to the number seven, etc., outlining the number with your finger on his forehead, getting him to focus his eyes and telling him he can try to open his eyes but he will not be able to do so until you reach the number "ten". When you get to ten, do not mention any focusing of the eyes. Simply say "Ten! Now you can open your eyes easily."

☐ Once you have gone through this with him and he is convinced that he not only cannot open his eyes but that the harder he tries the more firmly they stay closed, you can then go on to relaxation to the symbol "1000-3".

Start over from this point and there should be no more difficulty with 1000-1 and 1000-2.

Make it clear that he is to stay on the relaxation pattern while you go over the entire technique and that after you do this you will then have him proceed along with you on the rest of the symbols.

The wording for completing the expectation sequence is:

■ "It is easy for you to put yourself into a deeply relaxed state whenever it is safe and whenever you wish to do so. When you are in a safe, comfortable place, you will think first of the time you wish to be awake, and you will always wake up at precisely that time. You will think next of your suggestion. You will think of your suggestion in imagery of the suggestion taking place and in words describing what you wish to have happen. You will use words in terms of the second person, as if your conscious were talking to your subconscious. Your suggestion will go into effect as you put yourself deeper by thinking of the circle with the X and carefully erasing the X without touching the circle.

"After you think of the time and of your suggestion, you will think of 1000-1. As you think, over and over, of 1000-1, your eyes will instantly become heavy. When your eyes are nearly closed you will think '1000-2' over and over, and your eyes will close. Gently and firmly. Your eyes will stay closed until it is time to wake up. You will not be able to open your eyes until it is time to wake up. The only exception to this is that if there is ever any possible danger or any very important reason for you to be awake you will know of it instantly and you will wake up. This is not apt to happen. So, in the usual course of events you will not open your eyes until the exact time you have set for yourself to wake up.

"When you think of 1000-3 your body will relax and it will continue to relax deeper and deeper even after you can no longer feel it doing so. Deeper each time I work with you. Deeper each time you practice.

"When you think of 1000-4 you feel very peaceful, very tranquil. The only thoughts you have are pleasant, happy thoughts of things you have done or things you are going to do of a pleasant, happy nature. You will think only of the present and the future. The past is over and done with. You think only of pleasant, constructive things. You think of yourself doing, feeling, and thinking in an ideal way.

"When you think of 1000-5 you are so relaxed you have just enough awareness to think. There is the letter X in the circle touching the circle at four points. As you slowly and carefully erase the X without touching the circle, you go deeper. Deeper each time. Deeper than before.

"As you go deeper, the suggestion you have made goes into effect. Any suggestion that is good for you. Any suggestion that is right for you goes into effect as you go deeper."

☐ If your subject is obviously relaxed, breathing deeply and regularly and remaining motionless except, perhaps, for a slight fluttering of the eyelids, you can begin to talk about a suggestion as will be explained. If not, it will be a good idea to repeat the above instructions once more, to suggest that suggestions will work out well on the next session and then to awaken the subject by slowly counting from six to ten with instructions in between each count to the effect that on the count of ten he will be wide awake and feeling fine.

CONDITIONING OF NEUTRAL SUGGESTIONS

"Neutral" suggestions are those that have no emotional content. In other words, there should be no objection or resistance on the part of the subject in effecting such suggestions. Quite often a person may be so anxious to achieve certain results that his over-anxiety becomes inhibitive to progress. Many times this over-anxiety, or impatience, is an underlying cause of his problem, and resolution of it may go a long way toward alleviating the problem. However, resolving it may be difficult to do in a direct manner.

It is best to divorce the development of self-hypnosis from the purpose for which it is being developed until such time as the technique is firmly established. Then, and only then, can it be utilized to best advantage.

This is why we start with neutral suggestions. When the subject achieves the ability to put into effect increasingly complex suggestions of a neutral nature he can then apply this ability with increasing effectiveness toward suggestions that are more important to him.

Suggestions may often work best when you are assisting the subject. When this happens you should repeatedly suggest that your subject can do these things easily by himself. It is a good idea to walk out of the room occasionally after getting the suggestion started so that you can later tell the subject that you were not even present and he did accomplish the suggestion on his own. This should be done discriminately and over whatever period of time is necessary in order to convince the subject he can do as well alone, or even better, than when you are assisting him.

It is not unusual for suggestions to work well while the subject is in trance, only to have them diminish or disappear upon awakening. This difficulty, too, should be eliminated by suggestions that the subject can easily "carry over" suggestions into the waking state.

You must always be positive that suggestions are working well and will work even better the next time. This may seem ambiguous but it is necessary. The more positive you are, the better; however, if something doesn't work well or doesn't work at all, you must be prepared to minimize the failure and encourage the subject in every possible way.

One of the most difficult things about self-hypnosis is this paradoxical situation in which the subject must maintain interest enough to work and practice consistently and yet adopt an attitude that minimizes the significance of poor—or no—results. It is your job to keep his interest up regardless of what happens and to point out that the end result will be successful and worthwhile.

If your subject is obviously relaxed as described above and you intend to go through this conditioning session, or if this is the session following and you have again arrived at this point, you should consider the time involved, which will be approximately another half hour. If you feel you wish to proceed, simply follow the instructions below. If there is any doubt, you should awaken the subject, discuss what has happened and come to a mutual agreement as to whether to proceed or wait until the next session. If time allows, and if the subject reports that he felt completely relaxed, it is better to continue. In this case, the first steps must be repeated to the point of eye-closure and relaxation. Then as follows:

■ "We are now going to assume that you are at the stage of 1000-5 and that we have made the suggestion that your right hand is going to move up toward your face, and when your fingers touch your face you will go deeper than ever before. While you are very deep I will go over the pattern again, and from then on you will be able to put yourself into a deep trance whenever it is safe for you to do so. You will be able to go deep any time you wish. Quickly and easily as long as it is safe. Deeper each time.

"I want you to think about your right hand now. Notice how it feels. Everyone has sensations going on in his hands continuously, but usually we don't notice these sensations. We have no need to notice them. Now, I want you to notice your right hand. Think about how it feels. Think about whether it feels warm or cool. Think about whether it feels light or heavy. Notice whether or not you can feel the pulse beating in your hand or fingers. In a little while, perhaps already, there will be a sensation of lightness in your hand and arm. Your hand will keep getting lighter and lighter and it will be drawn up to your face. When your fingers gently touch your face you will go very deep. Deeper each time. Deeper than before.

"Keep thinking about your hand. Your fingers may have a tendency to twitch or move a little. This just means you are going deeper. This is what we want. Now I want you to think of your hand being a little bit higher than it is. Picture your hand a little bit higher and, as you do, it becomes that way. Now picture yourself writing the word 'lighter' on a blackboard. Each time you write the word 'lighter' your hand moves up higher, a little higher each time. It keeps moving higher and higher with each breath. Picture the image of your hand a little higher alternately with writing the word 'lighter' on the blackboard. Each time you do, subconscious impulses make your hand and arm lighter, and they keep moving up. Moving up. Higher and higher."

☐ The objective here is to keep the mind of the subject occupied with the idea of the hand moving to the symbols of the word "lighter" and the imagery of the hand being higher than it actually is. If the hand begins to move even slightly, the subject is either in, or close to, hypnotic trance.

You must use your own judgment at this point. If the hand is moving up it would be a good idea to continue until it touches the face of the subject and, as it moves, to make suggestions of the subject going deeper the instant it does so.

If the hand is not moving at all it would be best to go over the instructions once again with added emphasis that each time suggestions work more easily and each time the subject will be deeper. If the hand does not move up after the second time around, it would be best to slowly count from six to ten with suggestions of waking up feeling fine and each time going deeper.

If, on the other hand, the subject is responding satisfactorily, you would do well to take advantage of the situation of the hand moving up. The subject is in trance, and you can take as much time to think and plan your suggestions as you need. Your subject at this point is oblivious to time. Simply suggest that, as the hand moves up, the impulses are stronger and it will move more easily, become increasingly lighter, and when it touches the face he will instantly go deeper. Deeper, deeper.

At the instant the hand touches the face the suggestions of going deeper should be more authoritative and the word "deeper" repeated several times. After that it should be suggested that the hand is now getting limp and heavy and will fall back to the arm of the chair (or the lap) and that as it does so the subject will go even deeper.

You can then state very firmly that the subject will continue going deeper as you go over the pattern again and that from then on the subject will easily go into a deep trance whenever it is safe and whenever he so wishes. Tell him that any suggestions that are for his good will become increasingly effective and then repeat the pattern as before. Then slowly awaken him with suggestions of feeling fine.

This procedure of the hand moving up to the face is called hand-levitation and is fairly easy for most subjects, especially when they have someone assisting them. Even if it takes several sessions to accomplish this result, a major step will have been taken, and one that augurs well for further success in more important suggestions. The subject, definitely having achieved the trance state, now has the added advantage of post-hypnotic effects. The next session, whether one of private practice or one with assistance, should be quicker and easier than any previous sessions for accomplishing trance depth, relaxation and a simple suggestion.

There are some subjects who may not react to this hand-levitation suggestion. If this turns out to be so, there are several courses that may be taken.

During the particular session at which 15 minutes or more were spent on hand-levitation with little or no result, it would be best not to mention it further and instead to suggest that each time the subject practices, with or without assistance, suggestions will work better. Then, if time permits, go on with arm-rigidity, which will be described below. If pressed for time, it is best to finish the session with a repeat of the symbol-meanings and then awakening by counting slowly from six to ten.

ARM-RIGIDITY

This type of suggestion is a physiologic one (as is hand-levitation), since it involves control over a part of the body. It is an excellent means of convincing the subject that hypnosis is "working" and will also serve as a means for you to evaluate progress.

There are several factors involved that are all, according to their degree of effectiveness, indications of both progress and potential ability. These will be discussed in order of their increasing significance.

AUTHORITATIVE SUGGESTION is functioning when you bring about arm-rigidity by actually taking hold of the arm of your subject and placing it in the desired position, while suggesting in a firm voice that he will not be able to lower it nor bend it when you count to three.

■ Start off by saying, "I want you to imagine your arm as if it were carved out of wood and sticking straight out in front of you *stiff* and *rigid!* Imagine it is like a piece of wood floating in the water. When I take hold of your arm it will become like a piece of wood—stiff and rigid! You will not be able to bend it. It will feel as if it were floating in water and any attempt to lower it will only make it bounce back like a piece of wood floating in water. Stiff and rigid."

Take hold of the subject's hand by placing your fingers under his hand so your first finger is under the second joint of his fingers and your thumb is on top. Place your other hand under his elbow. Lift the arm slowly into position straight out in front of him at shoulder height while saying: "Your arm is like a piece of wood, stiff and rigid." Pull firmly on his fingers and push up under his elbow causing his arm to be firm and rigid. Then: "I want you to form an image in your mind of your arm being carved out of wood and floating on water. Keep thinking of it this way, stiff and rigid. Now, imagine that you are writing the word 'rigid' on a blackboard and that each time you write the word 'rigid' your arm gets stiffer."

Keep talking to him about the picture of his arm and writing the word "rigid" and, as you do, very slowly draw your hand out toward the tips of his fingers and slowly test his elbow to see if his arm remains rigid. Do not let go of his arm until you notice a stiffening each time you talk about it. Keep suggesting in a low but authoritative voice that his arm is getting more rigid each time he spells the word "rigid" and it keeps getting even more rigid to the point where "You cannot bend your arm! The harder you try the more rigid it is! When I count to three you can try to bend your arm but it will be more rigid. Even the thought of bending will make your arm more rigid. Keep thinking of the image of your arm and of writing the word 'rigid'. ONE...You cannot bend your arm! The harder you try the more rigid it becomes."

If the arm is now rigid and remains suspended as you gently remove your hand, you can go on with the count, and the chances are he will not be able to bend his arm. If, however, it looks as if he is not reacting well, then you must talk longer and try to get him thinking only of the image and of writing the word "rigid". If you cannot get a good response it is best to "back out" of the situation and take as much advantage of it as possible by saying, "Each time we do this and each time you practice, your arm will get more rigid. It is easy for you to see your arm like a piece of wood and to imagine writing the word 'rigid'. Each time your arm will get more rigid. So rigid you cannot bend it." You then lower his arm back to his lap or the arm of the chair and talk as if you were simply showing him what is going to happen later. Tell him to let himself go deeper, go over the symbol-meanings again, and then wake him up.

If the arm stays put and seems to get more rigid each time you talk about it you can say: "TWO...You cannot bend your arm. The harder you try the more rigid it is. It keeps getting more rigid until I touch it. Each time you think of the word 'rigid' it gets even more rigid. Keep thinking of your arm floating on water. You cannot lower your arm. It keeps bouncing up...bouncing up...like a piece of wood floating on water." As you say this you can hold the edge of your hand under his wrist, and as you say, "bouncing up...bouncing up...", you can lightly tap the top of his wrist so it hits your other hand and does bounce back each time. This is very good evidence that he cannot lower the arm and that he will not be able to bend it when you get to three. If he does lower the arm or bend it at this point you should simply say that he was not supposed to try until you got to three. Sound as if he were the one at fault (he actually is) and suggest better results each time you practice.

If everything is still working well, then: "THREE...You cannot bend your arm! Try!...Try hard...The harder you try the more rigid it is. *Stop trying.*" Quickly touch his hand and say, "Now your arm is relaxing. As it goes back to your lap you go deeper...deeper than ever before." Then go over the symbol meanings again and suggest he can do these things perfectly himself. "It is *easy* for you to go into a deep trance whenever you are in a safe place—whenever I am working with you and whenever you are practicing by yourself. Very easy...deeper each time."

You should also suggest that the arm will move "all by itself" the next time.

☐ **PASSIVE SUGGESTION:** When the subject can suggest that his arm will become rigid upon thinking of the wooden image and writing the word "rigid", and it reacts that way while in trance, he can then suggest that he will go deeper each time he touches it to release it. Causing any suggestion to go into effect while thinking of a symbol denotes a better trance ability than the successful "authoritative" suggestion.

Better yet, however, is **AUTOMATIC SUGGESTION:** When the subject can make the suggestion before going into the trance and it goes into effect as he goes deeper, he is demonstrating a high degree of suggestibility and control. Most any in-trance phenomena can be easily put into effect from then on. Many constructive suggestions can be employed with this degree of trance ability.

The ultimate, though, is **POST-HYPNOTIC SUGGESTION:** When a suggestion such as arm-rigidity can be carried over into the waking state so that any attempt to bend the arm only makes it more rigid, and this can be done to the point at which the arm is so stiff it actually begins to hurt, then any hypnotic phenomenon is assured of being possible for this subject.

It should be noted that in arm-rigidity the arm takes on a rather weird appearance which is impossible to duplicate in the waking state. This has been noticed by the author and by other hypnotists. It seems that muscles react differently upon hypnotic suggestion than they do ordinarily. Not only do the extensor muscles become rigid but the flexors too, and this is not possible under conscious control.

Many subjects will carry out this suggestion with amazing ease and speed, even on the first attempt. Failure to do so should not be discouraging, however, because any effect of rigidity experienced during the above procedures is also indicative of future success, even though it may take longer.

Remember, a great number of very worthwhile things can be accomplished by subjects who can go no further than relaxation. Besides, many of these subjects may be surprised at some point to find that, once they have stopped trying so hard, they suddenly have progressed to a more advanced stage without realizing it.

There are innumerable other suggestions of a neutral nature and some may work better with a particular subject than those mentioned so far. A number of them will be listed, and you and your subjects can decide if you wish to practice any of them.

Developing two or three suggestions of a "firm" nature and two or three of a "soft" or passive nature may be advisable if the subject wishes to accomplish things later that could be considered analogous to firmness and passivity. You might say that not only can the subject suggest that his arm will get rigid beyond conscious control, but that it would also be logical for him to plan some future activity, such as making a specific number of sales calls, and be compelled to carry it through with equal firmness and loss of conscious control.

The passive analogy can be made that, as he can cause his body (or part of it) to remain relaxed through suggestion and conditioning, he can with equal facility, upon suggestion, remain relaxed under the most trying conditions.

It is most important that means of releasing any suggestion be available to the subject so he will not have to go back into trance to obviate it. It might be best to start right out by suggesting that any physiological suggestion can be negated by some signal such as touching the area with the other hand. Any other suggestion will automatically be eliminated if something occurs unexpectedly that is more important for the subject.

You should also suggest repeatedly that only neutral suggestions, or those of benefit to the subject, will become effective.

In the two lists that follow are some "firm" and "passive" suggestions that may prove to be of use.

"Firm" suggestions:

Fist-clench: The fingers of one hand curl up into a tight fist and cannot be straightened except upon release signal.

Bent-arm: The elbow is bent and cannot be straightened.

Bent-leg: The leg is bent at the knee and cannot be straightened until signal.

Hand clasp: The hands are locked together and only get tighter until signal.

Vise-grip: An object is held in the hand and cannot be dropped or put down.

"Passive" suggestions:

Floating-arm: The whole arm is light and moves easily but cannot be lowered.

Limp-arm: The muscles remain so limp and flaccid that the arm cannot be stiffened until released.

Limb-body: Body is so relaxed it is impossible to get out of chair until signal.

Weak-fingers: Fingers cannot pick up even light objects.

Weak-leg: Impossible to stand on leg, it is so weak and limp.

There is usually a progressive achievement of any of these suggestions from working with an assistant to performing them alone, from doing them in trance to carry-over into the waking state and from using a symbol to cause them to happen to having them go into effect automatically at some time subsequent to the suggestion. Irreversibility is also an evaluating factor. The suggestion actually becoming stronger upon any attempt to resist it denotes better development, of course, than does a weakening of the effect as such an attempt is made.

The "challenge" described above, in which the subject is told that when you count to three he will not be able to bend his arm, serves to convince the subject that suggestion is working, and each time this occurs it increases the likelihood that the next suggestion will be successful. (This type of challenge would, of course, more properly be termed a suggestion.) The subject is probably not analyzing the situation at this time, and it is just as well he isn't. When you say "When I count to three..." the subject is really not sure that he should *try* to bend his arm *during* the counting, so almost without exception a subject will wait until you get to "three". If your subject is one of the rare exceptions and starts to try during the counting, you should immediately get his mind back to the imagery. You should *imply*, without actually saying so, that he is supposed to be thinking of the imagery and not of bending his arm until you get to three. If such a challenge is made properly the subject cannot "win". After a well-executed challenge the subject should have the impression that he had the opportunity to try bending his arm for an extended period yet was unable to do so. During the counting practically all the emphasis is on "you *cannot* bend your arm" and "the harder you try the more rigid it becomes." For a few seconds only, immediately following the count of three, do you say "try to bend your arm...try hard!" If he tries and cannot do so, you can be more emphatic and safely say, "Try as hard as you can...it is impossible...the harder you try the more rigid it is." After not more than a few seconds you should touch his hand and say, "Stop trying. Your arm is relaxing now. As your arm relaxes you go deeper...deeper...etc."

During the whole challenging episode, which may last three or four minutes or more, there are only a few seconds that are not used for strong *suggestion*. Then, even if he *does* evidence the ability to bend his arm, you should immediately minimize this by saying "We have *practiced* the suggestion that we want to have happen *later on*. As your arm relaxes you go deeper. The next time we do this your arm will become even more rigid."

Now all of this may seem like taking advantage of the subject in an unfair contest, but it is your job to help the subject understand that this is not a contest at all. If, rather than analyzing what is going on, he is following instructions and thinking of the symbols and imagery as you direct him, the suggestion will become effective. He may have "lost" the contest involving the challenge, but he has really "won" the ability to reach a highly suggestible state and this, after all, is what he is after.

There is another subtle but extremely effective device used in the challenge technique as described above, and it should be brought to your attention because the same principle may be used with any suggestion. This is the "tying in" or associating of a new suggestion with one already in evidence. When arm-rigidity or any other physiological suggestion is about to be released, the additional suggestion of going deeper will be "carried along" with it if it is mentioned simultaneously. For example, when you touch the back of the hand of the subject and suggest that the arm will now relax, you actually have the advantage of *two* suggestions that are "working"; first is the arm-rigidity itself; next is the relaxing of the arm, which at this point should be most welcome to the subject. Then, by suggesting that he will go deeper as the arm relaxes, you have a series of suggestions, each one of which increases the effectiveness of the one following.

Although this technique of self-hypnosis utilizes the principles of conditioned responses, it should be pointed out that conditioning becomes increasingly efficient as the subject achieves the hypnotic state. A response that in the waking state might require hours to evoke or to condition to a specific stimulus will under hypnosis require only a fraction of that time.

A time comes when the technique may be used to increase its own efficiency. In other words, the state of increased suggestibility is the logical point at which to induce suggestions that the ability to reach this state will be increased as well as any other desirable suggestions not associated with the trance itself. This is why the subject should be told during every practice session that he will go deeper the next time and that suggestions will work with increasing effectiveness. It pays to take advantage of every factor: conditioning, hypnotic trance, post-hypnotic suggestion and dissociation.

The term "dissociation" has not been mentioned before, and a few comments about it might be helpful at this time. To whatever degree you can keep your subject occupied with imagery or some neutral, mental task while you simultaneously make suggestions, those suggestions will be increasingly effective. This tends to keep any possible resistance from interfering. The use of the alphabet and the word "deeper", as described in chapter three, is an example of what we mean. Another very effective device is to ask the subject to think of the number "1000" and then to think of the next lower number, "999", etc., with each breath, and to continue counting down, to himself, as you make suggestions. After doing this several times—making suggestions that with each lower number he will go deeper, and reenforcing the symbols—it may be found that this is too easy for some subjects. If they do not report increasing difficulty in thinking of each lower number, then having them count down by "threes" or "sevens" may be effective. Inserting the word "deeper" between each number may be advisable. The task must be sufficiently difficult to occupy the mind of the individual subject.

CHAPTER 6

MECHANICAL AIDS

THERE ARE a number of devices which can help in varying degree to induce and deepen the hypnotic trance. These range from very simple and inexpensive to rather complicated and expensive.

A volume could be written on this subject, but for our purposes this fortunately will not be necessary. Mention of a few in each category that are known to be helpful will enable the reader to decide for himself as to whether or not he requires such assistance.

Fixation objects can be of help, especially at the start, in keeping the eyes focused. A simple object such as a thumb-tack, a paper star, a small fluorescent object, a tiny light bulb, a spot or crack in wall or ceiling will give you some idea of the things most often used. Trying a few of them will help you to decide.

One of the simplest yet most effective fixation devices is the flame of an ordinary candle. The gentle movement and changing shape have a fascination for most of us. Imagining yourself as a tiny figure in the flame is quite easy, and the fatigue of your eyes is hastened by the varying glow.

A more elaborate fixation device is the metronome used in musical instruction. The mechanical type with an oscillating hand that moves back and forth with a slight audible sound is fascinating to many, and setting it at a speed of forty to sixty beats per minute is the range found satisfactory to most people. There is also an electronic device of this nature that costs in the neighborhood of ten to twenty dollars. This has a tiny light that blinks synchronously with a sound that is adjustable in frequency and volume. In addition to its value as a point of fixation, any type of metronome can help if you think of your symbol each time you see or hear the stimulus.

One of the most famous devices is the "hypnodisc". Although made in an infinite variety of shapes, sizes, colors and complexities of construction, the basic idea is a disc with a spiral design that tends to pull your eyes toward the centerpoint as it revolves.

There is also the little glass ball with vanes that revolve when exposed to light or heat. This is called a radiometer, and many people find it intriguing to watch as it silently revolves in the faintest of light.

Any of these devices might help you to some degree, and if you feel the need it might pay you to look into them further. They will only be useful at the start, however, and your ultimate results will be better if you can do without them.

The idea that stimuli such as sound, intelligible or not, can influence you in a constructive way while you are sleeping has not yet been fully explored. It is, however, rather obvious that suggestions made by the human voice can help to induce the hypnotic state with resultant hyper-suggestibility. One of the means we use in distinguishing the hypnotic state from natural sleep is to evaluate the efficacy of verbal suggestion; it is evident, therefore, that if any degree of suggestibility exists during natural sleep, it is far exceeded by suggestion made in the hypnotic state.

In the author's opinion the most helpful device of this kind is a tape or record made of your own voice, or a voice of which you will not be critical, making appropriate suggestions that will contribute to your achievement and utilization of the hypnotic trance. A voice that can "think for you" and make suggestions while you allow your conscious activity to diminish can be most effective. The voice of an expert hypnotist is best, of a friend you trust next best, if the voice is intelligently stimulating you toward the hypnotic state while your responses are being observed simultaneously, that is, in person. Next choice would be your own voice making suggestions to you while you are going through the induction technique, and finally the voice of an expert making suggestions in such a way that they do not require synchronization with your responses in order to be most effective.

Tapes or records of this type should be kept in three distinct categories: induction, deepening and suggestive.

Following are examples of a script for each type:

SCRIPT FOR INDUCTION

Note: Subject should be in position as described in chapter on procedure. Any necessary tests on volume of sound and repeat or shutting off of equipment should have been completed. Subject should understand he is not to attempt to synchronize his thoughts or responses with those being voiced.

■ "Whenever you are in a safe, comfortable place it is easy for you to put yourself in a deep trance. (Repeat.) You will think first of the time you wish to wake up, and you will always wake up at exactly that time. You will form your suggestion with images of yourself doing, feeling and acting as you wish and with words or symbols representing your desired responses. You will think of these words as if you were talking to your subconcious. *You* will go deeper each time you practice. *You* are more relaxed each day.

"When you think of one thousand one your eyes immediately get heavy and heavier with each breath. (Repeat.) When you think of one thousand two your eyes close, and they stay closed until the time comes that you have set for waking up. (Repeat.) The only exception is that if there is anything of danger or importance happening you will know it even sooner than if you were awake and you will wake up instantly, wide awake and able to take care of it. This is not very likely to happen. In the normal course of events you will be unable to open your eyes until the time arrives that you have set. The harder you try to open your eyes the more firmly shut they are, as you go deeper. Each time you practice your eyes are tired more quickly than before. Each time you practice your eyes close gently and firmly at 1000-2. When you think of 1000-3 your body relaxes, and it continues to relax deeper each time. All your muscles relax deeper and deeper. When you think of 1000-4 you feel very peaceful, very calm, not concerned about anything for a little while. Just letting yourself go deeper, deeper each time, deeper than before.

"When you think of 1000-5 you have just enough awareness left to imagine a circle enclosing an X. (Repeat.) Your suggestion goes into effect as you go deeper. Your subconscious accepts your suggestions as you go deeper each time you practice.

"When you think of a large circle with an 'X' in the circle, you carefully erase the 'X' without touching the circle and you go deeper, deeper. As you go deeper your suggestion goes into effect."

□ This type of tape can be very effective if good diction and enunciation are used. It should be soft and smooth rather than dramatic. The example given is only to illustrate the general idea. Emphasis should be on repetition of various weak points of your pattern and the tape revised as these are corrected.

It is important that the volume be such that it does not interfere with the thoughts and imagery going on at the time. One way of effecting this is to time the start of the tape after the symbol of erasing the "X" and the idea of proceeding through the alphabet is being used. In this case you should keep your mind on the alphabet and the writing of the word "deeper" so that by keeping your conscious activity occupied, the taped suggestions are more efficiently conditioning your subconscious patterns.

A faint musical background can increase the effectiveness for some people if it does not have too much for them to identify with. The pieces should be such that they can be repeated without seeming to have a beginning or an end. One excellent number for this purpose is the first movement of Beethoven's *Moonlight Sonata*, a piano solo played appropriately well for our purposes by Paderewski.

SCRIPT FOR DEEPENING

Note: You should have all tests finished for volume, etc., and some easy means for starting sound as you get to the point of erasing the "X".

■ "Imagine yourself in a large room with a blackboard along one wall. On the other side of the room is a big window. There are several desks in the room. You are standing near the blackboard and have just finished erasing the "X" from a large circle. As you continue to hear my voice you will write in the first letter of the alphabet, then carefully erase it and write the word "deeper" off to one side; then the next letter of the alphabet and so on, as far as you can. With each letter you drift deeper and deeper. You let yourself go. Each time you do this you go deeper than before. It is easy for you to relax and go deeper. It is more and more difficult to think of the next letters, you are so deeply relaxed. It doesn't matter. You are going over to the window now and are looking at the tree outside. Beyond the tree is a wide lawn with a hedge around it. Beyond the hedge is a field with the grass moving in the gentle breeze. Way off in the distance is a forest, and in your mind you seem to be going toward the forest. As you approach it you feel very calm and relaxed. Not a care in the world. As you walk in under the trees you notice the shrubs and flowers there. It is darker and very comfortable under the trees. As you walk along you come to a hill, which you start to climb. You keep walking up and you begin to get tired, but pleasantly so. Finally you reach the top and you look out over the valley. You look up at the sky and watch the clouds float by. In the valley below there is a small village. You can hear the sounds of people going about their daily chores. The sound of traffic comes to you from the distance. You decide to lie down and relax for a while. You find a soft, comfortable spot. You sit down and lean back and you look up at the soft, fleecy clouds drifting by. As you watch the clouds you go deeper. Each time you watch the clouds you go deeper. The changing, moving shapes of the clouds. Deeper, deeper each time.

"Each time you practice from now on your eyes get very heavy when you think of '1000-1'. When you think of '1000-2' your eyes close and they stay closed until it is time to wake up. When you think '1000-3' you relax deeply and completely. As you think of '1000-4' you feel peaceful, tranquil. Only pleasant, constructive thoughts can enter your mind. You are thinking of the present and the future. What has been in the past is over and done with. When you think of '1000-5' you have just enough awareness left to think of the circled X, and then, as you erase the 'X' carefully, you go into a deep relaxing state. Deeper than before."

SCRIPT FOR SUGGESTIONS

☐ Any suggestion becomes most effective when it is "tied in" with one that is already effective. We often use a neutral suggestion for this purpose. That is a suggestion that has no particular significance or importance in itself. This will be explained in detail in the chapter on suggestion, but for the time being, let us take a suggestion such as "arm-rigidity" for the neutral suggestion and explain how a record or tape can help in tying in an important suggestion with it.

Let's say you wish to improve your ability to speak to a group of people. You would like to be more relaxed and at ease in such situations.

We must assume you have already perfected the arm-rigidity suggestion, which means that after getting to the point of erasing the "X" your arm moves into a position out straight in front of you and becomes so rigid you cannot lower it nor bend it until you touch it with your other hand. Upon touching it with your other hand the arm relaxes and as it does so you go deeper into the trance.

The following script could be used to tie in your important suggestion with the relaxation of the arm as you go deeper. Your free hand should start the sound device just prior to touching the rigid arm so that the voice starts at the same time your arm relaxes.

■ "As your arm relaxes you go deeper than ever before, and as you listen you continue going deeper. Each day you will speak to someone new and hold longer conversations with people you know. You will make it a point to find a little more to say to these people and you will say it with sincerity and increasing ease. You will feel completely relaxed each time you do this and you will find more and more interest in their responses to what you say. It is easy for you to talk with and to people of all kinds. You enjoy it. You feel better each time you greet anyone. You feel more relaxed each time you listen to someone and comment on what they have said with interest and sincerity.

"You will imagine now that you are at a luncheon or a dinner and you are the guest speaker. You remain deeply relaxed because you know this is really an imaginary scene and no possible harm nor embarrassment can come to you. You are speaking to these people and they are listening intently to what you are saying. You are relaxed and speaking freely and effectively. You make a humorous remark and they all smile and laugh in appreciation. You become serious again and they nod in agreement with what you are saying. You handle your topic well. Someone asks a question and you answer easily, feeling happy about being able to convey the information. In answer to another question you point out that the answer, to be given properly, would take too long for this particular occasion and that you would be glad to talk with the person later about it. You realize the audience does not expect you to know or answer everything at this time. You see yourself speaking, acting and feeling in an ideal way, and you know that as time goes on you will easily do this. Each day you are progressing toward this. Each day you are speaking to more people with increasing confidence in your ability. You realize you have been trying to do too much too soon. You would not reasonably expect to go from one floor to another in a building in one step. You also realize that to change rapidly into an accomplished speaker is equally unrealistic. As you would expect to go to the floor above one step at a time, you will now expect to achieve good speaking ability by little increases each day. You will do this easily, a little step each day. Meanwhile when you practice you will always see yourself as you soon will be, speaking in a confident, relaxed manner, to more and more people. Each time you see yourself in an ideal situation you tend to be more and more that way. Each time you actually speak to someone, you realize you are making progress and you speak with increasing ease. You think more and more about the importance of what you have to say rather than the way you say it."

☐ The above scripts are intended to be examples of the types of suggestions used in self-improvement. They should be gently persuasive rather than strongly authoritative. Whenever possible they should point out some reasonable way to achieve the goal in logical and gradual steps rather than to attempt some dramatic immediate change.

The script should point out that most people have problems of some sort and that in this respect you are no different from anyone else. You are doing something about it, and with patience and effort you will soon be the way you wish to be.

Positive imagery should be developed involving yourself doing, thinking and feeling perfectly in the particular situations desired: a kind of projected image of yourself in the near future performing perfectly in situations that formerly would have been difficult for you.

Ideally these records or tapes should be made especially for you because of the many individual differences of attitudes, concepts and goals that we all have.

At this point in the development of your self-hypnosis pattern it is probably a little too soon for you to evaluate your progress adequately and to determine whether or not you need any aid from such devices. They have been mentioned at this time simply because it seemed an appropriate place to do so.

You should complete the procedures outlined in the rest of the book and practice them as instructed. There will be a number of tests you can make, then, that will help you to decide whether or not you need any further assistance and if so, the kind that would be best for you and your purpose.

CHAPTER 7

DEEPENING AND TESTING THE TRANCE

ALTHOUGH A CONSIDERABLE NUMBER of hypnotic phenomena are possible in the light and intermediate stages, there are some that seem to occur only in the deeper stages of trance. Individual differences are multitudinous in this respect. What one person may experience or express at a certain "depth" is not necessarily true of any other person or group of persons.

There is a great deal of controversy among investigators in the field as to the significance not only of trance depth and the evocable phenomena, but also of the reliability of testing and evaluating procedures.

Many hypnotists put great emphasis on "depth scales" which are generally based on groupings of types of behavior of an increasingly complex nature, with a number assigned to each group. The idea then is that if a certain type of behavior is evocable, the subject is said to be at the depth representative of the numbered group in which this behavior falls. For example, one well-known scale uses numbers from one to thirty with a physiologic expression of behavior opposite each number. This behavior ranges from "fluttering eyelids" and "relaxation or immobility" at the lower end of the scale to "amnesia, post-hypnotic negative hallucinations and anesthesia" at the upper end. The types of behavior are then further classified, starting from number one, with five or six numbers representing increasingly deeper stages. "Zero" is considered "Insusceptible", "One to Five" is "Hypnoidal", "Six to Eleven" is "Light Trance", "Thirteen to Twenty" is "Medium Trance" and "Twenty-one to Thirty" is "Deep Trance or Somnambulism".

Another very popular scale uses six numbers with three types of behavior represented by each. This scale is considered less cumbersome and easier to remember and utilize.

Some of the difficulties arising from the use of such scales involve the manner or procedure used in inducing the trance, individual differences in subjects, variations in the length of time spent on a particular suggestion, and the observation that successful evocation of a suggested response is considered facilitative, not only for a subsequent suggestion but for increasing trance depth.

The question might well be asked, "If a subject responds immediately to a suggestion made directly and simply, should he be considered 'deeper' than one who responds only after the suggestion has been repeated in the same or more elaborate form?"

The concept of "depth" and the practical application of scales as used by this group of hypnotists is that if the subject meets the criterion for a specific depth he should then be able to experience or express behavior of a similar degree of complexity.

A considerable amount of time, ingenuity and effort are currently being expended in investigating these scales and procedures. Attempts are being made to "standardize" induction techniques, suggestions and responses, and to evaluative procedures.

Another group of hypnotists places little or no emphasis on evaluating depth of trance. The reasoning is that if the evocation of a certain type of behavior is desired, then that in itself becomes the goal and successful elicitation the criterion. This does not mean that the principle of progressing from simple to complex responses is ignored. It does mean that much more emphasis is placed upon procedures leading more or less directly to elicitation of the desired responses than upon procedures leading to an evaluative response of similar complexity.

Both schools of thought have merit. There are advantages and disadvantages in both procedures. It will not be necessary for the student of self-hypnosis to delve into this question any further than he deems advisable to reach a basis for resolution of his own problems or goals. The main thing to remember is the principle of successfully developing the use of suggestions by proceeding from the less complex to the more complex. This is true whether you make a direct or an indirect approach to your goal.

If you have been practicing the techniques and procedures as described up to this point, you may already have the ability to achieve your purpose in desiring to develop self-hypnosis. If your purpose is similar to or the same as any of those listed in the preface of this book, you may need no further depth and you could go on to the procedures outlined in the following chapters for helping you to attain specific goals. You can evaluate your progress by considering the following questions:

Are you now able to relax completely during the practice of this technique?

Do you notice a significant difference in your ability to relax during your normal activities?

Can you successfully put into effect the suggestion of arm-rigidity or hand-levitation and release it while in the relaxed state?

Can you develop reasonably good imagery, while in the relaxed state, of descending in an elevator, an escalator, or drifting along in a boat?

If your answer is "yes" to all of these questions, you can be reasonably sure that you have the ability to go on to the procedures leading more directly to your goal. If your answer is "no" to any of the questions, then you must practice further before proceeding with either this or subsequent chapters, especially if your goal is in the second group or of a similar complexity.

DEEPENING

One of the most elementary yet effective methods of increasing trance depth is simply to suggest, each time you practice, that you will go deeper the next time. This usually has an additive effect, and if you get in the habit of including this thought along with any other suggestion concept, you may be surprised to find, when you get to the point of testing, that you are going deeper than you had realized.

Another excellent technique is to "tie in" the suggestion of going deeper with another suggestion that is already working well. You can make the suggestion, for instance, of hand-levitation, and include the thought that when your fingers touch your face your arm will immediately become heavy and fall to your lap and that as it does so you will go deeper than ever before. This same suggestion is often very effective when included with the release of arm-rigidity. Once the arm is out straight and rigid you reach over with your other hand, and as you touch the rigid hand you think, "deeper...deeper...deeper". As your arm relaxes and falls back to your lap, just "let yourself go." Try not to analyze or evaluate at that precise moment. Use any conscious energy you have at that time to think of any concept of "going deeper", and sooner or later you will. Remember, as you go deeper your ability to evaluate is diminished. In a way you become less "aware", even of your decreased "awareness". You must wait until later to recognize and evaluate this fact.

An example of what can happen may, at this time, help you to better understand this loss of awareness. A man who had been instructed in self-hypnosis for an important reason had, in order to expedite his learning, also been shown how to condition himself to concentrate better while bowling. Previous to this he had been bothered by the "jibes" of his bowling competitors, and also by the surrounding noises. He reported to me later that "As soon as I let go of the ball there is an awful increase in the noise." I felt it inadvisable to explain this phenomenon to him, as he was greatly pleased with his increased scores (which averaged 21 points per string increase for the season over his previous yearly average).

Obviously, his awareness of "an awful increase in noise" as he let go of the ball was owing to the fact that he was no longer aware of the noise *once he picked up the ball* and also that he was *unaware* of his *diminished awareness!*

This same situation holds true as you go deeper. If going deeper means less awareness, how can you possibly evaluate it at the time?

One more deepening technique will be explained and then we will go on to ways and means of satisfying your curiosity about your depth of trance.

This procedure is called "fractionation" and is undoubtedly the best of deepening techniques. It simply means "splitting", or utilizing fractions, of the total trance period of time. Instead of practicing for one extended period of time on one trance induction, the period is split up, and several trance inductions, each one designed to facilitate the next, are practiced, one right after the other. Three or four such "fractions" are usually considered best.

For example, suppose you plan to practice for 15 minutes on your next daily session. You might first decide that you are going to use this method of deepening and that you will go through two sessions of three minutes each and a final session of nine minutes. The first two sessions will be for the express purpose of deepening the third one, regardless of the suggestion you wish to put into effect.

■ While you are in your "safe, comfortable" practice position, you think, "You are going into a very deep trance for three minutes. You will wake up feeling very sleepy and anxious to go right back, deeper than before. You will go much deeper the second time and wake up even sleepier and even more anxious to go deeper in the third and final trance. You will stay in the third trance for nine minutes, during which time your suggestion will go into effect."

☐ You can then proceed with the symbols "1000-1", etc., and when you feel it is time to wake up, you should count slowly from six to ten and, as you do so, think of being very sleepy. Your eyelids should feel very heavy when you get to ten but, whether they actually do or not, you should act as if they do and go right through the same procedure again. The second time you wake up there should be a significant increase in heaviness of the eyelids and after going into the third trance a greater depth should be achieved. Practice this procedure several days before testing, and then for several more days before testing again. The results should be very satisfactory and conclusive.

Any of the preceding techniques can be facilitated with imagery of riding down in an elevator or an escalator, lying in a hammock, watching clouds drift by, or any imagery of a relaxing nature that has a connotation of going "deeper". Counting down from "1000" by ones, threes or sevens, with a lower number at each breath and thinking of the word "deeper" in between each number, is another possibility. Any of these methods will be helpful, especially if you can, even temporarily, allow yourself to believe they will be.

The time required to achieve a deep trance state varies considerably with different individuals, especially at first. Anywhere from ten minutes to an hour or more is not unusual, but invariably this decreases gradually after once being achieved. With continued practice, a few minutes are all that are necessary.

If you feel at this point that you are not going deeply enough—or rather, after determining this by the following testing procedures—there may be an element of anxiety acting as an inhibiting factor. If this is the case, the anxiety may be alleviated through procedures to be explained in the next two chapters.

As with other hypnotic phenomena, deepening of the trance is more readily accomplished with the help of an assistant. The "outside voice" making deepening suggestions of the above nature while you are going through your practice sessions makes it possible for you to expand less conscious effort, and the deeper responses are more firmly conditioned at subconscious levels.

TESTING TRANCE DEPTH

As mentioned previously, any test for trance depth is dependent upon so many variable factors that the reliability of such tests as being indicative of specific depth is open to question. This becomes even more apparent when such tests are self-administered and self-evaluated.

There is, however, an increase in confidence that accompanies successful achievement of increasingly complex suggestions, and there is considerable value in the principle of developing suggestions along "neutral" lines before working on the problem of major interest. For these reasons we will list several phenomena the successful execution of which will be indicative, at least, of increased ability in the development of increasingly complex suggestions:

1. Inability to open the eyes after reaching "1000-2" and while going through the imagery of the numbers from six to ten as if seeing the numbers written on the forehead.
2. Ability to achieve significant relaxation soon after reaching "1000-3".
3. Ability to experience hand-levitation or arm-rigidity while imagining the appropriate signals (imagining the arm reacting and writing either "lighter" or "rigid" on the imaginary blackboard).
4. Ability to cause either hand-levitation or arm-rigidity simply by suggestions made before the trance, and after "1000-5" with no further conscious effort.
5. Ability to successfully suggest that arm-rigidity will carry over into the waking state and will not release until touched by the other hand.
6. Ability to successfully suggest that "glove anesthesia" will develop simultaneously with hand-levitation and carry over into the waking state.
7. Ability to successfully suggest amnesia for a previously written word or number and recall upon signal.

For all practical purposes the ability to accomplish all seven of the above phenomena should parallel or exceed the necessary ability for achieving any reasonable purpose with self-hypnosis. The ability represented by the first five will be adequate for a large number of purposes.

You should already be familiar with procedures for developing items 1 through 5. Some comments on 6 and 7 follow.

"Glove anesthesia" means the loss of tactile sensation in the hand from the wrist to the finger-tips. After developing hand-levitation the suggestion is made, during a number of practice sessions, that as the hand becomes lighter it will also become numb and will feel just as if it were enclosed in a thick glove. The suggestion should also be made that this loss of sensation will occur more quickly and easily with each session. Many people are able to experience this in one or two sessions. Generally, a feeling of "numbness" occurs in the first practice session and seems to become more profound with each subsequent session.

If you wish to develop anesthesia further, as for dental work, the glove anesthesia can be "transferred" to the area desired. Once the hand is readily made numb the numbness can be made to leave the hand by appropriate suggestions as the hand is rubbed against the cheek or jaw. When the jaw is completely numb the hand can be lowered as a signal for the dental procedure to start. This, of course, should be discussed with your dentist, and he quite probably will be able to help you develop the anesthesia, if necessary. You can also suggest that as the dental work is being done you can watch a movie or experience, through imagery, any other pleasant activity, and you will still follow orders from the dentist as he gives them. The numbness will stay in your jaw all during the proceedings, and there will be no pain or other after-effects. If it is so suggested, there is little or no bleeding from extractions or surgery when hypnotic anesthesia is used, and therefore healing takes place much sooner. The visit to the dental office can actually become a pleasant experience for the person who develops this ability. More detail on developing specific techniques is contained in later chapters.

To develop a temporary amnesia as mentioned in item 7, write a word or a number on a piece of paper before you start the practice session. Make the suggestion, in the usual manner, that as you go deeper upon erasing the "X" you will "see" the word written across the sky by an airplane, and once it is clear the wind will blow it away. Also suggest that as it is blown away it is also fading from memory, and you will not be able to speak it, after waking up, until you look at the paper and read it. You can suggest that at any attempt to think of the word later, you will again see it written across the sky, but each time you try to speak it, it will fade away as it did in your imagery. You must, as with any suggestion, want this to occur and leave the testing of the suggestion until the proper time.

Consistent practice each day with a minimum of expectancy will bring better and quicker results than over-anxiety or trying too hard.

It is possible to bring about a temporary amnesia, or inhibition, so to speak, for the person's own name. Having experienced this myself many times, I should be able to describe it quite easily.

The first time this occurred was eight or ten years ago during a trance induced by another hypnotist. Several experimental phenomena of a simple nature had successfully been suggested, and then the hypnotist told me that I could easily see my name being written across the sky and that as I saw it I would raise my first finger of my right hand to let him know. This readily happened. He then said that as he counted from five back to one the wind would blow my name away. As he said "five... four..." this occurred also. He then said, "After you wake up it may seem a little silly to you, but when anyone asks your name you will immediately see it clearly, as you just did, written across the sky. Yet each time you try to speak it, it will fade away and you will be unable to speak it until I snap my fingers." I recall very vividly thinking to myself that this would not be so. In fact, I thought I would make a special effort to prove him wrong. Nevertheless, as he continued to count backwards it did seem, in my imagery, that the wind blew my name out of the sky and I was watching clouds swirling around. After I had been awakened we discussed the events prior to the suggestion of seeing my name, and I remember thinking that the hypnotist was purposely avoiding the issue. During this conversation I occasionally "saw" my name in the sky and felt I would certainly be able to utter it upon being asked. Suddenly, however, the hypnotist said, "By the way, what is your name?" Instantly I smiled, as I could see my name very clearly, but when I tried to speak it faded away! For several minutes the hypnotist and others present tried to get me to speak my name but the more I tried, the more difficult it became. I kept turning my head slightly to the right, as it seemed to me that my name was written in the sky in that direction. Each time I did this I could see it clearly but, upon turning to speak, it was gone.

When the hypnotist snapped his fingers I immediately spoke my name and felt very much relieved that I could do so.

In the years since that experiment I have seen this happen hundreds of times and have experienced it myself both upon self-suggestion and hetero-suggestion, i.e., suggestion by another person.

I recently made this suggestion to a physician during a short trance session, and even though we had discussed it previously and he had agreed to try to avoid responding, upon my awakening him and asking his name he reached for his wallet, apparently to look at his name imprinted on a card therein. Yet he could not speak his name even while looking at it in printed form.

This phenomenon has been described in detail because it is so typical of what happens with many post-hypnotic suggestions. The subject often feels that it is not going to "work", only to find that it does.

It appears, too, that the building of imagery into a scene involving the "seeing" and "fading away" of the material to be forgotten is more effective than direct suggestion. This is a subtle point, but one that is indicative of trance ability or, if you prefer, trance depth. The less imagery and the fewer repetitions required to successfully evoke a post-hypnotic suggestion, the greater the ability, or susceptibility, of the subject.

You should also be aware that a period of latency often occurs immediately after the subject wakes up. In other words, if tests are made or signals given too soon after the ending of the trance, the post-hypnotic suggestions may not be carried out. If this happens, the suggestions may or may not be carried out later.

In a recent experiment conducted before a rather large audience of professional people, there occurred an excellent example of this period of latency. The subject volunteered to participate, but said he was a "poor" subject as induction had been attempted many times without success. Evidently the circumstances were ideal for him at this time, as he went into a trance very quickly simply upon my request that he stare at the far wall and imagine himself in a schoolroom writing numbers on a blackboard. After only three or four minutes of imagery of this type I suggested, in the manner described above, that he would not be able to speak his name until I snapped my fingers. In contrast to this, I also made the simple suggestion, once, that he would have no knowledge of the number "four" until I tapped on the desk.

Immediately after I awakened him I asked if he could tell me his name. He spoke his name without hesitation. I then asked him to count rapidly to ten and he did this perfectly, including the number "four." I turned back to the audience and rather sheepishly explained that this sometimes happened and only proved that hypnotic phenomena were not mathematically predictable.

However, I suddenly turned and in a rather commanding voice said to the subject, "Count on your fingers as rapidly as you can. Out loud!" He held up his hands and did as requested, but this time he skipped number four! He tried several times and each time he was puzzled when it appeared he had six fingers on his left hand (because he had left out the number "four") and eleven fingers in total. Then, when I asked him his name, he was further confused when he could not say it, no matter how hard he tried.

Upon snapping my fingers he responded by speaking his name rather spontaneously and loudly, and with obvious relief that he could do so. We then had a rather humorous discussion in which he tried to explain his concept of a square having either three or five sides (the number four was still lost to him) until, upon my tapping the desk with my fingers, he suddenly recalled the number four and seemed anxious that everyone know he could speak it.

It was interesting to discover later that this man is a professor who teaches psychology in a nearby city college and that he was delighted with the success of the experiment.

I am sure that the audience believed I had purposely conducted this experiment to demonstrate the period of latency. The truth of the matter is that I was as disappointed as anyone when the subject showed he could recall his name and the number four. It was only by a fortunate coincidence that I happened to think of the latency principle at that precise moment and decided to see what would happen. The attempt could, just as easily, have ended with completely negative results.

Developing this ability to experience temporary amnesia is far easier with someone else deciding the material to be forgotten and with someone else describing the imagery and making the suggestions. It can be developed without assistance, however, and when it is done in this way, is indicative of a higher degree of ability.

From a practical viewpoint the value of this ability lies in the fact that if amnesia can be developed for "neutral" material it will be easy to condition relief-responses to stimuli involving previous traumatic experiences, thereby decreasing anxiety-responses by "reciprocal inhibition". This will be explained in detail in the chapters on anxiety and reduction of anxiety.

CHAPTER 8

TIME-DISTORTION

TIME DISTORTION is one of the most interesting, and may prove in some instances to be the most useful, of all hypnotic phenomena. There are so many ways in which it may be utilized to facilitate other phenomena that anyone interested in self-hypnosis should also be interested in learning about and possibly developing this ability as well.

Although the name "time-distortion" is appropriate in a general way, it is not accurately descriptive of what takes place. A person who experiences time-distortion is actually experiencing a distortion of his *perception* of elapsed time. It is quite possible, by suggestion, for a person to perceive either a greater or lesser number of events during an interval of distorted time than he would normally expect to perceive during a comparable interval of actual time. This sort of thing is commonly experienced in dreams in which the dreamer feels that a number of events have taken place at a reasonable rate of speed and over an extended period of time only to wake up and find he has only been asleep for a few minutes; it not seem possible to him that all those things could have happened in so short a time. Most of us have had experiences in which time seemed either to "drag" or "fly". The former usually occurs when we are anxious for something to happen, as when someone we wish to see is late for an appointment. The "watched pot that never boils" is another example. When we are suffering, in danger, or experiencing anything unpleasant, it often appears that things are not happening as fast as usual. Yet the fact that the opposite is true when we are occupied with pleasant activities should help us to realize it is not the rate at which these events take place that is varying. It is, instead, our desire that changes. When we are happy we are not likely to be "conscious" of time passing by. The desire, if we are aware of it at all, would be for the pleasant experience to continue. On the other hand, if we are dissatisfied with what is occurring, the desire for escape or for the activity to cease would be strong. We would be very much aware of it.

"Time" is a nebulous concept. Most people take it for granted that when they look at a clock or a watch, or even an hour-glass or sun-dial, they are looking at instruments that measure time. This is not quite so. These instruments actually measure space. Let us consider the true significance of the movement of the minute and hour hands of ordinary clocks and watches. First of all these hands are geared together in such a way that when the minute hand makes one complete revolution the hour hand makes one-twelfth of a revolution. The minute hand, therefore, must make twelve complete revolutions in order for the hour hand to complete the circle once. Starting with both hands at the figure "twelve" we have, if the clock is correct, a reading that means twelve o'clock, noon or midnight. Let us say, for the sake of this explanation, that it means noontime. Then the minute-hand must go through twelve revolutions and the hour hand one complete revolution to reach twelve o'clock again, but this time it means midnight. Now, it is obvious that this instrument is more or less synchronized with the revolution of the earth. When the sun is directly overhead the hands indicate twelve o'clock noon, and when the earth turns through one complete revolution the hands of the clock will be once again at twelve, after having shown twelve once before at midnight. The hour hand, then, is a pointer which makes two complete circles each time the earth turns once. The minute hand makes 24 such revolutions as this occurs. The instrument is therefore really measuring *space*. The hands of the clock or watch move over the face of the instrument in such a manner that we can determine approximately how much the earth has turned since the sun was directly overhead. This is called the "spacial" concept of time. The rotation of the earth is taken as a constant and reasonably uniform occurrence to which other occurrences may be compared. When the earth makes one complete revolution we consider that a day has gone by and we have become used to synchronizing our various activities to this repeated occurrence. To convey information regarding a certain event to someone else, we often wish to include "when" it happened. To do this, it is necessary to use some means by which other people can compare the event to occurrences with which we are mutually familiar. The most familiar instance of this, perhaps, is the use of the event of the birth of Christ. We say something occurred before, after or at the time of this well-known event, which is mutually understood as having taken place about two thousand years ago. The number of years, however, actually means that the earth has made a certain number of revolutions since that event took place.

Events that we wish to describe as having a short duration require that fewer revolutions or fractions of a revolution be used as the mutually recognized constant. When we say it takes five days to cross the Atlantic we mean that the trip can be made during five revolutions of the earth. When we say an event occurred a week ago we mean the earth has turned seven times since that happening. The use of minutes and hours is simply a way of comparing the duration of events, or the interval between which they occurred, to partial revolutions of our planet.

The almost universal acceptance of this method of describing the sequence of events and the duration of certain happenings is evidence of acceptability, but it is still a system in which the movement of certain objects through a certain amount of space is the criterion for comparison rather than actual measurement of "time" itself.

There are other concepts of time but they all have to do with comparisons of the phenomena to be measured or described, with phenomena considered uniform or standard in rate or duration of occurrence.

It is not necessary to delve too deeply into the theoretical aspects of time in order to understand what occurs during time-distortion under hypnosis. In fact, many people have observed and experienced these phenomena with little or no appreciation of the fact that different concepts exist. The reader who is not particularly interested in "why" such things happen but wishes to know "what" happens and how he may develop and utilize this ability can easily go on to the descriptions that follow and skip the next few paragraphs.

If we accept the spacial concepts of time as being sufficient for most practical purposes, we can then consider time, as measured by the clock, "actual time". This actual time then becomes the standard to which we can compare a concept of "experiential time" in which we have events that "seem" to occur at normal rate yet may vary in total duration between one episode and another under certain conditions.

The perception of time is just as much taken for granted as is perception of space, motion, color, etc., and, as we attempted to show earlier in the book, our perceptions can be altered without our being aware of any such change. Although we continuously perceive events as occurring before, after, or simultaneously with other events, our judgment of the intervals between certain events can be tremendously varied. This judgment is affected to a considerable degree by the nature of what we perceive, if anything, in between certain occurrences and by the "actual" interval duration. For example, two sharp clicks with an interval of silence in between will be perceived as being closer together in time than if a series of clicks continued throughout the same interval. It can also be demonstrated that we tend to overestimate short intervals of time and to underestimate longer intervals, everything else being equal.

Many of us are familiar with the changes in perception of time that occur as we repeatedly travel a particular route by car or on foot. When we go over a route for the first few times, it seems to take much longer than when we become used to it. We actually may save time owing to familiarity with various factors en route, but this still will not account for the change in "seeming" duration. The same phenomenon can be observed in the case of any intervals that become less "filled" with other activity. Traveling a new route exposes a person to many unfamiliar stimuli, each of which may be perceived as a new experience, so the time interval is "filled" with impressions. Upon repeating the similar experience, the same stimuli evoke fewer lasting impressions to "fill" the interval, and so it seems to require less time.

To a person trying to stay alive in shark-filled waters it may seem that a rescue boat is taking hours to get to him, and yet it may be only a few minutes. On the other hand, the person who is saying "good-night" to a loved one may perceive an hour or more as if it were only momentary.

These are all more or less conscious experiences, and they seem to indicate a sort of contrariness of our mental processes in which time goes against our wishes. We often cannot see how time could have gone by so quickly. Yet, under different circumstances, we cannot see why time drags on so slowly. What actually does happen to "time" under circumstances such as these? It is, of course, unreasonable to think that all the clocks and watches and even the earth itself can speed up or slow down depending upon the circumstances in which one individual finds himself while desiring to be in a situation entirely different. This is especially so when we discover that someone else may feel that time is dragging while we ourselves know it to be flying by. The answer, then, must have to do with changes in our perceptions of this elusive entity, time.

Many of us are prone to think of mental processes as if they were of a mechanical nature and therefore limited to the same restrictions imposed upon other physical phenomena. The ease with which the average person can bring to consciousness any one of thousands upon thousands of thoughts or ideas should be conclusive evidence that the mind is not encumbered by such limitations. Even the speed and efficiency of the finest electronic devices yet devised fall far short of being worthy of comparison to even a tiny part of the human brain. The rest of the human organism is in many ways much more restricted in speed and efficiency that the brain. We can think, for example, much faster than we can talk. We can think of doing anything much faster than we can actually do it. Now when we think of doing something of an active nature we know that a certain amount of activity goes on in the muscles that would be employed if we actually performed the act we were thinking of. This, to be sure, is a slight amount of activity, but it is enough to be measured by instruments attached to the muscles so involved. We also have good substantiation for the concept that an idea tends to generate its own actuality. If an idea in the form of mental imagery can be made to occur with great rapidity of repetition, it would seem reasonable then that, even though the organism cannot perform with such speed, the idea would be more capable of evoking appropriate responses upon subsequent manifestation at a rate to which the muscles could respond.

The amazing possibilities of such procedures have been only cursorily investigated. Yet some of the results already seem promising, as the following examples will indicate.

It is not unusual to have a person who has been hypnotized report, upon waking, that a suggested experience seemed to be of longer duration than the length of time actually elapsed during the trance. This happens many times with no intended suggestion to that effect. The hypnotized subject may be told, for instance, that he is watching a movie, and then, after only a minute or two, he is told to wake up. Now, in my experience, the subject who shows signs that he is watching the movie as suggested invariably reports afterward that he saw a movie for approximately the time allowed, in this case only a minute or two. But if the subject is one who remains immobile, or who has been trained to remain so, he will invariably report that he saw anywhere from five minutes to half an hour or more of the movie, even though the total time of the entire trance may only have been one or two minutes. This is with no suggestion of any alteration of experiential time.

Before we go on to what happens when time-distortion is specifically suggested, there is another interesting way in which the phenomena may be induced. While a subject is in trance he may be told that at a given signal, such as a snap of the fingers, he will be in a fruit orchard and will pick several pieces, examine them carefully and place them into a container; he will count the number he picks up until the giving of the second signal, at which time he will slowly wake up. The time between signals is carefully noted, as is the reported number of pieces of fruit the subject picked. During a subsequent trance the subject is instructed to experience other imagery and then, in addition, he is given the identical instructions about picking fruit. This time, however, the actual time between signals is a few seconds less. Usually the subject will report the same, or even a larger number of pieces. By having the subject experience different types of imagery in which counting takes place, it is found that a considerable increase can be developed in experiential time. The subject reports that everything seems to occur at a perfectly normal rate, and yet it is not at all unusual to note increases of sixty to one, or experiential time of, say, one hour in actual time of one minute. These subjects are very much able to describe their experiences in detail and they report that it seems as if they were really doing the things suggested. Only when a person has experienced time-distortion himself, however, can he truly appreciate the "actuality" of the experience. Especially during the interval immediately following the trance is it difficult to realize that you were only experiencing imagery and were not "right there".

When a person is trained or trains himself to experience time-distortion, the results can be most fascinating. It is almost an everyday occurrence now for subjects to experience hours, days, weeks or even months of imagery in actual times of minutes or seconds. One of the most startling examples of this happened several years ago when a lady who had developed self-hypnosis had come to my office for a final session. She had already accomplished the major purposes for which her doctor had referred her to me, and she wanted to know if there was some way she could facilitate her practice on the piano with the use of self-hypnosis. As I had worked with a number of other people who had been using time-distortion very successfully for similar purposes, I had every reason to expect that she too would find this helpful. After she achieved a self-induced trance, I explained to her that she would see a movie that she had seen years ago, that it would be very clear and vivid and that she would see it upon a signal of snapping my fingers. I made a mistake, which had to do with the realization that I had neglected to give her certain instructions, and inadvertently snapped my fingers before explaining to her about the second signal. Imagine my surprise when she immediately woke up! I felt rather provoked with myself until I noticed her amazed expression, and she said, "Why, that's the most interesting thing that ever happened to me!"

"What happened?" I asked, not knowing quite what to expect.

"I just saw *Gone with the Wind*," she replied, laughing.

"How much of it did you see?"

"I saw the whole thing from beginning to end. It was even better than I remembered."

While I was still trying to figure out what had happened, she was telling me at great length about the picture. I found it hard to believe that she had really seen the whole picture, or even a small part of it, in such a short instant of time. But she convinced me by describing every detail of the opening scenes and dialogue, and continuing with vivid word-for-word reproduction as if she had just come from the theatre. Better, in fact, than if she had. It was clear that she had experienced imagery of the most vivid kind imaginable of a two-and-one-half hour picture in the time it took to snap my fingers—not between two signals; just during one snap!

I thought I had experienced and witnessed some fantastic things before, but this exceeded any previous experience I had had in hypnosis or anything else. Since then there have been many other instances of similar time-distortions, but probably because this one came as such a surprise it has stayed with me all these years. I'll never forget it, nor, as indicated on her last Christmas card, will she.

Although some people who have developed self-hypnosis have to a certain degree been able to induce time-distortion imagery without assistance, it is much easier, and the results are far superior, when someone else gives the instructions to the subject while he is in trance. Once that is established, the subject himself can then induce the effect by incorporating the appropriate ideas in his suggestions.

Anyone who has good visual imagery while in trance seems to respond well to suggestions of time-distortion. I have had no success whatever with subjects who have poor visual imagery, even though they were excellent in other ways. My work on this has been limited to less than half a dozen people, so it is by no means conclusive.

Although time-distortion cannot be utilized in learning new material or practice of anything not already experienced, it can greatly facilitate practice, retention and expression of material that has been read or performed only briefly. For instance, a person who has developed the ability can read a chapter or more of study material, listen to a lecture or practice on a musical instrument while in the waking state and then put himself into a trance and review these experiences in vivid imagery that seems to proceed at a normal rate of speed; yet the entire trance may take only a few minutes. If, however, the person does not understand what he has read or heard, there is very little likelihood that time-distortion practice will help him to do so; but it will help him to retain and recall, and upon subsequent conscious review he may then achieve a better understanding. In the practice of musical or other instruments, manual dexterity may be increased significantly, and coordination of muscular activity with reading may be improved. This is supplemental to practice in the usual way; nothing can be expected through time-distortion alone.

As imagery proceeds at such a rapid rate under time-distortion it is impossible for other physical activity to keep pace with it. This fact makes for a very unique therapeutic situation in which traumatic events may be reviewed with no physical manifestation of abreaction. It is also possible to keep all or any part of the reviewed material below conscious level. Several instances of the therapeutic use of time-distortion are described later in the book.

Regardless of the subject's purpose, time-distortion should be developed with imagery of a neutral nature first and then, only after it is working well, adapted to the original purpose. Overanxiety to achieve a specific result is inhibitive in this, as it is in other areas of hypnosis.

One who wishes to develop this ability should have someone else study the instructions that follow. This assistant can then repeat these instructions to the person and help him through the various stages by keeping records of the actual time of each episode, the experiential time and the "actuality" of the imagery as reported by the subject. A time-distortion ratio of at least thirty to one should be achieved before utilizing the ability for a specific purpose. The following instructions are typical of those given to train the subject, first for neutral imagery and then for specific purposes.

A young woman who had developed self-hypnosis as a means of maintaining a proper diet told me one day that if she could improve her ability to operate a particular business machine she could get a better job. She mentioned this rather incidentally, as if she felt there was little chance of her accomplishing it. She went on to explain that a test was to be conducted one week from that day and that she had been practicing for two months but still made mistakes so frequently that her grade for accuracy would be poor. She appeared to understand the operation of the equipment from both the mechanical and the mathematical aspects, but in trying to achieve speed her coordination declined. She agreed to put herself into a trance with the suggestion that her right arm would become heavy and slide from the arm of the chair into her lap as a sign that she had reached the symbol "X". In a matter of seconds her body relaxed, and in less than one minute her arm slid limply into her lap. She was then instructed:

"You are in a very tall building. Everything is perfectly safe. You are walking toward an elevator. The door is open, and there is a light on inside. You step into the elevator, push the button, the door closes, and you very slowly descend. As you ride down in the elevator you keep going deeper...deeper. There is a window in the door of the elevator, and as you slowly go by each floor you can look out and see what is there. On one floor you will see furniture. On another floor you see appliances and people...salesmen and people buying, talking and moving around. As you go deeper, these scenes become very real to you. You can see everything vividly. You can hear what is going on. You look around you in the elevator and you notice a panel with a number that lights up. It is the number 'ninety-six'. You know you are just passing the ninety-sixth floor because the number goes off, and number 'ninety-five' flashes on. You look out the window and you see lots of clothes...dresses, coats ...lots of people moving about and looking at all the clothes. At each floor you pass, you go deeper than the time before. You keep going deeper. In a little while I will give a signal of snapping my fingers. When I snap my fingers the first time the elevator will stop, the door will open, and you will find yourself in a scene which I will describe to you before I snap my fingers. As I describe the scene to you, you will keep riding down in the elevator, going deeper and deeper. But when I snap my fingers the first time, the elevator will stop, the door will open, and you will be within the scene I have described. Everything will be very clear and vivid to you. You will actually be there. You will actually be doing the things I describe. Although your body will remain motionless in the chair, you will feel in every way that you are really doing the things I describe, and you will complete each scene before I give the next signal. When I give the second signal you will instantly be back on the elevator going deeper. Now, when I give the first signal the elevator door will open and you will be in a movie theatre watching a movie, a pleasant movie that you saw years ago. You will be watching a pleasant movie that you saw years ago. Vividly...clearly...watching a movie... Now!" Snapping my fingers, I looked at my watch, waited about 45 seconds and then said, "Now back on the elevator, going deeper. Back on the elevator, now!" (snap). "In a little while I will give another signal. This time you will be playing the piano. You will be playing a piece that you haven't played for years. You will have a little difficulty with it at first, but you will start over and play it all the way through perfectly the second time. You will be very well pleased with yourself. You will not hurry at all. You will do everything at a normal rate and you will be all finished playing when I give the second signal. When I give the second signal this time, you will be back on the elevator going up. Going up this time when I give the second signal. And when you reach the top floor the door will open and you will wake up. Now, the first signal...you are playing the piano...a piece you haven't played for years...now" (snap). I again checked my watch and waited for 30 seconds. Then, "Now you are back on the elevator...going up...now!" (snap).

After a few seconds she slowly raised her head and after a few more seconds she opened her eyes and gently smiled. I asked, "How did it go?"

She nodded her head, still smiling, and said, "Just fine. It's amazing, isn't it?"

"How was the movie?" I asked.

"Clear as a bell. It was a movie called 'Beat the Devil', and Humphrey Bogart played in it. It was very funny. There was a scene where these men...let's see...Peter Lorre, Humphrey Bogart and two men, I don't know their names, but they were all so evil it was actually funny. They were riding in this very odd car..." She went on to describe this and several other scenes in great detail, mentioning, in passing, that she had seen one scene twice. She got to laughing so much as she talked that the rest of us laughed too, and we spent about half an hour listening to her description of what had been, obviously, an enjoyable experience. Now, this girl had experienced so many hypnotic phenomena that she was not at all surprised, at first, that everything had happened as it had. She was so engrossed in telling us all about the picture that I don't think she even considered the actual time in which her experience had occurred. In fact, she acted just as if she had stopped by on her way home from the theatre to tell us about a movie she had just seen. Finally I asked her how much of the picture she had seen, and she said just about all of it, but there were several parts missing. Not wishing to go further into that at the moment, I asked her about playing the piano. She brightened up, for her brow had been wrinkled in thinking about the movie, and she said, "That was very good. I haven't thought of that piece for years. Why do you suppose I picked that particular piece?"

"What piece was it?" I asked.

"It was called 'Star of the Sea.' My mother used to play it and sing it too. I used to play it when I was a little girl. I haven't thought of that piece for years."

After discussing the experiences for some time, it became evident that both scenes had been very vivid, as was the ride in the elevator. The rate at which she experienced seeing the movie and playing the piano seemed normal to her, and as we talked about the differences between actual and experiential time, she became aware what an amazing affair she had gone through. She increasingly realized that the entire episode had taken no more than six or seven minutes, yet she had perceived at least on hour and a half of events.

She again put herself into a trance, but this time I explained that she could experience any secondary imagery herself simply by thinking of it in her pre-trance suggestion. I told her that when she suggested she would be riding down in the elevator, the ride would always start right after she got to the "X" and that when she was deep enough the elevator would stop "of its own accord", the door would open, and she would be within the scene she had previously chosen. I also said, "From now on, the secondary scenes will increase to such a rate that even though they seem to happen at a perfectly normal pace you will always complete any scene you wish within the time you have allotted for your trance. You can repeat experiences and practice anything as many times as you wish to between the time you leave the elevator and the time you get back to the top floor. These scenes will be clear and vivid, and when you practice you will do everything perfectly." I then told her she would now ride down again in the elevator; when the elevator stopped she would be in her office practicing the operation of the machine for about an hour, and then she would be back on the elevator, going up to the top; she would then wake up. About a minute later she woke up and, as expected, she reported having been working on the machine and doing everything perfectly. She was advised to practice for two or three minutes, four to five times each day, and to do as much actual practice as she could.

I wish I could report, after all this, that she got the top grade in the examination and was given the coveted job. This did not happen, but she did come in third, out of sixteen girls who took the test, and she did get a similar job several weeks later with higher pay than the previous job had offered. This girl continued to use time-distortion in practicing the piano and is currently playing in a much more accomplished manner than her previous talent and subsequent, normal, practice would account for. This is the evaluation in the opinion of herself and of several music teachers.

Not everyone can develop time-distortion to this degree or with such ease. Even a few very excellent hypnotic subjects have not been able to do much with it. Indeed, some of the latter who have tried have had an apparent decrease in their regular imagery; this, however, is rare. Most everyone else who has developed self-hypnosis, if they have good imagery at the start, will experience very significant degrees of time-distortion and, usually, more vivid imagery.

One of the most interesting and gratifying cases I have ever worked with concerned a young man with a facial affliction. I was chatting on the phone one day with a doctor who specializes in cases of allergy. He had been a student of mine some years previously and, although he was an accomplished hypnotist, he quite frequently called me in to work with him on cases of asthma and dermatitis. We were just about to conclude our telephone conversation when he interrupted himself in the middle of a sentence to ask if I could get over to see him that afternoon. I asked him what he had in mind, and he said he had a patient coming in whom he would like me to see. This patient, whom he had been treating for hay fever, had an additional affliction known as Bell's palsy. Although I had heard of this condition, I knew little about it and had always rather vaguely associated it with tic doloureux.

At the doctor's request I reached his office about two o'clock in order to hear more about the case before the patient's arrival. The patient was 24 years old, married, and had been coming to this office for four years to receive treatment for his hay fever, which was pretty much under control by this time. At the age of eight the patient had suffered a severe case of mumps, and, as an apparent aftermath, the symptoms of Bell's palsy had appeared. In spite of considerable treatment over the years, it had continued to the present time. Unlike tic doloureux, the doctor explained, there was no pain associated with these symptoms. Instead, there were facial grimaces and contortions of the mouth whenever the young man attempted to smile or to speak certain words. The trouble seemed to be on the left side of the face, with the muscles pulling in that direction regardless of how hard he tried to control them. The doctor went on to tell me how much this condition was interfering with the boy's desire to become a teacher and that, although he was naturally very self-conscious about it, the boy was willing to cooperate with the doctor in anything he might suggest. At this point the secretary announced the arrival of the patient and his wife.

They were a lovely couple. The girl was not only very pretty but expressed a great deal of understanding and intelligence in her direct and yet gentle manner toward her husband. He, whose gaze I found I had a tendency to avoid at first, was strong-looking and had a ruggedly handsome face—until he tried to smile.

We got through the introductions and I found that they both had some idea of what the doctor had in mind. The young man requested that I not feel embarrassed for him, as he was anxious to demonstrate the extent of his symptoms, and to find out if we thought hypnosis could help him. The doctor very matter-of-factly had him speak various words and letters and made a running commentary on the muscular reactions. At first I could think of little else than the extreme changes in appearance that occurred. This poor fellow could not make any kind of facial movement without his pleasing features assuming the effect of a Halloween mask. Finally I overcame my shock and began working up a mental set for hypnosis.

We decided the first thing to do was to develop a trance and proceed from there. I had the patient focus his attention on his hand, and within a few seconds it was obvious that he was an excellent and cooperative hypnotic subject. Before his hand had moved up off the arm of the chair and upon brief suggestions of hand-levitation, he was in a trance, his eyes were closed yet fluttering slightly, his body was relaxing, the coloring around his temples was lighter, and his hand began to rise slowly but steadily toward his face. He was reacting so quickly and so well that I decided to deepen the trance right then. I told him that when his hand was halfway to his face he could try to hold it back but that it would only move more surely to his face the harder he tried to hold it back. At this point his hand was just about halfway, and the instant I noticed him testing I said emphatically, "Try...try hard to hold your hand back! The harder you try the more strongly it pulls toward your face." He tried quite hard but the hand kept moving up, so I told him that as his hand moved further he would go deeper. I told him to stop trying now and to let himself go deeper and that when his fingers touched his face he would go even deeper and would go deeper with each breath and not wake up until I told him to. I kept talking along those lines and suggested, as his fingers touched his face, that his arm would now feel heavy and that after it fell back to his lap he would find that he could talk very easily if he wished and still keep going deeper and deeper. His hand fell back to his lap and after some prodding I gradually got him to answer simple questions about how he was feeling. He felt fine. He felt relaxed. He felt more relaxed than he had ever felt before. His head was toward his right shoulder and he was facing downward, so, as I bent over to look at his face, everyone else including the nurse, who had come into the room, knelt down and crawled to various vantage positions. The thought ran through my mind that all of us made an amusing scene, fit for a cartoonist who wished to represent what goes on in the modern doctor's office during a scientific procedure.

I came quickly out of my reverie as I noticed a smile! Not a twisted grimace, but a nice, even, symmetrical smile. Apparently there were present intact nerves and muscle fibers which we could develop. I looked at the boy's wife who was kneeling on the floor looking up into her loved one's smiling face, and I saw the tears start to flow as she looked at me with an expression I will never forget. I stood up, quickly helped her to her feet, and said she and everyone else should now go out to the other office while the doctor decided what we should do next. After a brief consultation with the doctor, I suggested to the patient that he would go into a trance quickly and easily from then on whenever it was safe for him to do so and whenever he wished to do so. I then suggested he would slowly wake up feeling fine in every way, and this he did. Upon waking up he stretched and he smiled, but his smile was the same old grimace. This came as no surprise to the doctor and me, and was the main reason I had got the wife and nurse out of the room. We talked at some length and came to a mutual agreement that the results were encouraging and set up an appointment for the following week. This was not an unusual procedure for the doctor and me to follow, since we both felt it worthwhile to spend a few days in discussion and investigation rather than to jump quickly to possibly erroneous conclusions. It was, however, no easy task to explain this decision to the wife, and I felt most relieved that the doctor assumed most of this responsibility. Her anxiety was understandable. After all, it was the first time she had ever seen a true smile on the face of her husband.

The following week the patient came in alone. During that two-hour session there were six short trances induced, with evaluations being made of the facial control before, during, and after each trance. The doctor explained to the patient which muscles were involved by tracing with his finger over the young man's face. The patient was trained to listen to either one of our voices—the doctor's or mine—and to follow instructions as they were given. The conclusion we came to was that during trance the symptoms completely disappeared, but in the waking state they immediately reappeared with little or no improvement regardless of the type, directness or indirectness of suggestions. It was decided during the next few days to see what would happen with time-distortion. The following week this was easily established, and secondary imagery of neutral material indicated a ratio of one hundred or more to one. This procedure took about an hour. We then suggested secondary imagery in which the patient would experience various social activities in which he was talking and smiling perfectly. And then we had him experience "seeing himself" practicing in front of a mirror for "four" hours and observing his image in a pool of water in a pleasant place in a forest. During the last two trance episodes of this session we began to notice some improvement in the waking state, and were very much encouraged. Even the patient felt he was improving after observing his image in an actual mirror. He was requested to practice three or four times each day using the imagery of social experiences and of mirror practice with time-distortion.

During the week following, the wife dropped in to see the doctor and elatedly reported that her husband was making "marvelous" improvements. The next (fourth) session proved that this was certainly so. The patient could smile perfectly and the only problem seemed to be in making "o" and "e" sounds. The patient's animated appearance was so markedly different that it was difficult to evaluate other characteristics accurately, but unquestionably he seemed more confident and assertive than before.

At the end of the seventh session the doctor, the patient and his wife and I had a conference. We mutually agreed that an improvement of at least 80 per cent had been made and that it was largely owing to procedure, on which the patient had more or less standardized, of practice sessions in front of a mirror for four hours of experiential time in actual time of three minutes, including trance induction, and this for three or four times each day.

This was the final formal session. The patient decided he could continue on his own. It was later found that his improvement continued, but at an apparently decreasing rate until finally, about seven months from the start, he felt and appeared completely symptom-free. He continued practice of one episode per week, on the average, for another three months and then discontinued. There has been no relapse whatever as determined through six-month check-ups over a period of four years. One of the doctor's children is currently a student of the former patient, and it is interesting to hear him remark about his teacher's friendly smile.

The possibilities for the therapeutic uses of time-distortion seem to be unlimited. Naturally there are complications and limitations. It must be understood that the previous accounts have not been given with full scientific detail; the purpose of this book and limitations of space do not allow for a full exploration of this phenomenon. There are books available to the interested reader that do go into elaborate detail in a number of extremely interesting and worthwhile case histories.

There is another case in the author's experience that seems worthy of mention as an example of the therapeutic use of time-distortion. The patient, a 22 year old male, was slender in build and moved in a very lethargic manner as he came into my office accompanied by his father. Whenever I asked the boy a question he would do and say nothing for several seconds and then slowly turn his head toward me and speak in a low voice with the words coming in regular but distantly-spaced intervals. The phrases he used were well-structured and indicated a high level of intelligence, but they seemed incongruous because of the exceedingly slow rate at which they were uttered. The patient's doctor had talked to me at some length a few days previously and explained that the young man had a morbid fear of leaving his house unless he was accompanied by at least one other person. He also had, as far back as anyone could remember, a seizure every morning just prior to awakening. These seizures, the doctor said, had been diagnosed as a form of epilepsy called *petit mal*, for even though they occurred every morning and lasted only one minute, they were rather intense while they lasted. He requested that I see if the patient could be hypnotized and, if so, if any psychogenic basis could be established for the symptoms. He cautioned me to proceed very carefully and to keep constantly in touch with him as to what was happening.

The boy's father said he had some things he would like to do and that if it was all right with the boy and with me, he would leave and pick him up later. The boy was agreeable, so we arranged for the father to return in about two hours. It became apparent, after two hours of conversation, that the boy was anxious to get rid of his symptoms; he appeared perfectly willing to answer any questions, and he had no apprehension regarding hypnosis. It was decided that his father would bring him in again the next day.

The doctor called a few minutes after the pair left and seemed a little provoked when I told him that all we had done was talk during the entire session. I reminded him that he had himself advised me to proceed with care and that, for my part, it might be several sessions before we got to hypnosis—if at all. He readily agreed that this was wise, and again asked me to keep in close touch with him.

The following day I explained and demonstrated the pencil, semaphore and pendulum phenomena to the boy, whom we shall call Neil, and he understood and reacted very well. I told him, as an indirect suggestion, that everyone in an hypnotic trance would always wake up feeling perfectly calm and relaxed if the hypnotist gently touched their temples with his fingers. I was really overemphasizing the controls and minimizing the drama of a trance-state in an attempt to avoid any spontaneous regression or abreaction in Neil as he approached the trance. Either this approach had worked perfectly or it had been unnecessary, because a few minutes later he experienced hand-levitation and went into a trance calmly and easily. I used almost continuously a technique of talking and getting him to talk, getting him to tell me what he thought about what was going on, how he felt and, finally, if he could experience imagery of both subjective and objective nature in writing on a blackboard and seeing himself walking across a room. This, apparently, he could do vividly.

That ended the second session, and I reported to his doctor in some detail. We arranged to get together that evening to discuss it further. As a result of this discussion we decided to hold the next session in the doctor's office where actually, and in the presence of the doctor, all the remaining sessions were held.

I had not as yet considered using time-distortion in this case, for I was more intent on establishing a good rapport with the patient and, if possible, finding out a basis for his symptoms. I believed it unnecessary to go back to original traumatic episodes, nor did I think that abreaction of them would be beneficial. I felt instead that if we could discover the stimuli evoking these responses we would be able to condition other responses to the same stimuli. I also felt that any erroneous beliefs, though they might originally have been conditioned during childhood, could be treated on the basis of their present structure if some way could be found to determine what they were.

During the next three sessions Neil talked more and more freely under hypnosis and, at the doctor's request, we began to explore what went on in his mind immediately preceding his seizures each morning. He described a very dramatic episode in which he was being seduced by a girl and, in telling about it, he showed agitation by squirming about in his chair. He also told us about various sexual episodes, and each time he reacted the same way. It was always suggested that he would not recall any of this upon awakening and he never showed any evidence of doing so. One of the episodes had to do with an act of a masturbatory nature which he said occurred when he was seven years old. Another had to do with going off on a drinking spree with an older woman and engaging in wild sexual orgies over a period of several weeks when he was 16. When questioned directly about his avoidance of going out of the house alone, he replied that he was afraid he might meet someone and not be able to resist having some drinks and indulging in sex.

Traditionally this type of case is often treated by the reliving of painful episodes and gaining insight at a conscious level of the infantility of the patient's attempts at adjustment in the light of his present knowledge. This is sometimes an effective approach, and it was what the doctor had in mind, but he was interested in discussing it further.

During waking discussions Neil expressed a broad and practical knowledge of sexual matters as well as a desire to be able to engage in such activity if and when the circumstances were appropriate. Upon questioning, he revealed no knowledge of what he had told us in his trance regarding his thoughts and dreams prior to seizures. But he did tell us about the episode with the older woman and several other incidents of a similar nature. When asked how he regarded the idea of going outside alone, he said he could not think about it at all. He would just begin to shake when the idea occurred; he could not bring himself to go out of the door alone.

The following weekend I was visiting the doctor at his home, and at this time we talked for several hours about different theories of hypnosis; I told him my theory about mental imagery being subject to principles of conditioning. I am always delighted to expound on this to a professional man to see if it can stand up under scrutiny. The doctor was intrigued with this concept and wondered how it might apply to the development of Neil's symptoms. I then mentioned time-distortion, a subject new to the doctor, and this we discussed for an hour or more. After dinner that evening we evolved a plan that included some elements of my theory as well as the concept of time-distortion. We reasoned that if Neil could remain relaxed during enough repetitions of imagery containing stimuli that normally made him anxious, then perhaps relaxation-responses would be conditioned to these stimuli in the waking state and dominate the anxiety-responses.

Whether or not this reasoning was correct we may never know. But, correct or not, the plan certainly worked.

Monday afternoon Neil's father dropped him off at the doctor's office. In a few minutes he was in a deep trance. We developed time-distortion, using very carefully selected secondary imagery that we felt would be of a neutral nature to Neil. He turned out to be one of those perfect subjects who can experience weeks of imagery in actual time of a few seconds.

It only took about three quarters of an hour to establish this fact, and all three of us were pleased with the results. Neil was more interested in this than in anything we had done previously. This was the first time he was allowed to recall any of the trance events, and it fascinated him completely.

We then put him back into a deep trance (we never did, of course, teach him self-hypnosis), and the doctor and I took turns talking to him and explaining exactly what was going to happen. We told him that there would be three signals and that he would actually be doing the things we would suggest immediately upon each signal. We spent a good half-hour going over the instructions of how vivid everything would be, how long and over what periods of experiential time, how relaxed his body would remain. We also said that he would not remember anything upon awakening but would feel as if a great weight had been lifted from him and he would feel really wonderful from then on. We went over the instructions in minute detail, but *we did not describe the secondary imagery*...until I said, "Now, when I give the first signal you will review everything that ever happened that made you feel guilty, ashamed or fearful, and you will look at these things, then, in the light of your present knowledge. NOW!" (snapping my fingers). I said this distinctly but very rapidly and then started to look at my watch, but a motion of Neil's body caught my eye. I was startled and then concerned as I noticed his body stiffen. His breathing was normal but his arms were stiff at his sides and his legs had straightened; this was most unusual, as he had always previously remained limp and relaxed during every episode. The doctor was watching him intently but seemed more interested than concerned about him. We had planned to wait three minutes on this phase, a prolongation which was really the doctor's idea and a concession on my part because of the abreaction similarity. I was somewhat upset by Neil's appearance and I didn't wait any longer. It probably was no more than a minute after the first signal when I said, "Now, when I give the next signal you will relax and go deeper. Your mind will be a blank and you will feel wonderfully relaxed. NOW!" (snap). He relaxed immediately. And so did I. I looked at the doctor and he smiled and nodded his head. I could tell by his expression that he had been somewhat amused by my concern.

After a wait of two minutes I said to Neil, "Now, on the next signal you will experience six months of pleasant and normal activity including sleeping, dreaming, waking each morning feeling fine, going out to all kinds of places with others and alone, doing everything you would like to do each day for six months, and when you have finished you will slowly wake up. NOW!" (snap). There was no change in Neil's appearance that I could observe for over three minutes. He then began to stir and gradually woke up.

He was smiling as he stretched his arms and looked from me to the doctor, who asked him how he felt. Neil nodded and said, "Just wonderful!", and he said it quickly and emphatically, as he had never done before. He then asked, "What happened?", as he smiled and looked from one to the other of us again. I asked him what he thought had happened, and whether or not he remembered anything at all. He answered, "I don't remember a thing, but I sure feel as if a great weight has been lifted!" The doctor and I glanced at each other. This was one of the phrases I had used while he was in trance. I studied his face to see if he was joking with us, but he seemed to be sincere enough, so I asked him a few more questions, but he said he had no recall whatever of the trance events. The doctor asked him if he would like to know what had happened, but he said he was more interested in "drinking a coke or something." The doctor asked him if he would like to go down the hall to the coke machine and bring us all one. He responded by getting up and doing so. When he returned, his father came in the office door and we could see he was amazed to have seen Neil coming up the corridor by himself.

We set up another appointment, but it wasn't necessary. The doctor has been in constant touch with Neil and his family ever since, and there have been no seizures and no fear whatever regarding going anywhere alone. The doctor and I have often thought, though we have never done so, that it would be interesting to put Neil in a trance and have him tell us what happened.

Six months after the final session I received a telephone call from Neil, telling me, rather triumphantly, that he had taken and passed the test and now had his driver's license.

CHAPTER 9

IMPROVEMENT OF RECALL

SELF-HYPNOSIS may be used effectively as an aid to learning, retaining, recalling and expressing. There are, however, certain limitations, and it is just as important to have a clear understanding of what may not be expected as of what may reasonably be expected to occur upon developing these techniques.

First of all, a major characteristic of the hypnotic state is a selectively uncritical acceptance of suggestion. The abilities to evaluate and to reason are inhibited. Creativity, although it may seem to be tremendously enhanced, is generally confined to knowledge and concepts that have already been learned. New combinations and perhaps applications may be discovered for the elements of recalled material, but, as is true of the waking state, true creativity is usually contingent on the acquisition of new and unique elements. This does not mean that self-hypnosis cannot bring forth worthwhile results; quite the contrary. It can help to release talents and abilities that the person may never have realized he possessed. It can also help to develop better expression of those abilities. The point is that the knowledge, talent, ability or whatever material is being affected, must already be there. Self-hypnosis, then, can greatly facilitate the resynthesis, recall and expression of this material.

The student who wishes to improve his study habits and increase his grades will find self-hypnosis of tremendous help if he uses it properly and does not expect unrealistic results in areas where the techniques do not apply.

Self-hypnosis should be developed for use at some future and indefinite date. Those who suddenly decide they are going to develop it and "try it out" for the exam "next week" will invariably be doomed to disappointment. It is absolutely imperative that self-hypnosis be developed with no pressure for accomplishment by any deadline or date. The development procedures must be practiced as unallied activity until neutral suggestions are evoking the appropriate responses. Then and only then can the technique be applied to the specific purpose with reasonable predictability for success.

Almost always the student will experience some benefit as soon as relaxation responses carry over to his study and classroom periods. To suggest this or become over-anxious about it will only inhibit over-all progress.

Once the pattern is developed, there is a logical and systematic procedure to follow. This may be thought of as three distinct phases. Learning, Recall and Expression. "Learning" as intended here means not only absorbing knowledge but also "learning how to learn".

Interest is an important factor in this first phase. There must be sufficient incentive to learn each individual subject in the course so that interest is initiated and maintained. If the student recognizes a lack of interest in one or more subjects, he should find, if possible, some way to correct the situation. Revision of the curriculum may be possible. If not, emphasis should be placed on as many attractive elements as possible: the credits carried, the associative value to subjects of more interest, possible future value, even the value it has as an obstacle to be overcome, looking forward to the relief of having finished it. There are all sorts of ways, both positive and negative, by which interest may be developed, and each one can be enhanced with suggestion through self-hypnosis. Both direct suggestion and imagery of the attractive aspects should be used.

Attention is another important factor. This includes devoting sufficient time and energy to learning as well as concentration during study and lecture periods. Again, direct suggestions and imagery for a few minutes each day can eliminate procrastination and compel the student to follow through on the following day and night with the schedule he has set for himself. Students who do this have reported to me that even the most disturbing distractions have little or no effect. Some have told me that any such persuasions only make them adhere more firmly to their suggested schedule. It is not at all unusual, if so suggested, for sounds, peripheral activities and all stimuli not pertinent to the subject under study not only to fade from perception during specified periods, but actually to increase concentration-ability during such periods.

Understanding is next. It is possible to "learn" material without understanding it, and with certain types of information this may be sufficient. Lists of items which must later be recalled with little or no requirement as to meaning can be read or otherwise studied and then reviewed over and over by means of time-distortion in the trance. This will facilitate retention and recall but will add nothing whatever to understanding. To whatever degree meaning and understanding are essential to the material under study, these must be accomplished by waking study. Understanding, itself, facilitates retention and recall, as there are then more association patterns to reenforce the conditioning. It is often helpful, however, to learn smaller amounts of material to the point of understanding and then to review them under hypnosis. Segmented practice such as this makes it much easier to understand each segment, and then the total material can be reviewed more effectively.

In "rote" learning there is usually much less understanding involved than in trial-and-error learning, problem-solving and the learning of skills. Although the principles of conditioning responses can be shown to apply in each of these types of learning, there are major differences in the manner in which the responses become conditioned, and differences are also apparent in the manner in which such material is recalled.

In rote learning, such as of a list of names, recall is dependent upon an initial stimulus that will evoke imagery of the first item on the list. This item then becomes the stimulus for evoking the next item, etc. Repetition is the major factor in this type of learning, and if the list is extensive the technique of segmentation mentioned above will be most helpful. As each item on the list becomes interchangeable as a stimulus-response entity, the material is considered "learned" even though there may be little meaning associated with it. We are all familiar with situations in which a person reciting such material must "start over" if he has trouble part way through the recitation. This, obviously, is because he has lost the stimulus value of one or more items, and the response of the next item cannot be evoked without it. With repetition the entire list becomes increasingly evocable as a response to the initial stimulus, and parts of it can be "held" intact while the lost item is being sought for and the continuity resumed when it is found.

In the problem-solving type of learning there are usually logical procedures and formulas to be committed to memory along with concepts for applying these to different problems and situations. Practice under hypnosis will help to establish and retain the memory "records" of this material so that recall is easier, and more mental energy, therefore, can be devoted to the application of this learning in the waking state. The discovery of new applications for such material while in hypnotic trance is possible with some subjects, if there is sufficient experiential material to which the newly acquired learning may be compared.

Trial-and-error learning is a situation in which the student is exposed to a variety of stimulus patterns and has no way of telling which is correct until he tests or tries one pattern or part of one pattern at a time and progresses through the available patterns until he "guesses" the correct one with more frequency than the others. This too is conditioned-response learning. For example, the instructor may have a number of cards on which there are several symbols. He may arbitrarily choose the "correct" stimulus to be that evoked when the symbol is on the right-hand side when shown to the student. Now, there is no possible way for the student to solve this problem with one exposure. If he happens to pick the right or "correct" situation on the first try, it can only be a guess, and he has nothing to compare the situation with until successive exposures are tried. After a number of exposures the correct response to the "correct" stimulus-pattern must occur with sufficient frequency to make this pattern stand out against the "wrong" responses in order for the student to know he is correct. If the student says "wrong" to the "correct" pattern he must be told his answer was wrong in order for him to gain anything from the exposure. If waking practice has proceeded to the point where sufficient numbers of exposures have been made, and yet the student is not yet positive about the correct answer, then practice under hypnosis can be helpful. This help would not come as a result of using reason or logic, however. It would be owing to the increased conditioning through repetition of the correct response to the correct stimulus pattern—that is, saying the pattern is correct when it is correct and saying it is wrong when it is wrong—until recognizable contrast develops.

We have already touched upon the learning of skills in the case of the girl practicing the operation of office equipment and that of the girl who uses time-distortion for practice on the piano. As skills involve coordination of sensory stimulation, or imagery, and muscular activity, it is obvious that time-distortion practice should be very helpful. The ability of imagery to evoke neural activity in appropriate muscle groups is well substantiated. Even though the activity is a "miniaturization" of that which would occur during actual practice, the great number of repetitions possible with time-distortion has an additive effect during shorter intervals of actual time.

Under hypnosis and later in waking practice there is much less inhibition of expression. Although this fact may be more pertinent to our later discussion of expression, it is also important here to the extent that improvement of expression may be considered part of learning.

Many people use imagery while in a self-induced trance for repeated practice of recently acquired knowledge and partially-developed skills. As long as they know what they wish to achieve, to the extent that they can include the improved concept in their suggestions, the practice will be effective. After the use of imagery in which ideal performances are experienced, practice in the waking state reflects improvement toward the ideal ability evidenced in the imagery. If the person has not learned enough about the particular skill he wishes to develop to know what constitutes an ideal performance, he cannot very well make appropriate suggestions for this type of practice.

Learning is much more efficient when the student is wide awake and alert than when he is tired and drowsy. Wider ranges of concepts can be perceived. Logic and meaning are more easily understood. Attention is more easily maintained.

Consideration should be given to adjusting waking habits for the greatest assimilation of knowledge along with self-hypnotic suggestions that these new habits will be easily acquired and engrained.

Recall is the next area for discussion, and it too is interrelated with and interdependent upon other factors. In the learning of complex concepts, recall ability plays a major role. The greater the ease with which conceptual elements can be brought to mind, the more energy is available to manipulate and construct the concepts. Although learning, as stated above, is more efficiently acquired in a state of full awareness, recall is more efficient in relaxed states. Tension and over-anxiety are inhibiters. Confidence and relaxation are facilitative.

In the use of self-hypnosis for developing recall, the suggestions should first be toward relaxation under specific conditions, as during exams, and then toward recall of simple and neutral material. Knowing that the material has been learned and believing that it can easily be recalled will help in developing relaxation during recall periods. This statement may seem ambiguous, but it is true. The more confidence a student has, the more relaxed he remains during tests and recitations. The more relaxed he feels, the better the recall. When practice is performed under hypnosis, the recall suggestions should be for neutral material, since there would then be less inhibition owing to over-anxiety. As the ability for recall develops in this type of material, confidence should increase proportionately so that more and more essential material can be recalled. This initiates a positive cycle in which each factor contributes toward facilitation of the other factors.

Finally, expression of the recalled material is essential. The student who tightens up during exams or recitations can benefit from ideal practice with time-distortion and waking practice of speaking out loud, in private if necessary, and then gradually developing more assertiveness by speaking to other people in increasingly larger groups.

Increases in these abilities generally occur slowly or in random fashion. That is, there may be slight improvement noticed almost daily or more dramatic improvement at times when it is least expected. Suggestions made for recall of specific material may not seem to work for a few days and then will spontaneously occur with increasing frequency and under better control as to suggested time of recall. Many students report having made suggestions for recall of material for a specific examination with little or no success only to have the material "pop into their minds" a day or two later when they no longer needed it. When this happens, it will usually occur with increasing proximity to the time suggested until it is finally under full control.

I have had many people come to me seeking aid to the recall of specific information: forgotten names, dates, combinations to safes, locations of various objects, and events of different kinds. The percentage of successful recall, in my experience, is approximately fifty per cent during the first session, sixty-five during the second, and seventy-five to eighty during the third. From then on, due to a number of factors, further efforts seem to be wasted. Sometimes, however, those with more than three sessions have called later to tell me that the information "came to them" at a subsequent time.

The use of self-hypnosis for improving recall abilities associated with sales talks, lectures, sermons, scripts and acting, involves the same procedures as outlined above. The salesman may also wish to overcome procrastination. This he can do by making suggestions each day for following a prepared schedule for the next day's activities: the time he will start out, the number of calls, the type of sales talk, etc. Many salespeople report that they not only make more and better sales calls and talks, but also feel more refreshed and confident during the working day and when they finish at night.

When self-hypnotic ability reaches the point that arm-rigidity can be successfully carried over into the waking state, it is helpful to create an analogy between this and the firmness of resolve needed to carry out a desirable program. The subject reasons to himself, "When your arm, by suggestion, becomes so rigid that you cannot bend it no matter how much conscious effort is expended, the suggestion that you will not be able to deviate from your suggested schedule will be equally effective."

Another type of suggestion that helps to overcome procrastination is one in which some act, such as picking up a book, is involved. The subject simply suggests that after he comes out of the trance he will not be able to resist picking up a certain book. With practice, resisting this suggestion becomes close to impossible; that is, upon waking up, the subject tries as hard as he can to resist picking up the book, but invariably he finds he must do so. When his suggestions are working this well, he can then be sure that if he suggests in the same way that he is to make eight calls the next day, he is going to find it equally difficult not to do so.

A number of law-enforcement agencies throughout the country are now using hypnotic techniques to obtain factual information from witnesses and to aid amnesia victims in recovering their memories. In the former cases, the recalled material is not admissible in most courts, but this often does not matter. Frequently the recovery of information that is not needed in court may facilitate gathering other material that is admissible yet previously had not been known or available. We must remember that the truth is not always the essence in recalled material, since a person may fantasy or lie as easily as in the waking state.

A frequent occurrence of recall under hypnosis is typified by the following case. A local businessman recently requested that I help him recall the combination of his wall safe at his home. He had recently changed the combination and for a few days had no difficulty remembering it. One day, however, he attempted to open the safe and, upon failing to do so, realized he was trying the old combination. After that he could not recall the correct one. He had recorded the old combination by writing it backwards on a slip of paper, but he had neglected to do this with the new one.

That he was an excellent subject for hypnosis was evidenced by his achievement of a medium trance within a few minutes of induction. I suggested that he would "see" himself working out the new combination and opening the safe several times by using it. He indicated that he had completed this suggestion by raising his hand, as we had previously agreed upon. After I awakened him, he promptly wrote down the new combination and was extremely pleased that it had been so easy. He called me later in the day to say that he was very much puzzled because, although he was certain the combination was the correct one, it wouldn't work. I was equally puzzled, and we arranged for him to come in the following day to try again. Instead, he called the next morning to tell me that during the night the answer had come to him: The combination was correct except that, for some reason, it was reversed. He had gotten out of bed to try it and had immediately opened the safe. This event still troubles him, as he is positive the combination was as he first recalled it. Clearly, he is mistaken; some trace of the thinking that prompted him to write down the old combination in reverse order was probably interfering with his recall. This sort of thing happens rather frequently.

Occasionally there is a seeming "contrariness" in certain suggestions made to some subjects. I was working with an elderly lady at one time for the purpose of helping her to recall where she had hidden some papers. During the induction I noticed that each time I suggested lightness of her hand, it seemed to become heavy instead. I then used Erickson's technique of "confusion" in which a number of suggestions are repeated and then, as if by mistake, some of them are reversed. This is done rather subtly until the subject is, without realizing it, using his own resistances to the advantage of the hypnotist. After suggestions that her right hand would continue to get light, her left hand heavy, her body lighter, her legs heavier, and that she would have difficulty keeping her eyes focused on her hand, I casually said, "Your right hand is very *heavy* now, your body lighter, legs heavier, etc." Finally her right hand slid off the arm of the chair into her lap and her eyes closed as she went into the trance. I made suggestions that she would easily go into a deep trance again, if she wished to, and then, to see what would happen, I told her that after she woke up she would have no particular interest in recalling where she had hidden her papers. Afterwards, this seemed to be so. She told me she had changed her mind and, as she was leaving the office, she casually remarked, "If I happen to run across the papers I shall let you know."

Several days later I called her to ask how she was feeling. She said, "Very well, thank you." Then, "Oh, by the way . . . I found those papers I was looking for."

"That's interesting," I replied. "When did that happen?"

"One-half hour after I left your office," she answered, rather crisply. In a surprised tone I said, "You told me you would call me if you found them." Very matter-of-factly she declared, "I figured if you were interested enough you would call, sooner or later." And that, as far as she was concerned, was that.

CHAPTER 10

OBESITY

• IN THEIR NATURAL STATE most animals are not able to acquire food easily or continuously, yet to sustain life the metabolic processes must go on without interruption. For the animal to survive and to continue functioning adequately during periods when food is unavailable, some sort of reserve is necessary in the form of either consumed or unconsumed food. In order to accumulate this reserve, nature endowed all animals with the ability to consume and store internally more food than is required at any given moment. This is what is called a physiologic reserve, and it consists of internally stored energy and sources of potential energy.

Man, to a greater degree of efficiency than any other animal, has acquired the additional ability to store *external* reserves of food. In human cultures where obesity is considered a problem, it is usually the case that the acquisition of food reserves is not so much of a problem. Unfortunately, in cultures where obesity is not a major problem, the acquisition of food reserves generally is.

Although it is obvious that the ingestion of food is highly correlated to body-weight, the problem of controlling obesity is not solved simply by controlling ingestion. The problem is far more complex than that. Due to a number of factors that may not be so readily apparent, the person who is overweight usually experiences great difficulties in effecting and maintaining weight reduction through changes of diet only. Those factors which were responsible for the increased desire to eat are often overlooked, yet, unless these too are changed, the results from dieting are rarely satisfactory. The common-sense attitude that "If caloric intake exceeds caloric output, a person will gain weight; and if the process is reversed, weight will be lost," is an oversimplification of a complex problem and does not take into consideration the reasons *why* the caloric imbalance occurs.

It seems evident that the person who eats too much must have developed stimulus-response patterns associated with eating that dominate those associated with maintaining normal weight and size. Changes in these patterns, then, are essential in addition to any changes in diet for the accomplishment of weight reduction, if it is to be significant and if it is to be satisfactorily maintained over a prolonged period of time. Stimuli must be found that will evoke responses associated with weight reduction that can dominate those associated with excessive eating. The *desire* to lose weight must be strengthened, and the desire to overeat must be diminished.

Although there is considerable controversy over the exact causes of obesity, it is generally agreed that most overweight persons do have underlying emotional problems. The question arises: Are the emotional problems caused by the excessive weight, or is the excessive weight caused by the problems?

The belief that glandular dysfunctions are largely responsible has diminished considerably in the last few years, with much greater emphasis now being placed on caloric intake. There are infinite numbers of reducing drugs, diets and "methods" being advertised, ranging from chewing gums and candies, day-by-day menus and liquid meals of specific caloric value, to various means for providing "effortless exercise", such as rowing machines, vibrators, motionless bicycles and gadgets that electrically contract the muscles.

Unfortunately, most reducing methods concentrate on one factor to the exclusion of other factors, and the one emphasized may have little or nothing to do with the real basis for the excess weight in a particular individual.

To alter one's diet indiscriminately because of a newspaper or magazine article is a serious mistake, and in any case the attempt will very likely prove ineffective. Such articles usually describe a "miracle" diet by which some individual or group lost weight in a certain number of days. Rarely, if ever, are there any follow-up articles to show what happened six months or more afterward.

The most inadvisable of all the methods are those involving the eating or drinking of one specific preparation. To expect a candy, pill or reducing "cocktail" safely to bring about long-term weight reduction is most unrealistic thinking. Such highly-touted remedies often contain drugs that may actually be detrimental to physiologic processes, and even if they are perfectly safe they do not affect the psychologic factors that invariably are associated with such conditions.

Methods involving effortless exercise may be a good way to stimulate muscles in a person who is physically incapacitated, but as a means of weight-reduction for a person who is able to walk about, they are close to being ridiculous. There is little possibility of harm from such devices, but approximately the same possibility exists for obtaining any significant loss of weight.

Weight-reduction is, to repeat, a problem involving many factors, and any method that does not include consideration of these factors on an individual basis is fairly apt to fail.

Now, even the most ardent exponent of methods advocating exercise or emotional stabilization will not argue against the fact that food intake must have some relationship to weight. After all, if we do not eat, we cannot gain weight; but without food, we cannot live, either. It is rather evident, then, that we must continue to eat. The question naturally arises as to whether excess weight is related to the total intake of food or whether it is more closely associated with the amount of nourishment the body absorbs from whatever food is eaten. As the nutritional value of different foods is known to vary greatly, it would appear that certain foods can be eaten in larger quantities than others, and yet the nutritional value would remain the same.

It is also recognized that volume or "bulk" is an important factor, not only in providing sufficient mass adequately to stimulate the various functions in passing through the alimentary system, but also in producing "substance" that is associated with reducing feeelings of hunger. Many diets overlook this latter principle. Their nutritional value may be sufficiently low to bring about loss of weight, but the bulk is also low and insufficient to satisfy hunger and emotional needs. Many overweight people like to eat "to have something to do". In others, overeating may be largely an automatic response, a sort of compulsive form of behavior that is actually a futile attempt to satisfy some other drive.

There are many people of normal weight or less who eat tremendous quantities of food without gaining weight. They cannot put on even a pound, no matter how rich or "fattening" their diet may be. There is only one possible answer to this paradox: Their bodies are somehow metabolizing the food at a rate sufficient to dispose of the energy consumed without storing it as fat.

The obese person has just the opposite problem. He does not utilize all the energy he consumes. Yet he is in a way more fortunate than the thin person. The solution to his problem is relatively simple, whereas the problem of the thin person who wishes to put on weight may not be so. I stated that the solution of the problem of excess weight is simple, and it is: *Stop eating excessively.* That's simple enough.

What is not so simple is finding some satisfactory way to assure that this be done for a sufficient period of time. When someone remarks that no matter how little they eat they cannot lose weight, they are only deceiving themselves. This is absolutely impossible. It may be undiplomatic to say so, but in my experience I have found it true that overweight people are the biggest prevaricators in the world when describing their ineffective attempts to lose weight. I have had people look me squarely in the eye while giving me elaborately-detailed descriptions of the tiny morsels of food they allegedly ate during the week, a tale decidedly contrary to reports from other, more reliable sources, of what they actually had consumed. And then, when I have called them on it, they held their ground relentlessly until forced by unequivocal evidence to concede, bit by bit, that they had "forgotten" *that* piece of cake, or that they "deserved" some little token after being "good" for so long.

In employing direct hypnosis I have often used a "lie detector" technique of first conditioning the subject to think of "red" each time he is lying about something. The subject thinks this is fun, as the items used in the questioning are unimportant, and he feels that he can tell me or not, as he chooses, whether or not he thought of "red" when he answered a certain question. The answer is usually truthful, but later on I suggest he will not remember that it was I who told him, but that any time he thinks of a color he will briefly lift the first finger of his left hand. This often becomes a little humorous when I ask, in the patient's waking state, about the diet for the previous week. Unknown to the subject, the finger twitches each time he tells me a fib, and there is usually a great deal of amazement about how I happen to know so much about what truly had occurred.

The best way to keep a person on a diet is to get him to want to stay on it. This is why self-hypnosis is so effective. It not only serves to keep the person on a suitable diet, but it helps to alleviate any underlying anxiety-responses that are mobilized.

As the problem of obesity control is closely related to drives for satisfaction of other drives, the solution might be stated as a method of getting *more* enjoyment while consuming *less* of anything. The increased enjoyment may derive partly from food and partly from increases of other activities, or from an increased appreciation of present activities. One way to get such increases is by contrast. Greater appreciation of "good" things may be obtained when it is easy to compare them with "bad" things. So self-hypnosis is used to make the desirable perceptions more frequent and more desirable and the undesirables more undesirable. The contrast then is more readily appreciated.

The first step is to consult with a physician and get a suitable diet worked out. To select a diet in any other way is avoiding vital issues, and the attempt might just as well be forgotten. The diet should bring about two to three pounds of weight loss per week, or less than this if the doctor feels it is better to go easy.

Next, a little "scenario" should be planned that includes: (1) a list of favorite, fattening foods, associating these with undesirable situations related to obesity and (2) the items on the new diet, relating these to "the new look", that is, the rewards in beauty, vigor, attractiveness and health obtainable as and when weight is lost. Several examples of how hypnosis and self-hypnosis are used will help make the procedures understandable.

Ellen (we'll call her) was 37 years old, a public stenographer. She was five feet three inches tall, weighed two hundred pounds and was rather pretty in spite of so much extra poundage. She was bright, cheerful, had a well-modulated voice and seemed perfectly at ease with people. She had an eight year old daughter, but had divorced her husband five years previously. She had had very little social life thereafter, as she preferred to stay home with her daughter. Taking the girl to a movie once each week and to Sunday school, where Ellen was a teacher, were about the extent of her outside activities. She had one or two girl friends who visited with her on an occasional evening, but no male friends. She mentioned this as if she felt she were not missing very much. Later I found out why. She had divorced her husband for infidelity and later discovered that he had once been married to "the other woman". After the divorce he and his former wife got married again and then moved back to the town, in another state, where he and Ellen had both lived previously. This, of course, made it difficult for her to go back to visit her former friends. She had done so once or twice, but had been so upset that she had decided never to go back again.

She had been about 15 or 20 pounds overweight before her marriage. In high school, she recalled, she had been heavy too, but not so much so that it interfered with dating. She remarked with evident pleasure that she used to have dates every weekend and would go to dances and parties. She had gone steady with one boy, after graduation, but he had been killed in Italy during the war. After that she had decided to go to college in the city where she now lived, and it was there she had met the man who was now her ex-husband. Although she had heard his name mentioned, she had not actually met him in their home town. It was not until later that she realized he must have been married to his present wife at the time he had been dating her. She recalled that he went away for a trip; later she had realized it must have been then that his divorce was arranged.

After Ellen's divorce she began to put on weight. She readily admitted that there was probably some emotional basis for her weight problem.

She said, however, that she had never really tried hard to follow the diet her doctor had prescribed. She had twice stayed on it long enough to lose twenty pounds, only to gain it gradually back as she deviated from the diet. She had a habit of picking up a few candy bars on the way to work in the morning, putting them in her desk drawer and munching on them as she worked. She was currently, she added, consuming six candy bars per day. I found out later that the number was ten. She felt guilty about her penchant for sweets and for hoarding candy in her drawer and sneaking a bite now and then. The habit appeared silly to her. Yet she continued.

At home she had the problem of cooking "nice" things for her daughter and then eating most of what she cooked before her daughter had a chance to appreciate her culinary artistry. She would hide cookies and cake from her daughter and then eat them herself after the girl had gone to bed. She admitted, too, that she attempted to justify many of her actions by telling herself that she wouldn't want her daughter to get fat. Her daughter, incidentally, was a well-adjusted, intelligent little girl of slender but healthy build.

Ellen credited her overeating to the fact that she was hurt because of what her husband had done to her. She never again wanted to be in a position where she could be hurt. Her self-esteem had been shattered by the realization that her husband preferred someone else to her. She had been used to an active, satisfying life with the satisfactions derived from long-term hopes and plans, as well as from day-to-day reductions of normal drives. Most of this was changed. The drives continued, but the means for reducing them became limited.

A brief mention of drives and drive-reduction is in order here, as it will help to clarify the reasoning that led to the particular procedures followed.

There are many connotations applied to the term "drive" when used in a psychological sense. Rather than attempt to distinguish between them, I shall define "drive" as I see it: Potential energy in the central nervous system so patterned as to evoke behavior intended to reduce such potential. For example, when the body requires nourishment, various organs stimulate the nervous system in such a way as to cause feelings of hunger. This stimulation increases to the point that appropriate action is initiated. The stimulation, in this case, is the hunger "drive". The appropriate action is eating. So eating is "drive-reduction".

We develop many types and intensities of drives. Some reach conscious awareness; others do not. In order to survive, we must have a certain amount of satisfaction. The great source of satisfaction available to us is *drive-reduction*.

We often develop long-term drives, or goals, and derive satisfaction from thinking about them. But it is the imagery of their being achieved, or reduced, that evokes satisfaction. We have imagery, too, of short-term drives that may evoke anxiety responses, but imagery of reduction of these drives will evoke relief responses. We may question why achievement sometimes does not result in the expected satisfaction. This situation may be owing to the presence of other drives which have not reached the same degree of awareness, or there may be a gradual reduction of the drive in question over a period of time so that upon achievement of its object, the drive is already nearly reduced.

There are also negative drives, or those of avoidance, in which drive-reduction occurs upon each episode of avoidance or upon imagery of avoidance.

To elaborate fully on this subject would mean defining and describing secondary or acquired drives and a wide variety of interrelated factors beyond the scope and purposes of this book. It is hoped that the above discourse will be informative to the reader interested in some of the underlying reasoning in selecting corrective procedures.

Up to the time of Ellen's divorce her behavior was directed toward reduction of social, prestige, security and sex drives as well as an infinite number of secondary drives developed through interrelated patterns of the others. From then on the drives for security and prestige increased, inhibiting her behavior and thus resulting in less reduction of other important drives; in consequence, there were increased anxiety and a level of satisfaction far below normal.

For several weeks after her divorce she did very little except to take care of her baby. She had trouble eating and sleeping, and she had no desire to see her former friends. Seeing them reminded her of her loss of security and prestige. Finally she had to think about getting a job. This she was able to do very easily. She arranged for her child to be taken care of during the day and picked her up on her way home at night. She began to eat and sleep better. We might say that she was systematically developing and reducing hunger and fatigue-drives and that this was some source of relief, along with drive-reductions associated with her job.

We could speculate that her mental imagery involved reviews of what had happened, resulting in drives to avoid a recurrence of her tragedy. This necessitated dissociating herself from men. Scenes of the future were mainly of security for herself and her daughter. Her moral code prohibited any reduction of her sex drive.

Her major sources of satisfaction, then, were eating, sleeping, working and, gradually, the development of new drives connected with her child.

But the greatest satisfaction was in eating. This she could do with the greatest ease, and in her desire to raise her level of satisfaction she kept on eating. Naturally, she began to put on weight, and this partially reduced her "avoidance-drive" because if she became fat she would be protected from men. No man would want her, and that was just fine with her. The drive-reduction from eating no longer depended on hunger. She ate whether she was hungry or not—for the relief of being protected, for the impossibility of being hurt again, for the sheer joy of a full stomach.

Once she became sufficiently overweight, her drive to make herself unattractive and hence undesirable to men was reduced considerably. There were few sources of pleasure remaining for her. As tension mounted she continued overeating in a futile attempt to relieve that tension. She craved other satisfactions. The reason she had seen her doctor, by the way, was not for weight-reduction, but to see if he could give her something to "pep her up". The medication he prescribed did this temporarily, but she had no way to expend her "pep", no direction to take in which she could satisfactorily expend this unaccustomed energy. The resulting letdown offset any benefit she had received.

She had read a few articles about hypnosis and thought that in some way it might make her "happy". When she mentioned this to the doctor he suggested instead that she get psychiatric help. Her immediate reaction was that the doctor thought she "had something wrong with her mind". When he reassured her that he felt she needed only advice and counseling, she accepted the idea. After further pondering, she decided against long-term psychotherapy because of her financial situation. She finally convinced the doctor that she wanted a consultation with someone about hypnosis, but would not go ahead without his permission. The doctor had explained this to me at some length when he called.

After listening to Ellen's story, I answered the usual questions and corrected the traditional misconceptions about hypnosis. I explained that one does not lose consciousness nor fail to hear and sense what is going on around one. There was an increase rather than a loss of will power, and there was no possibility of one's not waking up again. The main thing she would experience was a more relaxed feeling than heretofore, and with self-hypnosis she could possibly increase her confidence, assertiveness and feelings of well-being.

She wanted to know if she could be made to forget the past, and I told her that we would have to see later on if this was what she needed, or if, instead, she could learn and benefit from past experiences. I suggested that she could, if she wished, come to a relaxed and sort of neutral state in which she could view her situation more objectively.

Then she could think better and plan some activities that would satisfy her to some degree while she decided what she wished to do for her long-range activities.

I told her something of my experience with people who had similar problems of obesity, and I asked if she would be willing to follow a program that I would suggest for several weeks, with the idea that at the end of that period she would better be able to decide on future activities. She agreed, and we set up an appointment for the following week with the understanding that if she did not hear from her doctor before then she could assume his agreement also.

I had lunch with her doctor the following day, and I familiarized him with my techniques and arranged to continue the discussion at his office that evening. Though a diversion from our patient, I am tempted to elaborate on events that followed which indicate how fascinated even professional people become about hypnotic phenomena.

I arrived at his office to find that he, a young physician friend and his entire staff were eagerly awaiting a demonstration. During the next few minutes each person present made some remark about having a date or an appointment for dinner, and therefore it would be nice if we could go quickly through a list they had presented to the doctor, of hypnotic phenomena they wished to see demonstrated. This was at five-thirty. We were all still present at eleven-thirty! In fact, the group had two additions who had arrived as the result of telephone calls made by those present to explain why they couldn't keep their dates.

Except for the doctor, every other person present (each of whom volunteered as a subject) turned out to be an excellent experimentee. The doctor's interest, however, was mainly in observing and analyzing the behavior of others. We might mention in passing that over the following years he himself developed a high degree of self-hypnotic ability.

During the evening the thought had occurred to me that I might be able to get Ellen interested in a special experiment on developing self-hypnosis without first being hypnotized by another person. I thought this might be a way to make her feel she was participating in something more important than simply trying to help herself. I mentioned this to the doctor, and he agreed that it was worthwhile and asked me to keep him informed of any progress.

Ellen liked the idea too. She agreed to come in for an hour each day after work, and she also agreed to type up notes as we proceeded. I started then to explain the pencil, semaphore and pendulum phenomena to her, and she was quite fascinated with the proceedings. I explained the procedure of thinking about the time for each practice session and the manner in which to formulate suggestions. After finishing the explanation of the first two symbols and "eye-closure", she said she understood thoroughly and would practice that evening. She came in the next day as planned, but she had not yet developed eye-closure perfectly, and, as she was to do this on her own, I simply answered a few questions. She left with the understanding that she would call me when she felt she was reacting well to the symbols. Two days later she telephoned at noontime to tell me she had accomplished her task perfectly. She sounded very pleased with herself and anxious to come in that night to demonstrate her new ability.

She was right. She had done well and had every reason to be proud of herself. She left that evening, after I explained the process of relaxation, promising to call when she had accomplished the next step.

More than a week went by before she called. She wanted to know if I wanted her to come by that night after work. I could tell by the tone of her voice that she was teasing me when, in reply to my query as to how she was doing, she said, "Oh, just fair." But when I retorted seriously, "Well, you'd better wait a few days, then," she hurriedly said, "I was only joking. Wait until you hear what happened. I can't wait to tell you about it." But she wouldn't answer my questions, saying, "No, no, not now. I want to be there when I tell you. I'll see you tonight. OK?" She sounded pleased and animated.

She came in that night a bit early, sat in the reclining chair, and without saying a word, adjusted herself to a comfortable position staring straight ahead. Within a few seconds her eyes were closed and her body began to relax. She had a "Mona Lisa" smile on her face that quickly faded as she relaxed. There was a slight, barely perceptible quivering of her eye lashes as she relaxed even further. She was taking deeper breaths and swallowed several times. I thought to myself, "She is in a trance and doesn't realize it as yet. Did I help her in any way? How much benefit has she derived from reading the instructions rather than my giving them to her verbally?" I walked over, picked up her left wrist, which was limp and heavy. She was, without a doubt, profoundly relaxed.

I wondered if I would have to awaken her, but decided against it; I did not want to interfere unless it became absolutely necessary. It proved not to be necessary. She woke up by herself as I was thinking about it. She smiled, stretched, and said, "How did I do, Mr. Svengali?"

I laughed and replied, "Perfect. But where did you get that Svengali stuff? You did it, not I."

"That's right. I sure can relax myself, can't I?"

I debated as to whether or not to tell her she had been in a trance.

To give myself more time to consider it, I asked, "What were you going to tell me?"

"Well," she said, "last Thursday night I was sitting in the front room, and I made up my mind I was going to practice for half an hour. I knew I could relax myself, but I wanted to see if I could wake up in exactly a half-hour. I went into the bedroom and got the alarm clock, which gave the time as five minutes to nine. I wanted to be exact, so I set it ahead to nine o'clock and then I put it on the table and sat down to practice. I thought about waking up at nine thirty, and then I suggested I would relax deeper than ever before. I went to '1000-1' and '1000-2', and my eyes felt as if they were glued shut. I 'saw' '1000-3' as I usually do, on a big billboard, and then I felt as if I was floating on a cloud. I was sort of riding along on waves of clouds. Is that what it is supposed to feel like?"

I was absorbed by her description. "Yes, many people feel that way. What happened then? Did you wake up at nine thirty?"

"Wait," Ellen resumed. "I was riding along on this cloud. I was lying on my back, and I could see through the clouds and there was an outline of a clock in the sky with the hands pointing to nine twenty, and I could hear someone talking to me. Trying to wake me up. I knew someone had come in and that I wasn't dreaming it. I even knew who it was. Clara, one of the girls I used to play bridge with. I didn't want anyone to know what I've been doing, but I didn't want to wake up until nine thirty either. I remember thinking that I would tell Clara I was just sleeping. Then I looked back at the clock in the sky and, so help me, it said nine thirty-five!"

"Well, that isn't..." I started to tell her it was not unusual to go over at first, but she impatiently put her hand on my arm and said, "Wait a minute, will you? Wait till I finish!" I smiled and nodded.

"As soon as I noticed it was nine thirty-five, I started counting, and I wasn't in the clouds any more. I was right back in my chair, and when I reached ten I woke up." She was quite excited and full of her story. "Clara was there," she continued, "and she had been trying to wake me up. She asked me if I was tired, and I started to say no, but then I said I had been but was glad she came in. She said she had shaken me and actually yelled at me to wake up but I wouldn't budge. But the most amazing thing of all was this: I looked at the clock and it said nine thirty. So, I thought to myself, you woke up at nine thirty after all. Then, when Clara saw me looking at the clock she said, 'Your clock was fast, so I put it back five minutes.' Now how do you figure that out?" she asked me, with her eyebrows raised and her head to one side.

I had decided to tell her she had been in a trance, not only there in the office, but at home too. The question of the five minutes was just a coincidence, as people vary, especially at first, as to the preciseness of this ability.

In another month Ellen had developed most of the hypnotic abilities, including time-distortion. Best of all, she had done it on her own. I decided it was time to start working with her to begin developing other drives. I was, in the meantime, teaching her physician hypnotic techniques on the basis of two evenings a week, with both nurses acting as subject-students. He told me at one of our sessions that he thought it would be a good idea if we could get Ellen interested in more activities outside of her home. I mentioned Ellen's former interest in bridge, and after a few days of investigating and planning, we evolved what turned out to be an ideal arrangement involving a women's bridge club which met every Saturday afternoon at one of the church recreation halls.

To have proposed bridge to Ellen in the waking state would only have evoked other traumatic imagery of the past. Instead, I suggested a "pleasant scene of playing bridge" as the third item in a total of five scenes, while she was cooperating in an experiment on time-distortion. The other four scenes were of "neutral" content which, it was reasoned, would make the bridge scene stand out by way of contrast. I also allowed three minutes of actual time between signals on that scene and only one-half minute for the others. In previous experiments I had always emphasized vividness and remembrance of detail and had then discussed each scene with Ellen immediately after she woke up. I made the same suggestions this time, too, but rather than discuss the scenes with her in the waking state, I explained that for purposes of an experimental nature I wanted her to "forget" these particular scenes, if possible, before the next session. This was like asking someone who smoked a good deal to forget about smoking. As Ellen reported one week later, the more she had tried to forget those scenes, the more she thought about them, especially the one in which she was playing bridge. I asked her if any of the scenes disturbed her in any way. She replied, "No. They are rather pleasant."

The foregoing series was typical of a number of experiments in which scenes of activities were suggested because we knew of Ellen's having participated in such activities in the past and in which she would be seeing herself as she was then, happy and not overweight.

She began to expose herself to opportunities of participating in these activities, and one day she mentioned rather casually that she had joined a bridge club. I treated this information with equal casualness, but I was really very pleased about it. Some months later, when she had overcome most of her problems, Ellen smilingly accused the doctor and me of having "rigged" some of these situations. She thought that we had arranged to have various invitations presented to her and had asked some of her friends to drop in to see her. We had actually thought of doing some of these things, but it hadn't been necessary. The only things "rigged" were the time-distortion scenes.

During the weeks following the initial directive session she became much more active in everything that had been suggested. She showed increased interest in church affairs, in taking her daughter to museums and parks on weekend excursions and in teaching her to play the piano on two evenings each week. She had developed an interest in reading and had compiled a rather extensive list of books, mostly historical novels and works on religious concepts. She had even resumed working, with the intention of obtaining credits toward a degree, on a correspondence course she had previously discarded. Although most of her drives were toward short-term goals, this interest in a school degree was certainly indicative that long-term drives were beginning to develop.

She called one day to ask if she could arrange for a longer appointment that evening because she had many things she would like to discuss. When she arrived, she lost no time in going over a number of items, one by one, that she had obviously been thinking about and had, for some time, planned to talk about. She had reached some conclusions and wanted advice and reassurance as to the soundness of her reasoning.

One of the items had been initiated by an incident at the bridge club. It seemed that one of the "girls" had just gone through divorce proceedings and appeared to be so unconcerned about it that Ellen had thought, at first, she was being very callous or perhaps trying to conceal her genuine emotions behind a façade of gaiety. She discovered, however, that the woman was relieved and happy to be rid of her husband, who had been maintaining another intimate relationship. She had known this for years, the divorcee had explained to the bridge partners, and she had put up with it as being a more-or-less accepted part of the modern social picture. But when her husband had allowed his "hobby" to interfere with their marriage to such an extent that she was made to look ridiculous, and the children were being hurt, she had decided to "ring down the curtain" and start a new scene.

This gave Ellen much to think about. Here was a woman with not one child, but three. She was older than Ellen and not as pretty as she used to be. Yet she seemed quite happy about the divorce and was letting everyone know that she "had her eyes peeled" for another man.

"You know," Ellen went on, "I gave that a lot of thought. I made up my mind that I was going to try to adopt the same attitude. Not that I intend to get interested in another man right away, but the more attractive I am, I figure, the better chance I'll have of getting a good one if he comes along."

"That's pretty good figuring," I retorted. "How do you intend to go about it?"

She looked at me and pursed her lips as she said, "The first thing I'm going to do is get back to the way I used to be. I'm going to make myself as attractive and as happy as I can. I'm going to do things and have fun, and I'm going to show my daughter and everyone else what I can really be like."

In a somewhat more serious tone she went on, "What I really wanted to talk to you about is using my self-hypnosis to lose weight. I think I can put the past behind me. In fact, I think I already have. But taking off fifty or sixty pounds won't be easy, will it?" As she said this, she first looked at me and then held her arms out and shook her head as her gaze traveled from her arms to her body.

Her arms were three times the size they should have been, and her body and legs were in proportion. Her face, though full, was not unattractive. She was actually pretty, and it was discernible that she probably had once had an excellent figure. I said, "You already have the most important ingredient of a reducing formula."

"What's that?"

"Desire. If you really want to lose weight, you can do it. Perhaps not by next week or even in several months, but if you want to, you can do it."

"OK," she said. "I want to. I don't care how long it takes. If it takes time, perhaps it will mean more to me. What do we do?"

"Put yourself into a deep trance, and I'll be back in a few minutes." I watched her settle down in the chair, and then I left the room and closed the door.

Fifteen minutes later I was back. She was apparently in a deep trance, so I talked to her in a conversational tone:

"As you go deeper you will listen to my voice, and the scenes I describe will be very vivid, very real to you. You will actually be there doing the things I describe. You are in a large room and there is a long table in this room. To the left there is a doorway and a large mirror on the wall. At the far end of the room is another doorway and a large mirror there too. Near you, on the table, there are all sorts of rich foods in attractive dishes. There are pies, cakes, cookies and all sorts of rich foods with syrups and sauces. You sit down at the table and you eat some of these rich, sweet foods. You feel very full and uncomfortable.

You have difficulty getting up, but you do, and you walk through the doorway to the left. There is a desk there in the next room. You are sitting at the desk eating a candy bar and looking around to make sure no one sees you. You look rather silly, like a little girl getting away with something. But you are not little. You are big and fat, and you look silly eating the candy that way. You get up and walk to the other end of the room. There are lots of people there, and they are all enjoying themselves, but you feel out of place. You cannot enjoy yourself because you are overweight. There are many things going on, but as you walk around the room you find you cannot enjoy any of these things. You go back through the door and you look at yourself in the mirror. You look very fat and unattractive. You look over at the table, and the rich food has been replenished. As you look at these foods they look very heavy, rich, sticky and greasy. They remind you of your own heavy, fat body. As you look at some of the sauces you see something you did not see before. You see that they are covering raw oysters. All these rich sauces are covering raw oysters. As you look at the pies and cakes and cookies you can see that they are actually made of raw liver. You start to walk past the table and you can smell the liver. You look at the rich food and it is all ground up raw liver—uncooked, cold, raw liver. You hurry past this rich food, and you sit down at the other end of the table. There is nothing on the table. You feel tired, awfully full and heavy, and you put your head in your arms resting them on the table, and you go to sleep."

Waiting a few minutes, I then began again: "As you keep going deeper now, you find yourself still in that room. You are awake and looking at the table. There are attractive dishes with fruit, salads, meats and vegetables in them. Everything looks fresh and colorful and attractive. These foods look tasty and light and healthful. You are very hungry. You eat some salad and it tastes so good you chew it for a long while. You take a long while to chew it because it tastes so good. You take a little bit of each food and you chew each bit with satisfaction. It tastes wonderful, and you feel clean and good. You feel perfectly satisfied with this small amount of simple, light, healthy food, and you stand up easily, feeling full of energy. You look in the mirror and you see yourself very slender and pretty. You are smiling. Your eyes are sparkling, and you are pleased with your pretty dress. You like the way your hair is done. Everything is perfect. You go into the room on the right, and people look at you and smile in friendly greeting. They admire you. You feel very proud. You spend lots of time in this room doing interesting things with gay, interesting people. You are admired by everyone. They all like you and want your attention. Everything is perfect, just the way you want it. After a while you go out to see yourself in the mirror. You look radiantly happy, confident and proud. You see your daughter looking at you with adoring eyes as she comes from the room. You are going out together. There are many things to do outside. Things you are going to do with pleasure. You look forward with pleasure to all the things you are going to do as you are slender, confident and proud."

After a minute or two, "From now on when you see or smell any rich, fattening foods they will immediately remind you of raw oysters and raw liver. There will be no appeal for you in these heavy, rich, repulsive foods. As you even think of eating any such foods they will become more and more repulsive to you. Each time you decide you do not wish to eat these foods you will immediately feel clean and good and proud. Each time you eat a small amount of salad, fruit, meat or vegetable you will enjoy it and feel just wonderful. These images will grow stronger each day now. You will feel better each day. It is easy for you to get great pleasure and enjoyment from small amounts of light, crisp food, and each time you eat you will chew longer to get more of this wonderful taste and think of yourself as slender and pretty as you do."

After suggesting that she would go through this imagery once each day and that as she did the feelings and emotions would grow stronger, I slowly woke her up.

She said, "Boy! That was really something. I don't think I'll ever be able to look at a piece of cake again."

I reached into my desk and got a chocolate bar I had put there for the occasion. Offering it to her I smiled and said, "Well, one last piece of candy before you..." She looked as if she were going to be sick. "Oh no! That's awful. Just the sight of it makes me feel awful!" She drew away as if I were threatening her with a live snake.

We set up an appointment for one week later, but on the day she was due to come in she called to postpone it to the following week. She said she had lost six pounds. She had practiced every night and she was "thrilled" with the results. I warned her to keep in touch with the doctor, to let him know about her diet, and not to proceed too fast. She promised she would follow my advice.

I saw her only once after that. Although she called every week or so, to let me know how she was doing, she always had some reason for not coming in. About six months later I met her at a New Year's party. I had several conversations with her and even danced with her twice, but I didn't recognize her until she laughingly told me who she was. Practically everyone knew but I. When she had heard that my wife and I were to be there she called her friends and arranged the ruse of being called by another name to see if I would notice her.

She was slender, well-dressed and attractive. Best of all she was, very plainly, enjoying life once again.

All cases of obesity do not work out as well as this. In my experience four out of every ten achieve excellent results, and two or three more obtain something less. There are a number of different techniques that may be utilized, but they do not seem to differ as far as effectiveness in weight-reduction is concerned. What are much more important, apparently, are the other factors involved. Anxiety must first be reduced to a reasonable level before any effective weight loss can occur. But even if this is done, there must still be motivation of considerable strength, or the person will not stick to any procedure even though it is proving effective.

CHAPTER 11

ALLEVIATION OF PAIN

THE REMOVAL or alleviation of pain is one of the few areas in which hypnotism can be dangerous. A number of very important facts should be clearly understood before any attempt is made in this direction.

The existence of pain or unusual discomfort indicates a malfunctioning of the organism. The accuracy with which the person can describe these sensations is a major factor in diagnosing the underlying cause. Even an experienced physician may have difficulty in localizing the causative factors from the patient's description of pain sensations that he is experiencing at the time of the examination. Yet this is the time when the description is most accurate. The next best description of an ailment is from the patient who, though he is not suffering at the moment, has a clear remembrance of sensations recently experienced. How, then, can a patient give a clear and accurate description of his painful symptoms if they have been removed through the use of hypnosis or other means? The removal of discomfort may make diagnosis, which is essential to effective treatment, much more difficult, if not impossible, to achieve.

More serious still is the removal of incentive to have a diagnosis made. When a person stops suffering he is likely to postpone doing anything about his problem. Consider the individual who unknowingly has a tumor and begins to experience slight pain that he can describe to his physician. After he has given the doctor a clear-cut description of pain sensations that have not been blurred by anodynes, his tumor is very likely to be discovered and removed. But suppose, on the other hand, he begins taking pills which alleviate the pain to the extent that he puts off seeing the doctor. The pills he takes may relieve the pain, but they will not retard the development of the tumor. If he then finds the pain cannot be controlled by his self-prescribed medication and has his symptoms removed by hypnosis, the tumor could continue to develop until his condition is beyond the point where even major surgery could do him any good.

Hypnosis is a marvelous means of effecting and maintaining a pain-free and symptom-free state of being, but the fact that it must never be used for this purpose until the exact causes of the symptoms are determined cannot be overemphasized.

Once the causes are clearly understood there are a number of different procedures that may be used. These may be classified in a general way as suggestions for: well-being, anesthesia, analgesia, dissociation, and symptom-substitution.

Suggestions made to a subject while in trance are usually in the form of words that are intended to convey ideas. But a word or group of words may convey a different meaning to the subject than is intended by the hypnotist. For example, if the hypnotist should ask a number of people who are in the waking state if they would mind raising their right hands, the chances are many of them would do so. But the hypnotized subject upon being asked this question is quite likely to do nothing or perhaps, if he is used to talking while in trance, will reply, "No."

Those in the waking state are signifying their cooperation and suggestibility to what is actually an inferred suggestion. The question is, "Would you *mind* raising your right hand?" The hypnotized subject takes such questions literally. When he doesn't raise his hand or when he says "no" he means that he doesn't mind, but he has not been *told* to do so. If the hypnotist says, "Raise your right hand," he would undoubtedly comply.

Suggestions for *well-being* will be taken quite literally too, depending upon the meaning the words convey to the subject. It is important that such suggestions be well thought out so as to convey the intended ideas of exact feeling of sensation or lack of sensation, duration, etc. Otherwise the subject may feel one way in the trance and differently upon awakening or at some post-hypnotic period.

Suggestions made through self-hypnosis do not require such careful consideration, since the subject himself usually knows what his purposes are, and he is used to placing his own connotations on the words and ideas he uses to formulate his suggestions.

If a person is concerned about a specific pain or ailment, a suggestion of well-being may mean to him that only that specific pain or ailment will be alleviated. The suggestion could also mean, however, that as long as he experiences feelings of well-being he can have no sensation of pain or discomfort regardless of any pathological condition that may develop.

There is a great deal of merit in making positive suggestions; that is, in refraining from the use of such words as "pain" and "discomfort" and, instead, using suggestions for responses that are antagonistic to the undesirable ones. Rather than saying, "You will not be anxious," it is better to say "You will always be relaxed;" instead of "You will feel no pain," say, "You will feel healthy and wonderful in every way unless a condition exists where pain will serve as a warning to you."

In some circumstances, usually in a medical emergency, the suggestion may be used, "You will feel perfect now in every way and you will have a strong, unavoidable urge to see a doctor at the earliest opportunity." Thus the symptoms may be removed, but the equally strong suggestion is made that something will be done about their causes.

Anesthesia means the cessation of sensation to any type of stimulus in the area wherein it is developed; it is often neither necessary nor practical. The most effective uses of suggestions of anesthesia are in dental and surgical procedures. Here is where hypnosis and self-hypnosis are far superior to any other method. The patient can remain relaxed and free from apprehension and pain before, during and after the procedure, and yet be cooperative and helpful to any extent the doctor or dentist desires. Sometimes chemical anesthetics are used along with hypnosis, as they would have been used without it. Many times smaller dosages are required and, of course, there are cases where no chemicals are needed at all. In every case the use of hypnosis will provide additional benefits, but the results are most ideal when it is the sole modality used.

Self-hypnosis is an excellent means for inducing and maintaining a pain-free state, but this use is often difficult to develop without assistance. Pain itself is inhibitive to trance induction because of the inability of the patient to think of anything else. Drugs also interfere because in a state of even partial narcosis, the patient does not understand nor follow instructions as well, and the degree of hypnosis becomes more difficult to evaluate. More mentally-alert states, whenever possible, are desirable for successful induction and effective use of suggestions of any kind.

Anxiety tends to intensify pain and to inhibit the development of hypnosis. If the patient can be made to "project himself" forward with imagery of the immediate future in which he sees himself feeling better, enough relaxation may be obtained to make induction possible. As the ability to utilize suggestion is developed, suggestions for "glove-anesthesia" may be tied in with those already working well. The glove anesthesia may then be transferred to other areas as desired.

It is interesting to note that "glove anesthesia" has a great deal of significance, as it does not follow any neural pattern actually present in the hand. This is true of any inhibition of sensory perception induced through means of suggestion, but it is especially discernible in glove anesthesia. Whereas most people have either experienced or have heard descriptions of anesthesias produced in the jaw (as in dentistry), the experience of other localized anesthesias is not so common. It is easy to understand, then, how suggestion will induce a very satisfactory result in the jaw where it seems to follow existing neural pathways. But, since equally satisfactory results can ensue where no such pathways exist, it is evident that painful sensations can be blocked by inhibitive processes accomplished through suggestion.

Analgesia is a condition in which all sensations are perceived except those of a painful nature. This term is often used in describing the inability to perceive any noxious stimulus, such as that causing an itch.

The use of *dissociation* techniques is becoming more popular in both medical and dental procedures since, with good subjects, they require less time and effort. This means that suggestions are made to the subject that part or all of his body is displaced to another location and that he is engaged in other activity.

Two or three typical examples of each technique will now be described along with explanations of how and why the particular ones were used. Both hetero-hypnosis and self-hypnosis will be covered.

To develop anesthesia in a localized area, such as for dental work or minor surgery, one of the easiest and most frequently used techniques involves hand-levitation. Once the subject has developed the ability for either hetero- or self-suggestion to cause his hand to rise up and touch his face, suggestions are then made that as the hand rises it also becomes numb. This procedure is repeated until the hand does not react to a painful stimulus, such as a strong pinch of the fingers or light jabs with a sterilized needle. If these stimuli are felt, but no pain is experienced, then analgesia would be considered as present. If the stimuli are not felt at all, then total anesthesia exists. For dental work, even extractions, analgesia is generally sufficient. Once the hand tests satisfactorily, the condition is transferred to the jaw or other area involved, with suggestions that the numbness will leave the hand and pass into the other area. These effects may be heightened by the use of contrast. This is, while suggestions are made that one hand is becoming insensitive to touch or pain, the other hand is suggested as feeling hypersensitive. All of these procedures were used in the following case.

This case is so typical of hundreds of others that factors such as age, sex, etc., are relatively unimportant. In the initial interview, the patient explained that she was very apprehensive about dental work and had been avoiding the ordeal of seeing a dentist for so many years that she was now in need of having eight teeth extracted and 17 fillings inserted. She had finally worked up enough courage to see a dentist on the promise that he would do nothing but examine and evaluate her condition. Having found out what had to be done, she could not face going through with it. As for hypnosis, she was afraid it wouldn't work, that it might "wear off" during the dental procedures, that it might "affect her mind" or her "will power," etc.

I went through the usual explanations and then asked her to forget about the dental work until she felt like going through with it. I told her she could decide for herself when she was ready and how much work she would have done at each visit.

During the first session she was able to induce a trance by causing her hand to float up to her face as she visualized writing the word "lighter" on a blackboard. As her hand started to move up, her eyes would close, and when her fingers touched her face she would go into a deep trance. She agreed to practice this once or twice each day and to come in again at the end of the week.

On the second visit she reported that she could put herself into a trance in about three minutes and that she felt very relaxed upon doing so. I asked her to go through it again and told her I would talk to her as she proceeded. I waited until her hand started to move and said, "As your hand becomes lighter now, it is growing very numb. There is a tingling sensation from your wrist down through your hand to the tips of your fingers. By the time your hand reaches your face it will be completely numb. Your hand feels as if it were in a thick leather glove, and anything touching it feels as if it were touching the glove." I repeated these suggestions as her hand moved up to her face. When her fingers gently touched her face I went on, "Now your hand is heavy and, as it slowly goes back to your lap, all feeling is leaving it. You can feel nothing touching your hand." Once the hand was back in her lap I took a small, sterile needle and lightly tested her hand several times while I repeated suggestions of no feeling. There was no reaction to this stimulus. I then said, as I did the same thing with the needle on the other hand, "This hand is becoming very sensitive. Each time I touch it, it hurts and twitches from the touch. It is very sensitive. But," shifting to the first hand again, "this hand has no feeling at all." I repeated this procedure several times until her right hand showed no reaction to a severe test with the needle and her other hand jumped upon being touched with my finger. I then suggested she could wake herself up, and the numbness would become even more pronounced. This turned out to be so. She tested each hand herself and found there was no sensation that could be evoked in her right hand even upon pressing the needle into it quite deeply.

Many people will lose the effect upon awakening, but it is unimportant, as there is no need for them to wake up until after the dental work is completed. And strangely enough, when they wake up after the actual work has been done there is no return of sensation to the area until much later. These suggestions always turn out to be more effective during the actual work than while they are being developed.

This patient found she could make these suggestions herself and obtain "glove-anesthesia" quickly and easily. I then asked her to go through it again but this time, when her hand reached her face, to transfer the numbness to her jaws by rubbing her hand around her cheeks and lower jaws until they became numb and her hand became normal. I told her that each time she did this the numbness would become more profound and each time she lowered her hand that would emphasize it also. I suggested too that this numbness would grow deeper no matter what she thought or did until she released it by touching her face with her other hand.

By the end of the second session she could do this very well. I tested her gums with a needle and her teeth by placing the tip of my finger on the top of each tooth and pushing from side to side, all the while making further suggestions. I suggested she could be watching a movie or go into a deep sleep when the dentist worked with her, that she would follow any of his instructions, that any sounds would only make her go deeper, and that she could feel nothing in her teeth or jaws until she touched her face with her other hand. I also told her she would not wake up until the words "all done" were spoken by someone else.

When she came in for the third session she told me she had made her appointment with the dentist and had no anxiety whatever about it. She "knew there could be no pain."

We went through the procedure again and agreed that the lowering of her hand would be the signal for the dentist to begin and that he was to tell her, when he finished, that he was "all done."

She had not told her dentist that she had acquired the skill of self-hypnosis; his surprise can be imagined when his patient, formerly so apprehensive, walked in, waited her turn by reading a magazine, sat in the dental chair, looked up at him and said, "There will be no need for any anesthetic, doctor; just give me three minutes to put myself in a trance and then do as much work as you have time for. I will signal you when to start by lowering my hand from my face. I will do whatever you tell me while I am under and will not wake up until you say you are 'all done'. Be sure to use those exact words, 'all done'."

To the amazement of the dentist she proceeded, without another word, to do just as she had said. He had heard that the doctor who had referred the patient to me had been using hypnosis, so after she had gone into a trance, he called the doctor and told him what was happening. The doctor, although he knew the patient had been developing self hypnosis, had not realized she was ready so soon. Nevertheless, he told the dentist to go ahead as she requested, and to let him know the result.

The dentist extracted one tooth, then three more; excavated and filled two cavities; then finally decided, while he was at it, to extract the other four teeth. He reported to the doctor later that he was more nervous than the patient, who had remained apparently asleep all through the entire procedure yet had leaned over to spit, "opened wide" and followed his every instruction to the letter.

Variations of this type of result are occurring every day. Dentists report that the hypnotized patient is ideal in every way. There is even some control, through suggestion, over the amount of bleeding. The patients feel fine in every way, the wounds from extractions or surgery heal quickly and well, and the patients return faithfully on time for their appointments.

Some people can do this with only a single session of hypnosis. Some require ten sessions or more. Still others cannot achieve any significant degree of hypnotic anesthesia and require chemical anesthetics as usual. But even these latter cases derive some benefit in the form of increased relaxation and lessening of apprehension. To whatever degree hypnosis can be utilized, it always appears to be worthwhile.

A slightly different technique is for the patient to develop imagery of "wires" running from the area to be anesthetized and controlled by a "switch" near the temple that could be "shut off" so that no sensation can reach the brain. Either of the above techniques may be used with equal facility and may be developed by the person himself (which usually takes longer) or with the help of the assistant, physician, or dentist.

Also excellent for use with dental and medical procedures is the dissociation technique. The patient simply develops the ability to be "somewhere else" during the operation. He can be experiencing imagery of a trip in a car, boat or plane, or simply sitting or lying out in the other room, or walking around outside. When this is suggested, the person feels nothing because, in his mind, he is doing something else and is in some place other than the dental chair; in consequence, he cannot experience any sensation associated with the procedure that is actually occurring. This technique is fast and effective but, again, is most easily developed with some assistance.

About a year ago I received a request from a physician to call on a patient who had lost his leg in an accident. The man was forty years old, had a wife and three children and was reasonably well-off financially. He had not, as yet, been able to make any significant emotional adjustment to the traumatic effect of the amputation. He had tried to go through the procedure of being fitted for a prosthesis, or artificial leg, but the pain of any pressure on the stump was more than he could endure. He was on massive dosages of morphine derivatives which were having diminishing effectiveness against his pain and itchiness. To him the sensations were coming from the limb he no longer had! This is a condition known as a "phantom-limb" sensation. It is very common in amputations and also occurs in various types of paralysis.

This particular pain was occurring with increasing frequency and intensity, and each time it came his whole body would become rigid with agony. The itchiness was driving him frantic and was seriously interfering with his sleep. The usual procedures employing hand-levitation were used successfully, and direct suggestions were made that he would feel fine in every way from then on. He was told that he could easily induce self-hypnosis and use it to make suggestions of relaxation, deep sleep and continued well-being. When he woke up, he smiled and said he felt relaxed, free of pain and happy. After some further discussion and explanation he was able to put himself into a trance and wake up at a precise, predetermined moment.

The following week he reported that the effect had worn off a little. The pain had not returned, but the itchiness and insomnia had to some extent come back. It required three additional sessions to establish the pattern to the point where it appeared to be permanent.

Close contact has been kept with this patient for over one year, and he has had no relapse whatever. Neither has he required any further help. He uses self-hypnosis once a week. He now has his prosthesis and gets around as if he had no problems at all. His adjustment, both physiologic and psychologic, is excellent. He feels rather deeply and has said that with the aid of self-hypnosis he has recovered his pleasure in living.

It should be noted that no suggestions were used in which the word "pain" was mentioned. A successful suggestion of "feeling fine" would mean that no pain would be experienced. As this patient was being dominated by a specific type of painful sensation, the suggestions were interpreted by him to apply only to that. He since has shown that he reacts normally to other painful stimulations. If this had not been found to be so, additional measures would have been taken to correct the faulty reaction.

Mention was made earlier of *symptom substitution* as a means of alleviating pain. This technique is often used with patients who are expressing some form of undesirable behavior. Suggestions are made to the effect that this behavior will cease and be replaced with behavior that will provide the person with adequate relief for his compulsion or obsession and yet be less obvious or debilitating than the old conduct. A similar approach may be made to problems involving painful symptoms in which relief is desirable, but in regard to which some means of evaluating the underlying cause must be retained.

There are, for example, many cases in which the causes are known but treatment is expected to continue for some time before the condition is corrected. For the patient to continue suffering, or for narcotics to be used, is not necessarily practical nor essential. Suggestions may be made that the underlying condition will continue to evoke sensations but that they will not be perceived as painful.

A woman with a prosthesis in her right hip had been advised by her physician that a certain amount of exercise would be beneficial and, painful though it might be, was the only way she could hope to achieve maximum use of the leg. Ideally the exercise would be the greatest amount possible without increasing irritation at the joint. However, movement of almost any nature evoked excruciating pain, and it had begun to look as if drugs would be necessary if she was to move about at all. Since the use of drugs would make improvement difficult to evaluate, hypnosis was considered as a possible solution.

This patient turned out to be extremely resistive to hypnosis. Although she expressed a willingness to cooperate and had an intelligent understanding of the purposes intended, she was making little or no progress toward induction after more than twenty hours of instruction. These sessions were over a period of five weeks. Finally, she and I both arrived at the conclusion that any further attempt would be futile. We had no sooner agreed on this when I was amazed to see her go into a trance as we were discussing some of her childhood activities. She told me later that the conversation evoked imagery of some of her most pleasant experiences, and while this was going on she suddenly realized that this was what we had been trying to do all this time. She also said she knew I would recognize what had occurred and she felt secure in the knowledge that she could "let herself go", and I would tell her to wake up when the time came to do so.

Although I recognized that she had slipped into the trance, I had not immediately grasped the reason. I watched her for a few minutes and then softly suggested that she could, from then on, put herself into a deep trance easily and quickly whenever she wished and that she would go deeper each time she did so. I also suggested that whatever signal we agreed on would, after she woke up, cause her to go right back into the trance again. I then told her she would slowly wake up.

She smiled rather sheepishly and said, "I guess we finally made it."

From then on there were no further problems. The signal we decided upon was her imagery of a particular scene. I had no sooner nodded agreement than, with a slight smile, she went right back into the trance.

I then set up the usual pattern for self-hypnosis with additional suggestions that she would be able to walk and feel perfectly well, but there would be a slight feeling of numbness until the area around the joint had healed and strengthened. I also suggested that if she exercised too much she would know it by a return of slight pain, which would subside upon resting adequately.

That the procedure worked perfectly was manifested by her ability to walk around the room with only a feeling of numbness in the joint. It took four more sessions for her to reach the point where everything seemed to improve, which is always a good indication that suggestions are working the way they should be. She reported that the numbness gradually diminished over the next six months and on the few occasions that she experienced pain it was easily traceable to over-exercise.

Cases have been reported in which similar techniques were used to bring about "symptom intensification". This was supposed to have caused regression to original traumatic episodes with a form of abreaction through which the patient was supposed to have gained insight into the basis of his symptoms. That concepts of regression and abreaction are of any real therapeutic value is seriously open to question. There is evidence that, in many instances, they bring further anxiety and subject the patient to unnecessary emotional experiences from which he attempts to escape by telling the hypnotist whatever he thinks the hypnotist expects to hear.

No special psychoanalytic theory can validly be applied to hypnosis. The hypnotized subject tends to behave in the manner he interprets as that expected of him. If no direction is given him he is going to behave according to what his own concepts of therapy happen to be. If it is suggested, even through inference, that he must have episodes of regression, abreaction, sexual release, etc., before he can be cured, these are what he will have.

Moreover, under no circumstances should any suggestion ever be made, with either self-hypnosis or hetero-hypnosis, that any symptom—painful or not—will become intensified.

Pain which is thought to be of psychosomatic, hysteric or hallucinatory origin is best handled by developing insight into its nature. If the underlying cause is obvious to the physician, he may advise that hypnotic procedures be initiated and simultaneously treat physical malfunctions, if any exist medically.

The wife who has a genuine headache that happens to coincide with events objectionable to her that have been planned by her husband, may find a "headache" a convenient means of avoiding such events in the future. This type of "symptom" is considered to be one having a secondary gain for the patient. Such manifestations are of little concern to us here. The person who feigns a symptom but suffers no actual pain can decide for himself whether or not it is worth the effort to continue putting on the act.

A condition that is much more relevant to our present discussion is one in which the symptom may or may not have started out as painful but has in any event become so upon repeated "use" by the patient to gain some end. Sometimes the patient recognizes what has happened yet can do nothing about it. The pain may occur upon exposure to the original or similar situations, or it may be generalized to any and all situations in which the person wishes to get his own way or to avoid doing something disagreeable. The pain may even be evoked by simply thinking of these things.

The patient may not perhaps realize what is happening. The painful response may easily have become conditioned to stimuli no longer associated with the original episode. This type of symptom can be identical to one of strictly organic origin and should be treated in the same manner. Hypnosis will then be of no possible harm and may be of considerable benefit.

A very attractive young lady came to me because of severe migrainous headaches which had been bothering her for five years. Her doctor had given me some of her background, including the information that she had been married for five years to a man who was coarse in appearance and mannerisms and seemed most unsuitable as a mate for this obviously intelligent, soft-spoken and well-mannered girl. The doctor had been treating her for over a year, without success, for symptoms of severe headaches, vomiting, nausea and disturbances in vision. A thorough medical check-up revealed no organic basis for the symptoms, so the doctor had 'concluded that emotional factors were involved. He said he strongly suspected that her husband was in some way contributing to the condition in spite of the fact that the patient expressed great love for him and that the condition had existed for over a year prior to the marriage. The headaches occurred nearly every day and lasted for one to three or four hours. He had been able to find no correlation between the time of onset and any specific behavior or situation on her part or that of her husband.

During the first session I took down the information I needed for my records, answered the questions she put to me about hypnosis, and made the pencil, semaphore and pendulum test. The indications were that she would be an excellent hypnotic subject. I had asked her to submit to a psychological test, the Willoughby Personality Schedule, as a way of getting more information regarding neurotic components in her personality. She had readily agreed; her score turned out to be quite high for a person who claimed, as she did, that her life was happy and satisfying except during the experiencing of her symptoms. The test indicated a high level of anxiety arising from social events, as well as an extreme degree of shyness and frustration.

When I inquired about her marital situation, especially her sex life, she blushed and rather hurriedly told me she was happy and satisfied and felt that her husband was too. We had no time to go further that day into these questions, so we set up another consultative appointment.

Two days later she came in as agreed, and her husband was with her. Never have I seen a couple so ill-matched in appearance. This incongruity extended into other areas, I discovered as the second session progressed. As I have mentioned, she was attractive, well-dressed and capable of answering questions intelligently. Her husband, though well-dressed, was sloppy in his grooming. His tie was askew, his belt-buckle off-center, and his trousers needed cleaning and pressing. His fingernails were dirty, and he had several large blackheads on his face which were in need of attention. His voice was gruff, and he spoke ungrammatically. It was clear that, in addition to these unpleasant characteristics, he was very belligerent. "No one," he said, "is going to 'hypnose' my wife unless I watch. I don't think it'll do her any good anyhow unless you can make her give up some of her fancy ideas."

I realized I was developing an intense dislike for this person, but I also knew it would be useless to argue with him. Instead, I asked, "You want your wife to get over these headaches, don't you?"

He evaded my question by grumbling, "These headaches are all in her mind. If she'd start acting like a woman, she'd be all right." As he talked, his wife blushed and seemed to wilt. She obviously was afraid of him.

Looking straight at him, I asked, "Do you feel that these headaches are not genuinely painful?"

He sighed and shook his head. "I don't know. Maybe she hurts when she has these spells, but she brings them on herself. She acts as if I was going to slap her around or something. All she needs is a little guts. I'd straighten her out myself if she'd only listen to me instead of cry-babying all the time."

I asked, "Does she have reason to be afraid of you?"

As if puzzled by such a stupid question, he queried, "What do you mean by that?"

"Well, you mentioned she acts as if you were going to slap her around." Then I added, "*Do* you slap her around?"

"Sure," he replied arrogantly, "when she needs it."

"When does she need it?" I asked, as if what he had just said was reasonable.

"Oh, she's always acting as if she's better than anyone else. If I bring anyone home she acts like a damn fool. If anyone says one damn thing, she goes into her room and locks the door. She used to, I mean, but she doesn't any more. Her idea of being a wife is to put on the dog all the time."

During this exchange his wife had said not a word. She looked as if she would like to escape from this embarrassing scene. Turning back to the husband I asked, "When was the last time you straightenend her out? What had she done?"

"The day before yesterday," he replied, glancing over at his wife, "I came home with a couple of guys I work with. We had a few cans of beer, and we called up some other guys and was going to have a little poker game. I told her to get us some grub, and she started to, and then she disappeared. She locked herself in the room and wouldn't answer. She got fooled, though." Turning to his wife, "Didn't she, baby? She really got fooled though. Didn't she?"

"How was that?" I asked.

"I broke the goddam door down. I slapped her a couple of times and told her to get the hell out to the kitchen. I don't think she'll do that again in a hurry. I give her a good home, and I bring home plenty of grub, and what the hell does she do if anybody looks cross-eyed at her? She runs to her room and cries just like a little kid." He looked at me as if he knew I could understand and was agreeing with him about such sorry treatment.

I asked, "How often do things like this occur?"

"Practically all the time." He looked disgusted as he went on. "She likes to act as if she's better than anyone else, but she's nothing but a thief."

I looked, and felt, surprised.

"I may not be a brain, and maybe I don't go in for all them fancy ideas but, by Jesus, I don't go around taking money that belongs to other people." He looked at me and then, looking at his wife, he drew back his arm as if he were going to strike her from all the way across the room. She drew back and looked away, blushing and seeming on the verge of tears.

I felt that the girl had had about all she could take. I said, "Perhaps we had better postpone this until later. I have someone coming in soon." Looking at the husband, I continued, "I'd like to talk with you again, and I'd like to see if we can get your wife feeling better. These things are not usually all one-sided. None of us is perfect." Then, acting as if he and I were on the same side in our understanding of women, I said, "Women look at things differently than men, you know. Perhaps if we talk for a while we can find a way to get everything straightened out." Then, attempting to appeal to his vanity, I said "The biggest men are those who will listen to reason and accept advice if it is reasonable. You look to me," and here I stretched the truth a good deal, "like a man who has principles and doesn't mind listening to a few suggestions if they're offered in a friendly spirit." I asked if he would be willing to come in alone within a few days. He said he would, and we set up the appointment for the next evening. He then turned to his wife and said, "I'm willing to do anything that's reasonable. I'll even forget about the dough you took. I'll come in and yak with this guy tomorrow night, but if this isn't straightened out by tomorrow night, you can either start acting like you're supposed to act, or you can get the hell out." He emphasized his last remark with a truculent shake of his head: "You can either start acting like a goddam woman or you can get the hell out...and I damn well mean it!"

As he started for the door I said, "Call me tomorrow...", but I was looking at his wife as I spoke, and she nodded her agreement. Then, as her husband turned back to me, I finished as if I had been addressing him: "...if you can't make it."

I had assumed, until his last statement to his wife, that he had no intention of a separation. It was so obvious to me that in this marital "grab bag" he had drawn the better package. It was hard to imagine that he could actually think his ultimatum would be regarded as a threat. I later wondered how she had come to marry him in the first place; the next day I found out.

The patient (whom we shall call Marian) called the next morning and, although she was quite apprehensive about her husband finding out, she requested an appointment for that same morning. She came in, as we had arranged, at eleven o'clock. She didn't want me to have the wrong impression of her, she said, but she had not dared to speak up when her husband said she had stolen some money. "I took the money all right," she explained, "but I felt it was as much mine as his. My folks gave us five-hundred dollars as a wedding present, and we used it as a down payment on our car. Since then they have sent us five-hundred dollars every Christmas, and Jack always makes me endorse the check, and that's the last I ever see of it. He says that he pays all the expenses, and I should be willing to contribute this money to partially repay him."

"Do your folks know about this?" I asked.

"No." She shook her head. "My mother and dad were very much against my marriage to Jack. My father especially. He said he couldn't understand what I saw in him." She shrugged her shoulders. "I don't know...I guess I didn't want them to know about some of the things that happened." She started to cry, softly. "I guess what Jack says is right. I haven't any guts. I need someone to help me all the time. Just like a baby."

She looked so unhappy. "Would you rather not talk about it right now?" I asked gently. "Would you prefer to wait, or not talk about it at all?"

"No. I'd like to see what you think." She wiped her eyes and took a deep breath. Then, "I decided last night that I am going to talk to you, if you will listen, and I've made up my mind to do whatever you suggest. I can't go on this way. I'd rather be dead. Maybe that's the answer. I don't know..."

"Let's do this," I interrupted her. "Make believe you are talking about someone else. You'll find it easier that way. If you wish to, you can start right from the beginning. From the time you first met Jack. But just imagine you are talking about another girl entirely. Can you do that?" She nodded, then looked up at the ceiling in the typical gesture of one who is trying to recall.

She had gone out with Jack, the first time, just before graduating from high school. It had been a double date and, although his manners and speech had repelled her somewhat, she had been impressed with his honesty and straightforward admission that he lacked some of the social niceties. She did not like to think of herself as a snob or an unfair person and found herself, on subsequent occasions, defending him to her friends. She had felt she might be good for him, be able to help him in various ways; but she had had no thought of falling in love with him. She hadn't noticed at the time that some of the young men she had been dating were not calling her any more. The only boy who was calling, and with whom she had dates, was Jack. She had been asked, some time previously, to go to the senior prom with another boy, and she had accepted. She had had no idea, she said, of Jack's serious intentions until the night of the prom. She had not mentioned it to Jack, but had simply refused him a date for that night. The other lad had called for her, taken her to the prom and then disappeared after intermission. She didn't find out until the following week that Jack and two of his buddies had waylaid her partner, beaten him badly and told him to stay away from her. When Jack came in to say he wanted to speak with her for a few minutes, she saw nothing wrong in going out to his car. He had started the engine, remarking that he wanted to warm it up, and then, suddenly putting the car in gear, he drove off with her, ignoring her protests. He was furious, she recalled. He had driven for miles as fast as the car would go, finally stopping in a desolate wooded area. He had raped her and then threatened to harm her and her folks if she ever told anyone about it.

She was his girl now and anyone who tried to take her out would be "taken care of." He had forced her to submit to him twice more that night and then had taken her home after telling her she was surely pregnant and no one else would marry her.

For the following few weeks he had kept after her continuously with threats of what would happen if she talked or went out with another boy. But he also began to give her presents, to ask her advice about clothes and social graces and to tell her his actions had been dictated by his deep love for her.

Five weeks after the night of the prom they were married.

During the following year a number of significant events had occurred. Her father's company asked him to open a branch office in another state. He accepted the position and, as a result, the family moved to a city several hundred miles distant. Her husband had been proud and considerate of her most of the time and had taken evening courses as a means of self-improvement. Toward the end of the first year, however, everything began to change. Jack quit night school and belittled or ridiculed the value of formal education. He started going out with other women, at first secretly, then very openly. He apparently had convinced his wife that he was not to blame as he had a "normal sex drive" which she could not satisfy and he, therefore, was justified in obtaining satisfaction elsewhere. From then on she could do nothing to please him. Her every act was subject to criticism. He called her stupid, a "gutless wonder", frigid, etc. He even accused her of not being a virgin when he married her, knowing full well it was his own violent action that had made this so. He had said she "must have wanted it" or she would not have allowed him to have her. He always kept sums of money hidden about the house as a reserve for his poker games. It was some of this money she had "stolen". He had charged her with not dressing smartly, as the wives of his buddies did, yet he would give her no money for so doing. She had thought that if she bought a pretty dress and other things she needed he would be pleased, not only at her improved appearance but also at the evidence of her having the "guts" to take the money. This was the first time he had beaten her and called her a thief. She had run from the house, bloody and screaming, to be taken to the hospital by a neighbor. The next day he had gained entrance to her room at the hospital by appearing extremely concerned for her and also owing to the fact that she had told no one what had happened. He again used a combination of threats and promises to obtain her agreement that she would say she had fallen down the stairs. When she returned home from the hospital, his promises were soon forgotten. He dominated her thoughts and actions more than ever, always with ridicule and abuse. She finally left him, and it was during this time that her headaches had begun. She managed to get back home to her folks, but she had made it appear that nothing was wrong, that it was just a normal visit while Jack "was away on business."

It had taken Jack nearly a month to cajole her into going back with him.

This episode was, apparently, typical of the period over the next four years, until the time that she first came to see me.

It is clear that the emotional content of these headaches was not caused directly, as it might appear, by the treatment she had received from her husband. Nor was the cause associated with apprehension over the beatings. This is a very important point. If the treatment for her headaches had consisted of procedures so designed as to bring about a reliving of her original traumatic experiences with her husband, with abreaction of the associated emotions, the results would have been unpredictable, perhaps even disastrous. For this young woman was greatly in need of support and direction.

One might say that Marian's masochism was an important factor promoting her tolerance of maltreatment. But it was impossible to work on this element with her at the start. It was more practical to tackle another basic factor, her indecision. It was this that made it so difficult to determine the exact cause behind the symptoms. Her headaches did not seem to correlate with the traumatic episodes. She appeared to be motivated by a strong drive to do "right". If she had been able to feel that it was right to stay with her husband she would have continued to put up with anything he did, as many righteous women do. She was also motivated by a strong "negative" drive to avoid doing "wrong". She could not be sure in her own mind as to what was right or wrong. Her husband had tried to convince her that everything she did was wrong. But she was intelligent enough to know that this could not be so. "How could she be wrong for doing one thing and also wrong for doing the opposite?"

As we discussed the matter further, it became clear to me that headaches had occurred each time she had arrived at a point of indecision. Although the indecision, at the start, had to do with the "right" or "wrong" of leaving her husband and the "right" or "wrong" of staying with him, the headaches soon became conditioned as responses to any imagery associated with staying or leaving. For example, she could not understand why she had headaches after watching a happy woman walk past her house or a neighboring woman working hard scrubbing a floor. Such stimuli are easy to associate with "freedom" and "happiness" being right, and working hard about the house as being right too.

I pointed out to the patient that in my opinion she should first learn to clarify her ideas of what she really considered "right" and "wrong". She should then find some way of adhering to her conclusions and of remaining relaxed while doing so. She agreed to come in twice each week for a while so I could talk to her about how in my opinion other people make such decisions and in order that she could learn control and relaxation through self-hypnosis. I assured her I would do my best to see that she had nothing further to fear from her husband and that no harm would come to him either.

I intended to give her enough different interpretations to permit her to make up her own mind as we went along. I did not wish to impose my own views upon her, but only to help her to come to decisions of her own.

The session with her husband that night was in many ways exactly what one would expect. He attempted to show me what a "martyr" he was in putting up with such a woman. I led him into committing himself on various points such as "womanly virtue", "marital sexual obligations" and "fidelity"; then I proceeded to point out how shallow his thinking had been. He finally admitted he had only been "putting up a front" and that most of his behavior had been dictated by a desire to convince himself that he was "better than her", feeling all the while that this was not true.

We discussed several directions he might take to straighten out matters so he could be worthy of his wife, but he frankly stated that he did not think he could follow through with any of them. He felt he had made a mistake in the first place, and he now wished to live a carefree life of a kind that Marian could not share. He even expressed a willingness to continue to support her as long as she would require it and not to molest her in any way.

On the day following her husband's visit, Marian came in to see me to show me a letter she had received from him. In it he had said he was sorry to have caused her all the trouble, and that she deserved someone better than he was. She could, he said, keep the house and he would send her money each week as long as she wanted him to. The only thing he wanted to keep was the car. He had signed the letter: "Good luck. You deserve it. Jack."

While I was reading the letter, I noticed that Marian was sitting with her hands pressed tightly to her temples. She appeared extremely upset. Leaning back in my chair I looked at her for a few moments, then spoke her name rather loudly. As she looked up, her eyes met mine, and I said, "You agreed to let me help you, didn't you?" She nodded, without speaking. Holding her gaze, I said: "You are going to relax for a little while. It is not necessary for you to make any decisions or even to think of anything. You need to relax and forget about things for a few minutes. We can decide what to do a little later. Your eyes feel heavy. With each breath your eyes are heavier. You are breathing deeper now, and you are relaxing more with each breath. As your eyes close you find yourself in a garden looking at flowers." Her eyes closed and she began to relax. I wanted to induce a deep trance, but I also wanted to direct her imagery and avoid any anxiety response. I continued, "You are looking at beautiful red roses. Everything is pleasant and relaxing. When I ask you later on to wake up, you will feel very relaxed as you do so. Meanwhile you see only the things I ask you to see... pleasant, relaxing things. You walk in the garden examining all the flowers, smelling and touching them. You notice a lovely red rose and, holding it gently, you lean over to smell its fragrance. From now on when you see, smell or think of a rose you will relax and feel calm." I then went over the entire pattern for self-hypnosis, including several suggestions of arm-rigidity, hand-levitation, and imagery of drifting along in a boat. I told her that when she woke up she would think only of what we talked about and would go right back deeper as I described the scene of the garden or the boat. As I counted from six to ten she woke up with a slight smile on her face.

She said, "I feel more relaxed than I have ever been in my life. Can I do this myself?"

"Yes," I replied. "You can do it easily. But let's talk for a few minutes first."

My objective was to show her she could relax easily by putting herself into a trance and that any suggestions as to feelings or mood would be effective when she made them herself.

She had been amazed at the way her arm "floated up all by itself" and by the imagery of drifting in the little boat. I thought I would help her to develop time-distortion and use the boat as the primary scene. I explained this to her, answered her few questions and then suggested she go through the pattern herself, letting her arm slide off the arm of the chair to let me know when she got to the "X". She was an excellent subject. In less than two minutes her arm reacted. I then described the boat scene and made the suggestions for time-distortion to occur during a "pleasant scene in which you are doing something you always have wished to do." When she woke up she reported with obvious pleasure that she had, in her imagery, enrolled for a course in art at one of the nearby universities and had then spent the rest of the morning, accompanied by two girl friends, looking for an apartment.

After we talked about the various uses to which she could apply self-hypnosis, she said, "I guess I have lots of decisions to make." Then, "What am I going to do about Jack?" She was perfectly calm and obviously had no headache, even though no suggestions had been made to that effect. I said, "Jack will be all right for a while, I'm sure. You can decide later what is best as far as he is concerned. You must do, in a way, what he is doing."

"What do you mean?" she asked, puzzled.

"You must think of yourself first," I replied. "That is what he is doing. But I mean it in a slightly different way. This idea may seem selfish to you at first, but let me finish and you'll see what I mean." I thought for a few moments. I knew she had a strong desire to feel that whatever she did was fair and right; but I wanted to make it clear to her that this should apply to herself as well as to others. Finally I said, "Each of us, in order to help others, must feel well ourselves. We must do whatever is necessary to feel happy, to be as strong and healthy as possible and to think as clearly as we can. If we do not do this we are in no position to do anything worthwhile for anyone else." I could see she was listening seriously. This view of life was apparently quite new to her. I asked, "Does that make sense to you? Do you see what I mean?"

Nodding, she said, "Yes...that does make sense, doesn't it? If a person is sad or not feeling well, he could not do as much for others." She looked up at me as if she had just been startled. "If I had been strong and confident, I could have helped Jack get over his feelings of inferiority. Couldn't I?" Without giving me a chance to reply, she went on, "I must figure out what is right for me before I can tell what is right for others." She leaned back in her chair and stared off into space for a minute or two. "You know...I can think of many instances when I must have hurt him terrible. I was always correcting him. He came home one day, all excited, to tell me he and two other fellows were going into business. The repair shop..." She looked as if she was going to cry. "That's all right," she sniffed, and took a deep breath and then, smiling, she continued, "All I did was correct his grammar and pull away from his greasy clothes when he wanted to kiss me." She shook her head. "What a little snob I was! I didn't realize it, but I was. Do you think I should find him and tell him I'm sorry?"

"Now wait a minute," I smiled, "this is only part of it. There are many answers you must find to questions you have asked yourself already and to new questions that will occur to you from now on. I would suggest that we go over some of these now. You might then begin to plan your course of action more intelligently." She agreed.

As a result of this and several other subsequent discussions, Marian and I worked out several long-range plans. These included signing up, as she had done in her imagery, for a full-time course of study at the university. Taking in several girls as roommates helped defray expenses and provided her a means of enjoying stimulating social relationships. She also worked out programs for reading, sports, music and what turned out to be a very beneficial practice of visiting, twice each week, a local respiratory clinic where she talked with polio patients, helped them to read by turning pages for them, etc. This was a source of great satisfaction for her. To be able to help someone else often has a profound therapeutic effect.

She also had two long conversations with Jack. She told him very seriously and more or less calmly that she intended to go through with these plans. She wasn't sure, she said, whether she loved him or not. She was not interested at the moment in a divorce, but would agree to one if he wished it. She intended to avoid any romantic entaglements until she was sure about her feelings for Jack, but she did intend to go out with other fellows occasionally for dinner or to other social events. She also implied she would go out with him from time to time if he agreed to keep it on a "boy friend" basis. To this date the couple are still separated, the husband living up to his agreement and the patient better off for it.

For more than a year Marian has continued to use self-hypnosis in many ways. It has helped her to remain relaxed under all sorts of circumstances. It has been a major factor, she feels, in eliminating procrastination, obtaining high grades in school, facilitating her music practice and in resolving many other problems. She has had no more headaches since the time of her third visit. Her psychologic tests indicate a marked improvement in her ability to get along with other people and to face issues squarely as they arise.

Surely self-hypnosis was a major factor here, but there were other factors of equal importance: Developing a concept of temporarily putting things aside so one can reevaluate his goals, take stock of his personality traits and plan a realistic program for both short and long-term gain; getting to know one's self and how one compares with others in his own environment; accepting a logical and systematic procedure and then following it consistently; reflecting on the good qualities and putting them into practice—all of these are beneficial procedures that can be used alone or will be facilitated with self-hypnosis. To expect self-hypnosis to do the whole job, then, is not being realistic.

On the other side of the picture, responses of relaxation, of relief from pain and anxiety, of assertiveness, happiness and general well-being can be conditioned to the same stimuli that formerly evoked opposite responses by the use of imagery and direct hypnotic suggestion.

The physician who is not trained to do psychotherapy, or who has no time to work psychotherapeutically with a patient, should always refer a patient who needs psychotherapeutic help in addition to self-hypnosis to a qualified psychotherapist. In this way he can facilitate the patient's progress where improvement requires dealing with the personal conflicts.

CHAPTER 12

ANXIETY

NXIETY RESPONSES are unquestionably among the most frequently experienced of all human reactions. We respond with anxiety to specially charged events and thoughts of the past, present and future. Our anxieties are excited by almost any situation associated with a catastrophic feeling of helplessness.

We may feel anxious when certain things happen or do not happen, and we often have several types of anxiety affecting us simultaneously. The causes may be real and well-founded or completely without apparent reason. The anxiety responses may be mild and infrequent, or they may be intense and continuous. Usually there is a disruptive physiologic reaction accompanying anxiety, and this is followed by fatigue. The infinite psychologic and physiologic varieties of anxiety-responses are beyond description. Any attempt to delineate, let alone explain, all the ways in which anxiety affects our lives would require many volumes. This is quite evident from the vast number of articles and books that are available on the subject.

It will not, fortunately, be necessary to analyze every phase of this subject in order to achieve our purpose: a better understanding of how anxiety-responses are conditioned. By separating the various types of anxiety-responses into general groups and then classifying and discussing several examples in each group, there should be sufficient clarification for our needs.

Although two or more persons can experience anxiety evoked by a single stimulus-object, each individual reaction is an entity within itself and is influenced by the related characteristics of the individual personality. Anxiety is a conditioned response. Not only does it evolve through the same processes as other conditioned responses, it is also affected in many ways by factors of reinforcement and extinction. Anxiety may not always be manifested in the outward behavior because the individual may develop defenses to conceal it from others—and, indeed, from himself.

There is often an element of "remoteness" about anxiety that distinguishes it from other reactions, particularly when it involves imagery of either past or future events rather than current phenomena.

Let us first consider a hypothetical situation in which anxiety is evoked by a noxious stimulus of a physical nature.

Our subject, Nancy, is a housewife, let us say, with two children: a seven-year-old boy and an eight-year-old girl. Nancy is engaged in doing her household chores. Her husband, Bill, is at work and the children are off to school. At the present moment Nancy is debating with herself: Shall or shall she not get dressed and drive down to the Community Center? Her conflict involves the alternative of cleaning and ironing a special dress shirt that Bill is planning to wear this evening to a formal dinner and dance that they both have been planning and looking forward to for some time. Nancy feels guilty over the fact that she has left Bill's shirt unlaundered until now. Her gown is ready, and so is Bill's tuxedo. In fact, everything is fine except that Bill is so fussy about his shirts. This is his only dress shirt, and he gets upset if it is not laundered professionally. She should, she realizes, have taken care of it days ago. If she takes it down to the cleaners now, she may not get it back in time. She decides that the only way out is to drag out the ironing board and do the job herself. She is really not an expert, but, if she takes her time, she'll do a good job. Bill is too finicky about his shirt, anyway.

After setting up the ironing board and plugging in the iron, Nancy spreads the shirt out on the board only to find there is a smudge right on the front of it. She takes the shirt to the sink and breathes a sigh of relief when the stain is readily washed off. She then realizes that she has not put water in the steam iron so once again she spreads the shirt out and, with the iron in her right hand, reaches with her left hand to turn on the faucet. Unknown to Nancy is the fact that the electric cord is frayed, and the worn area happens, at this moment, to come into contact with her right forearm. As she touches the faucet, a whole series of dramatic episodes is initiated: she experiences a severe shock, drops the iron onto the ironing board right in the middle of Bill's shirt, and, in her haste to remove it, suffers a burn on her right hand. She goes hurriedly to the refrigerator to get some butter to apply to the burn and, while doing so, thinks of the burned spot she could only too plainly see on the front of the shirt. She "sees" Bill arriving home and, in her imagery, she is holding out to him his ruined shirt. He starts to get angry until she shows him where she burned her hand. His anger is forgotten, he takes her hand and, lifting it to his mouth, tenderly kisses the injured area. He puts his arm around her and gently guides her to a chair, telling her it isn't so important that they go to the dinner...Abruptly her imagery changes. The dinner! Well, if it isn't important to Bill, it certainly is to her! Let's see...After all, Bill hasn't had a new shirt for some time...he deserves a new one and his thoughtful, loving wife is going to see that he gets one. She can see the admiration in his eyes as she presents him with his new shirt, tonight. That's the answer. That old shirt was about ready for the trash bin anyhow. But...how much does a dress shirt cost? Does she have the money on hand with which to buy one? Are the stores open this afternoon?

Finally, after putting the ironing board away, she gets some scissors and, cutting out the burned area from the front of the shirt, she drops it into the garbage disposal unit. She then rips the shirt into several pieces and stuffs them into her rag bag. She starts to take ten dollars from the insurance fund in her bureau drawer, takes fifteen instead, gets dressed and merrily takes off in her little VW for the shopping center. Everything is back to normal. That silly incident of the shirt is over with. Her imagery now revolves around what a nice husband Bill is. He'll understand, later on, about the money she needs to balance her budget. This will not come up until next week, and meanwhile she'll show him what a good wife really means to a man. He's going to be pleased with his nice new shirt and, undoubtedly, he will also smile with pleasure when his smart, loving wife shows him her new hat!

Let us go back now to see if we can trace and isolate some of the factors involved in this hypothetical case, especially those factors possibly connected with anxiety.

Nancy's original desire to have a suitable shirt ready for her husband was probably motivated by some mild anxiety. This anxiety was evoked by imagery of a situation she wished to avoid. That is, she was anticipating Bill's reaction, upon coming home that night, to finding out that he had no suitable shirt to wear to the dinner. The thought of not going to the dinner was also objectionable to her, and again, anxiety motivated further thinking.

It is important to notice that the *original* stimuli evoking these responses were not in themselves associated with anxiety. They had to do with imagery of a pleasant nature, i.e., getting ready for the dance, Nancy and her husband getting dressed, Nancy's pretty gown, etc. Then, realization that Bill's shirt was not ready evoked imagery with an anxiety content. Imagery of Bill's negative reaction and imagery of not going to the affair were the major elements that cued off anxiety. What Nancy did in her attempt to avoid these disagreeable future circumstances was her "anxiety-response". The anxiety was provoked by anticipatory imagery and probably would not have been observable to anyone else if there had been others present at the time. Her imagery having to do with her plans of how she would go about providing a suitable shirt were also "anxiety-responses", as were her physical activities resulting from these plans. *Anxiety* then, is associated with imagery of unpleasant events, and these events can either be *real* or *fanciful*.

Anxiety is evoked upon learning or recognition that certain ideas, events or circumstances are or may be objectionable or dangerous to the individual involved.

Anxiety is not only a response but may also be a stimulus promoting further responses. Anxiety-responses may be in the form of imagery and physiologic and motor reactions.

Anxiety-responses may include withdrawal or avoidance-responses, attack or aggression-responses and a host of characterologic reactions, like dependency on an authoritative symbol. These reactions may in turn stimulate further anxiety.

Anxiety-responses, as with other forms of learning, may be conditioned to the point where imagery is no longer a part of the reaction.

So far we have considered only Nancy's responses to imagery. Let us now see what possibly could have resulted from some of the other stimuli.

The most drastic reaction described in our hypothetical series of episodes probably was Nancy's response to the electric shock. This, of course, would have been easily observable to others had they been present. It is not necessary for us to get involved with the effects of various types of electric current, so we will assume that upon touching the faucet with her left hand Nancy was completing a 110 volt a.c. current. This would cause an immediate withdrawal reaction due to the effect of the current, which would cause the muscles in Nancy's arm to contract, thus pulling her hand away from the faucet and breaking the circuit. Along with this contraction of the muscles Nancy would have experienced a strong sensation in the form of a massive vibration traveling through her body. Actually there might not have been any perception of pain, but the sudden, unexpected stimulus might at least have severely startled her and certainly would have been objectionable. If Nancy had never before experienced an electric shock, she would now know what one feels like and would undoubtedly wish not to experience it again.

There are all sorts of factors that now would enter into the situation, and to describe them all would be impossible. To investigate one or two possible responses, let us say that Nancy had no knowledge whatever of electricity and that she was unaware that the frayed cord had been touching her arm. Upon reviewing the episode later, as she would certainly do, her violent sensation upon touching the faucet would predominate. Her imagery would revolve around that scene. She would "see" herself reaching toward the faucet, touching it, jumping back and dropping the iron. She might even reexperience some sensation of shock, partly in imagery and partly in an automatic movement of her hand. This review would contain elements of curiosity regarding what had happened and what had caused it to happen, and then some anxiety as to the possibility of its happening again. Here we have anxiety induced by imagery and this in turn evoking further imagery regarding future events such as, perhaps, how this objectionable situation could be avoided. Nancy may decide that there must have been something wrong with the faucet, and in her imagery she may see herself telling Bill about it when he arrives home that evening. She may also see herself avoiding touching the faucet again. She may have imagery of herself going about her work to see whether or not she will be inconvenienced by being forced to keep away from the sink. There may, of course, be other forms of imagery with varying degrees of anxiety associated with other objects in the total scene, but her anxiety-evoking imagery would probably follow a pattern similar to the one described.

The electric shock itself thus evoked a violent withdrawal-response of a physiologic nature, but we could not consider this reaction "anxiety". In turn the evoked imagery, in the form of review of the incident, also is not "anxiety". However, the resulting recognition that something about the faucet could cause an unpleasant sensation can be considered a form of anxiety. A recognition or learning has here taken place: that a situation is objectionable, although in the particular case illustrated the anxiety involves erroneous learning since, obviously, the faucet alone could not be responsible for the shock. This points out a direct parallel to many situations in which anxiety and anxiety-responses may be strongly conditioned for which no actual basis exists.

Let us suppose that when Nancy's children arrive home from school she relates the episode to them. Her son may be able to explain what actually happened and convince her that she can touch the faucet without harm to herself. She may be skeptical at first, depending upon how much confidence she has in her son and how reasonable she feels his explanation is. She may timidly touch the faucet and then, finding her son to be correct, touch it again more confidently. As she does this she again has imagery, but this time it includes scenes of touching the faucet with no harmful result. The anxiey associated with the faucet is consequently lessened. As time goes on, and she repeatedly touches the faucet without experiencing a shock, the imagery involving anxiety is neutralized and the anxiety-responses are extinguished as far as the faucet is concerned.

Nancy may well go through a similar series related to the ironing cord. Her anxiety may lead to responses of getting a new cord, in which case the anxiety would again be extinguished, or she may continue to use the cord and avoid touching it and the faucet simultaneously. In this case she would retain some anxiety, and her anxiety-response would be one of avoidance.

Keeping in mind that imagery is a component part of anxiety we can now see if it ever serves a constructive purpose. It was anxiety that led to the anxiety-response which caused Nancy to avoid touching the faucet. As it turned out, there was really no need for her to avoid the faucet, so we could say that the anxiety-response served no useful purpose. This type of anxiety-response is called "unadaptive". The anxiety also evoked another anxiety-response, that of avoiding the use of the faulty cord. As it is very likely that a person could be harmed by such a cord or that damage to the electrical equipment could result from its use, this anxiety-response would be considered as one that does serve a useful purpose. Here the anxiety-response is adaptive, as is the anxiety that evoked it.

So far we have four classifications: *anxiety* and *anxiety-response*, both of which may be *adaptive* or *unadaptive*.

Adaptive anxiety not only is purposeful but may be extremely essential to continued well-being. It is adaptive anxiety that leads to all the protective devices and procedures we use: The safety gates on elevators, the railings around high places, fire extinguishers, windshield wipers, locks on windows and doors, traffic lights, gates at railroad crossings... all these precautionary measures and many, many more were the result of anxiety on the part of those who invented them and later, on the part of those who had them installed. When any dangerous situation is recognized it is adaptive anxiety that initiates ideas as to what might be done to eliminate or avoid the resultant harm to ourselves and others. If we can find some way to do this, the anxiety-response is completed as we carry out the protective measures. If we can find no satisfactory measures to take, the anxiety-response continues to be evoked each time we are exposed to the same or a similar stimulus, whether it is sensory or imaginary.

Generally speaking, any anxiety evoked by a real threat to our continued well-being is adaptive. But when the anxiety is evoked by a stimulus that cannot possibly harm us it is unadaptive. For example, when we learn that large, fast-moving objects such as automobiles can seriously injure us, we have imagery of being knocked down. This unpleasant situation creates further imagery in which we explore for ways to avoid such injury. We imagine ourselves looking both ways before crossing a street. We recognize the advisability of staying within the marked cross-walks at busy intersections. We imagine ourselves crossing when the traffic has stopped for us, when the light is green, or when the street is free of oncoming vehicles. At some point we reach the decision that if we adhere to certain principles and patterns of behavior there is little chance that we will be injured. As we put these patterns into practice, they become more or less automatic. We learn to respond to peripheral stimuli, and the pattern becomes so firmly conditioned that we inadvertently jump backward if an object moves rapidly into our visual field. So far the anxiety and responses to it are adaptive. But if we respond in the same way to objects that enter our field of vision but can do us no harm, such as clouds, people walking by, etc., then that part of the anxiety-response is unadaptive.

Excessive anxiety, or extreme anxiety-responses are also unadaptive. That is, if the feeling or behavior is out of proportion to the threatening situation, such as crossing the street. If we observe reasonable precautionary measures the anxiety is serving a useful purpose; but if extreme responses, such as refusal to cross a street when no traffic is in evidence, are evoked, then the anxiety-response is partly unadaptive. It would of course be unwise to completely eliminate this anxiety-response, as this might lead to the taking of foolhardy risks. The person might not exercise enough caution in potentially dangerous situations. It is clear that only that degree of anxiety resulting in excessive or extreme reactions is unadaptive.

Over a period of time, anxiety-responses can be firmly conditioned to stimuli that no longer evoke imagery, and the person may be unaware of what constitutes these stimuli. This we may call "pervasive anxiety". Now, this does not mean the types of anxiety in which the stimuli are known but appear to be of a harmless nature. That would be "specific" anxiety. Only when the stimuli are not known is the condition "pervasive anxiety".

If anxiety-responses are evoked by such things as colors, soft sounds, certain friendly animals or any harmless object or situation, it may be reasoned that there must be some underlying cause. This may be true, but, for our purposes, the anxiety-responses would still be considered "specific". Both pervasive and specific anxiety-responses can be evoked in the same individual simultaneously or at different times and in varying degrees of intensity.

This brings us to the final classifications of "intensity" and "frequency". The latter should require very little explanation. It simply means the number of anxiety-responses or episodes evoked during a given period of time. This might be based on the number per day, week or month, or it might be continuous. The intensity would be evaluated by the degree to which anxiety-responses interfere with other activities or the severity of physiological and emotional elements contained therein.

Anxiety may be evoked upon recognition of dangerous or undesirable elements in past events that were not recognized as dangerous at the time of occurrence. For example, a person might drive over a certain road during a storm and be told later that he must have driven over a bridge, the underpinning of which had nearly washed away. Reports of the bridge collapsing a few minutes later undoubtedly would evoke anxiety in the form of imagery of what "might have happened". If this resulted in the individual utilizing reasonable caution thereafter before crossing bridges, his responses would be considered adaptive, but if his responses were so extreme as to prevent him from crossing bridges even after observing other cars crossing in safety, they would be unadaptive, at least to some degree.

A common example of anxiety that is evoked by events which have not yet happened is that of a person with stage fright. Here the imagery is of the individual failing to perform well. He imagines himself looking ridiculous in front of a scornful audience. He is more concerned with how he will feel or how he will appear to the audience than he is with the importance of what he is to say or do. Although he may know very well that there is little or no possibility of any harm befalling him, and that once in front of the audience he will do a good job, he will still suffer from anxiety-responses in the form of nervousness, tension and irritability.

It may help at this point to outline the elements of anxiety:

1. Anxiety, when first evoked, is always associated with some form of imagery of a real or fanciful situation that is considered dangerous or undesirable. This may or may not be well-founded.
2. Anxiety is evoked only by the imagery preceding it, and not by direct physical stimuli.
3. Anxiety may be evoked by imagery of past, future or current events.
4. Anxiety is essential, initially, to any anxiety-response, but such responses may become conditioned to the point that the imagery is no longer required to evoke them.
5. Anxiety-responses may occur in the form of imagery, physiologic or behavioral reactions, or combinations of these.
6. Anxiety-responses may be adaptive or unadaptive, or combinations of each.
7. Anxiety-responses may be specific to stimuli that are actually or only fancifully of a threatening nature.
8. Anxiety-responses may be pervasive, in which case the stimuli are not known.
9. Anxiety-responses may be subjective, in which case they are

limited to imagery or sensations and physiologic reactions that are not readily observable to others.

10. Anxiety-responses may be objective and easily observable in the form of overt behavior: tremor, avoidance, blushing, rituals, lethargy, depression, fatigue, etc.

Another concept that is important to our discussion of anxiety is that of "drives" and "drive-reduction". The term "drive" is used to designate activity that leads or is intended to lead toward achievement of some goal. This activity may be physiologic, psychologic, behavioral, or a combination of these types. The so-called basic drives are those associated with bodily needs such as those initiated by hunger, thirst, discomfort, sexual desire, deprivation of homeostasis requirements, etc. The secondary, or acquired, drives have to do with the need for affection, knowledge, prestige, companionship, etc., and are considered by many investigators to be merely a generalized manifestation of the basic drives. A technical definition of "drive" would be "an excitation of the central nervous system that evokes behavioral patterns that, if successfully carried to completion, will reduce the need that originally initiated the excitation." In other words, the *need* is a form of deprivation (which may be real or fanciful) of a physiologic or psychologic nature. The need then, if physiologic, directly initiates excitation of the central nervous system. If the need is psychologic, it evokes imagery which then initiates the excitation. In either case the drive is reduced only upon successful execution of the behavioral pattern. In some instances, *imagery* of such successful execution may effect temporary or partial reduction of the drive, or it may result in an attempt to reduce the drive through some means other than execution of the behavioral pattern originally initiated.

Drive reduction is a major source of pleasure, and satisfaction and insufficient or incomplete drive-reduction can serve as a basis for anxiety. Everyone requires a certain amount of satisfaction, and if a specific drive is not reduced in order to result in adequate feelings of satisfaction, some of the energy of this drive may be deflected to a drive that is easier to reduce or to a form of behavior that may lead to further frustration. Such forms of behavior are usually considered abnormal and rarely have more than a temporary effect upon drive reduction, and therefore any resultant satisfaction is also temporary. In fact, owing to its abnormal nature, such behavior often leads to guilt and anxiety reactions.

A very obvious example of this is the person with a strong drive for affection who becomes a compulsive eater due to insufficient reduction of the original drive. This person is frequently one who has been conditioned over a long period of time by experiences in which affection drives were reduced in close temporal proximity to reduction of hunger drives. Such a person may have been used to going to various social affairs at which food was served, being at the same time accompanied by another person or persons who provided satisfactory reduction of the drive for affection. Then, too, there is always the conditioning that may have occurred during infancy and childhood in which feeding is associated with feelings of comfort, protection and security. As such a person grows older the affection-drive may become stronger due to increased feelings of insecurity, and reduction of the drive may be less frequent or less complete. In either case there may be such a decrease in satisfaction that the person attempts to maintain the established pleasure level by increasing the intake of food. This, of course, may result in obesity, which may in turn result in fewer episodes of expressions of affection. We now have the classic "vicious cycle" of excessive eating, excessive weight, guilt and anxiety feelings, increased affection-drive and back to excessive eating again as an ineffective and futile attempt to achieve satisfaction.

The attempt to reduce one drive through excessive behavior associated with a different drive is the most frequent means of all those we use in seeking satisfaction. Rarely, if ever, does it succeed.

One of the difficulties arising from a situation such as that described above is that the excessive eater is also depriving himself of the satisfaction that would normally ensue from reduction of the hunger-drive. He no longer gets truly hungry. There is so much food being stored in the overweight body that more food has little significance. It should be obvious that food will not replace affection; it will serve only to diminish the total sources of pleasure and satisfaction.

Many people will not face the fact that a drive exists, and the attempt to ignore or inhibit it may lead to serious consequences. This is most obvious in drives that seem to conflict with social customs and taboos, notably the sex-drive.

It is truly amazing how many people reach adulthood with erroneous knowledge—or none at all—regarding sexual matters. Many parents avoid such discussions and censure their children for asking questions about sex or for any expression of interest or natural curiosity or behavior. It is true that some improvement has been made in recent years, but problems involving sex are still a very major source of human ailment and dissatisfaction.

In a recent survey by one of the foremost national publications, a large number of parents were asked to describe the manner in which they educated their children on sex. Most of them reacted as if they would rather not talk about it and as if the subject of sex were in some way repulsive. Our children, evidently, are supposed to get this information from "someone else". Well, they generally do, but the difficulty lies in the fact that the ones who instruct them are no more qualified to give such instruction than are the children themselves.

There is no intention here to make an issue of what is proper or improper procedure in sexual education, but only to point out that such factors should be considered in any consideration of the underlying causes in anxiety.

Many anxieties are due to conflicts arising from a normal sex-drive and guilt-reactions evoked during drive-reduction or because of attempts to inhibit or divert such drives.

Incongruous as it may seem in this "enlightened age", there are great numbers of people who believe that masturbation causes "brain damage", impotence and a host of other undesirable consequences. What often happens is that people who believe this will either inhibit the sex-drive to such a point that its reduction is attempted in some other way, or they will go ahead and reduce the drive through masturbatory acts and then feel guilty for so doing.

One typical example of inhibition is the person who has been brought up to believe that sex is "dirty", a "sin", or simply that it should not be discussed or expressed in any way. This person then becomes very active in other ways of seeking satisfaction and may appear to be very prudish. There may even be an excessive avoidance of any situations remotely associated with sex. If these other activities prove satisfying, and if the sex-drive is not too strong, this may work out well. On the other hand, such a person may go to extremes in these other activities and appear to be abnormal because of his behavior.

In many localities there is no way for young people to meet members of the opposite sex except in places of business or perhaps in cocktail lounges and bars. What often happens is typically illustrated in the following case.

An attractive young woman who has recently divorced her husband may be struggling to provide for one or more children. Perhaps one of the reasons for the divorce was her prudish attitude about sex. As time goes on, a normal sex-drive may be inhibited to the point that this young woman begins to seek other ways of obtaining satisfactions from life. It might be supposed that her work, her household and her children should be sufficient, but, as we all know, what others think does not significantly affect our own evaluation of the amount of pleasure and satisfaction we feel we need. It would not be unusual for a girl such as this to inhibit her drives for a long period of time and then suddenly decide to drop into a cocktail lounge for "one or two drinks". The feeling of relief may well be so satisfying and seemingly unattainable in any other way that this girl could become conditioned to excessive drinking to the point of becoming an alcoholic. Because of the release of inhibitions she may decide to accept a proposal of a sexual nature and later be so overwhelmed by her "sinful" experience that she "blacks out" and has no recollection of the entire episode. There may be some hazy idea of what happened, or there may be an intense anxiety reaction to imagery of what might have occurred. In addition to feelings of guilt, there may be apprehension regarding possible pregnancy, disease, loss of social stature, loss of alimony, the children, etc.

The problem in such situations is that the person will not face the fact that such drives exist, or if they will face it, they feel there is no acceptable way they can reduce the drives. If a way is found for the person to reduce the drive over a period of time and in such a way that they retain control over the situation, periodic episodes of such an extreme nature would no longer occur.

There are many people, even those well past middle age, whose entire lives have been drastically affected because of erroneous beliefs regarding sex. One man in his late fifties, for instance, revealed to me that he "knew" his brain had been damaged because of masturbation when he was young. Here was a man who had a lovely wife, three grown children and several grandchildren, yet whose entire life had been shadowed by a mistaken notion. He had remained in one type of job for many years because he felt he was incapable of using his "mind" properly. He overcame this anxiety and went on to a better job, but only after he was able to be convinced that his beliefs had no foundation in fact.

Knowledge of the true facts of life and the ability to face them will go a long way toward reducing anxiety. We should clearly understand that all of us biologically and psychologically require a certain amount of satisfaction, and that a great deal of this satisfaction can come from reduction of basic drives. When we become tired from physical exertion, a drive to obtain rest develops and of course, resting reduces this drive. Everything else being equal, the reduction results in satisfaction. Reduction of any or all basic drives—sex, hunger, thirst, fatigue, freedom from pain, etc.—are all sources of satisfaction, but only when the drive-reduction is achieved directly rather than through excessive attempts to reduce one drive in order to affect another. Only when hunger exists does eating provide such satisfaction. Only when fatigue is present does rest prove beneficial. And only when affection is received will the drive for affection be reduced satisfactorily.

Many people do not obtain much benefit from drive-reduction today. They eat because "it is time to eat" rather than because of hunger. Sleep and rest conform to habit and custom rather than to need. Our modern culture, especially in this country, has tended to minimize the satisfactions obtainable from reduction of basic drives. Instead there is increasing emphasis on secondary drives. Unfortunately, however, there is little emphasis placed upon their reduction. Let us consider some of the most prevalent instances of secondary drives so we can see how such matters affect our lives and happiness.

It is quite evident that millions of persons in this country have strong drives to possess certain material things such as cars, houses, automatic washing machines, swimming pools, silver place-settings, corporations, etc. It is equally evident that many of these possessions represent different things to different people. Possession of an automobile may be associated with achievement of a means for reducing a basic drive or it may be associated with an image of prestige which would be part of a secondary drive. Now, secondary drives can develop in an infinite number of directions and intensities, but the more remotely they are associated with basic drives, the less probability there will be of drive-reduction to any significant degree. The possibilities of obtaining satisfaction are also diminished.

The person who buys a car solely for transportation purposes may derive considerable satisfaction from an old-model car because his motivation involves only the getting from one place to another more expediently than if he were to walk. This the car can do for him, and he is satisfied. If, however, the car is purchased as a means of obtaining prestige, the drive is then of a secondary nature and is not likely to be very much reduced. There may be considerable satisfaction derived from driving the car for a certain length of time and to certain places where the prestige value is evident, but in places where there are better cars, and after the newness wears off, there is more anxiety regarding the price and upkeep and less from possession. Even if the drive is partially reduced, it is tinged with anxiety, and when the new models arrive the drive continues with renewed strength.

One young couple who had consulted me professionally were searching for ways to reduce their anxiety regarding finances. They expressed concern over payments on their new car, their new home, their furniture, and hospital bills incurred in respect to their children. The husband made as much or more money than most of his neighbors, but expenses were exceeding his income. The young mother became quite upset when one of the children knocked over a toy which caused a scratch to appear on the leg of a new table. She wanted to know if "something could be done with those kids." It was pointed out that perhaps the parents of "those kids" had established a poor set of values. If the table could be thought of as a functional piece of furniture rather than as part of an over-all prestige pattern, it could acquire "character" along with the rest of the family and perhaps some day she would take pleasure in telling how "Jackie" had scratched it. It was possible to show these folks that they had been developing strong drives that would go on for most of their lives and that if they continued in the way they were going, they would rarely experience sufficient satisfactions, because reduction of such drives would not bring enough feelings of accomplishment.

This couple eventually moved into an older house. They not only balanced their budget, but began to accumulate savings which gave them feelings of security. Best of all, they began to enjoy their children more because they no longer let a scratched table assume tragic proportions.

This does not mean that all secondary drives are undesirable or that drives for prestige and ambition should be avoided. We are all different from one another in our personality structures, and our drives vary in type and strength as greatly as their reduction varies in providing satisfaction. Anyone experiencing anxiety might do well to examine such drives to see if their reduction will provide sufficient satisfaction to compensate for the necessary energy to be expended. They may possibly discover that by altering one or two such drives, reduction that might otherwise be impossible can be achieved.

Occasionally drives develop that conflict with each other in various ways. This conflict can involve drives that are toward desirable goals, or toward undesirable goals, or that are opposed to each other.

A man may recognize, for instance, a strong drive to achieve a closer relationship with a certain young lady and yet at the same time have a strong drive to avoid being tied down by marriage. If these drives assume equal proportions, a very difficult situation may evolve in the event the lady insists on marriage. The man may consider breaking off the relationship, which would satisfy his drive to be independent, but unfortunately, this mobilizes imagery of losing the lady and the opportunity for a closer relationship. The poor fellow then is right back where he started. Situations such as this can develop into very serious emotional problems involving high intensities of anxiety and can actually grow beyond the coping powers of the individual. Essential decisions may have to be imposed upon the person from external sources.

The "eternal triangle", for instance, always involves conflict in drives. Consider the case of the business man with an invalid wife who can no longer provide him with the satisfactions he considers essential. He may, without realizing it, begin to spend more time in town and have lunches and dinners with his secretary with increasing frequency until at some point he may feel he must make a decision. Now, this man really may be very virtuous. It could be extremely upsetting to him when he realizes he has gone as far as he has, though his utmost transgression may have been to stay away from home for several meals. He may be able to discontinue this activity or keep it from going further and begin to show more interest in his wife and home. He can, however, go in the opposite direction; paradoxical as it may seem, the more upright and honorable he feels he is, the more he is likely to become further involved with the "other woman". This may be owing to the increased significance he attaches to all his thoughts and behavior as compared to another man who would think nothing of such acts. In worrying about it, our "middleman" may worry himself right into the very situation he wishes to avoid. He may then arrive at a point exactly equidistant from the two perfectly balanced situations. As he approaches one, the other becomes more attractive. When he turns the other way the same thing happens. As he goes through these emotional acrobatics, he is only reinforcing both drives and making reduction of either increasingly more improbable. Only a firm decision on the part of one of the ladies involved can possibly affect the situation. He cannot resolve it himself. And if both ladies make their decisions at the same time and in the same direction, the results can be at least disturbing, and sometimes disastrous.

The man who becomes involved with two or more women simultaneously may be trying to prove his masculinity to others or to himself, and he will rarely keep his activities secret. He may do so for a time; in fact, he may feel he is going to great lengths to avoid "hurting" any of the people involved. He may even develop feelings of self-righteousness. He wouldn't wish to deprive anyone of the pleasure of his attentions; she might not be able to bear it! She might do something rash. However, if everything goes along smoothly for too long a period, he will eventually be unable to resist letting someone else know what is going on. He will not obtain the satisfaction he needs until he does so, and strangely enough, the person he is most anxious to have find out about the situation may be his wife. He may tell her himself. This type of "confession" is usually a means of letting his wife know that he is attractive to others; she should appreciate him more because of it.

The purpose in relating the above is not so much an attempt to explain specific emotional relationships as to show that secondary drives can be extremely complex and are not always what they appear to be on the surface. One who has a drive to appear strong may be attempting to compensate for feelings of inferiority or inadequacy. The excessively kind person may be trying valiantly to conceal a violent temper. The forgiving person may be one who would wish to be forgiven if it were he in the role of transgressor. This is not to say that everyone who is kind, forgiving or heroic is really just the opposite; on the contrary. Mature people are quite apt to behave as they truly feel; a mature person, however, is not one who is likely to have a high degree of anxiety. Since we know that high levels of anxiety exist among us, we must be able to face ourselves and admit our immaturities if we are to understand the basis for our anxieties.

If a "kind" and "considerate" person is behaving in what appears to be an adaptive fashion, it may not be desirable for him to change, even though his underlying drives are questionable. It easily could happen that such an individual can derive ample satisfactions from his compensatory behavior until his underlying drives are altered or diminished, and he behaves as he truly feels.

If, on the other hand, the kindly person recognizes an increasing tension and difficulty in maintaining such a façade, there is then a need for revaluation of drives and satisfactions.

Overcompensation of a different type is frequently observable in many people, for instance in those who appear to be "aggressive" and "unkind". Again, this kind of behavior may truly be representative of underlying drives, or it may be a means of avoiding feelings of inferiority, etc. Many times these drives develop because of erroneous beliefs or misunderstandings the individual has regarding himself or others. There are many people with excellent qualities and personality characteristics who simply cannot believe that they deserve the trust and affection of others, so they are continuously "testing" or doing things to provoke their friends and loved ones. They may or may not know why they behave as they do, but they invariably have high levels of anxiety and tend to keep others in a turmoil. They may even feel that if someone loves or trusts them, the person doing so is stupid or is only making believe that he feels the way he appears to feel.

Some years ago I met a man with a very interesting personality who had a tendency to speak a little more loudly than the occasion required. He was in the field of law enforcement, and the stories he related were extremely stimulating, but his loud tones were a little disturbing not only to me but to others of our mutual acquaintance. This was not due, as is often the case, to any impairment of his hearing, and eventually, when he had expressed an interest in self-hypnosis, he revealed the underlying reason. He began his explanation first by asking me to feel his biceps, which actually felt as "hard as a rock". He went on to tell me that, as a youngster, he had been rather short in physical stature (he was still below average) and not as strong as other children. He also had stuttered very badly and could find no one to help him with this affliction. Finally he had reasoned that if he could become "better" in some way than most other people, he would overcome his stuttering. He recognized that he had felt inferior owing to his being shorter than the other children. He began working out in a gym every day and, sure enough, as he became more muscular his stuttering had diminished. As he matured, he continued with his physical exercises and his desire to pass the examination for the police force was realized at approximately the same time as his stuttering ceased completely. He knew that he had simultaneously developed the habit of talking too loudly, but he felt he had to, or he would revert again to his stuttering. He developed the ability to use self-hypnosis and quickly overcame this habit without the slightest tendency to stutter. Utilizing imagery in which he "saw" himself in various situations talking normally, he was able to emphasize the favorable reaction of his audience to *what* he was saying and minimize his concern over his *appearance*. The ability to recognize and accept both his virtues and his faults allowed him to direct his drives in a constructive way and to achieve satisfaction as he attained his goals without weight-lifting or muscular gymnastics.

A fear of being considered in some way inadequate frequently is the basis of misdirected drives. This is seen in men who have become sexually impotent because of an excessive drive toward proving their masculinity to themselves or to others. Such a man may not understand women as thoroughly as he thinks. It is true, of course, that some women as well as men desire physical evidence and active expression of the passion they arouse in their partner. But these evidences and expressions may vary from time to time, and if erroneous interpretations are made of the other person's desires the results can be far from satisfactory for either or both. Most women at one time or another seek expressions of tenderness and wish only for gentle words and caresses to assure them that they are loved and wanted. Men often tend to think more of existing situations and hope to prove their love violently in "one fell swoop". It is traumatic to some men to perform inadequately sexually even once. They believe their manhood to be in jeopardy, and no one can convince them otherwise, regardless of logic. Their major objective from then on is to recoup their shattered self-esteem. Unfortunately, they will only be satisfied with a magnificent performance of which they have never been capable, whereas their partners would be satisfied with much less.

The reaction of the man who has "failed" provides a very interesting study. His wife may not have had the desire for a "bedroom cowboy"; as a matter of fact, she may for years have been hoping that he would slow down. But when she attempts to convince him of this, he thinks she is only feeling sorry for him. Because she is "being so nice about it" he decides he must try even harder to do better each time. These situations can generally be improved or entirely resolved through understanding and appropriate activity on the part of both involved parties. Too often there is a reluctance to discuss these matters or a tendency for one person to feel that the *other* should "know" how to act. The admonition to "know thyself" is an excellent one for people with problems, and in marital situations it is doubly important.

If anxiety is found to be based on erroneous drives, then changing the drives is mandatory. Coming to know yourself starts the process, a process which may not be too difficult.

Perhaps the most important single factor in reducing anxiety is knowledge of its cause. If it is felt that the cause is already known, the systematic procedures to be outlined should still be followed. Often "knowledge" about sources of anxiety may prove to be mistaken, particularly if self-acquired.

First of all, hypnosis or self-hypnosis should not be considered a means in itself. It may be true that hypnotic techniques can bring about reduction of high levels of anxiety, but it is more than likely that other psychologic influences are knowingly or unknowingly involved. Long-range results will be better served by seeking out possible underlying factors responsible for anxiety, and then if hypnosis is indicated, a positive outcome will be more highly predictable.

Although anxiety is a psychologic phenomenon, it invariably has physiologic concomitants. It is for this reason and to rule out coexisting organic problems that a thorough physical examination is indicated as a first step in the treatment of anxiety. Even though the anxious individual may feel physically fit, it is essential that he be further reassured after a thorough examination by a competent medical practitioner. The assurance that nothing is wrong, or that whatever is wrong will now be corrected, may in itself reduce anxiety. If the individual has some prejudices, misconceptions or religious beliefs that have kept him from consulting with a physician, or if he feels that his problem is one of "mind over matter", he should seriously consider the proposition that a medical expert in physiology will help him to correct his misconceptions but will not encroach upon his religious beliefs. He can liken his mind and body to a house in which he lives; what goes on in his house is his own business, as is what goes on in his mind. But if something goes wrong with the structure of his house, it is best repaired by an expert in such matters. If the heating system fails the expert can fix it, and the person is better able to carry on with his activities as he chooses. The expert has not interfered with his chosen activities, yet he has helped him to carry them on. By the same token the physician is the expert who can keep the body in good condition while the individual can cherish his private spiritual beliefs.

Very frequently there are people who have symptoms that do not respond to established methods of treatment. These are the conditions usually thought of as "psychosomatic". That is, there appears to be no organic basis for the symptoms, and the causes are therefore considered to be of a psychologic nature. This is often difficult for the patient to accept. He may feel that the doctor is implying that he is only "imagining" his symptoms, that they are all "in his mind". In this, of course, the patient errs. When a doctor says a condition is "psychosomatic", "psychogenic" or "hysterical", he does not mean that the symptoms do not exist or that the pain or disability is imaginary. What he does mean is that he can find no physiologic basis for the symptoms, and though they are identical to symptoms that usually have a basis, in this case there is an underlying emotional reason that initiates the symptoms. Occasionally a person who is told that his symptoms must have an emotional cause can accept the diagnosis and disclose the underlying conflict. Much more frequently the person can see no possible reason for his symptoms. This is understandable, as most everyone thinks of pain and discomfort as physical rather than psychologic. The phlegm of the asthmatic, the inflamed skin of eczema, the throbbing, nausea and visual disturbances that often accompany various types of headaches certainly appear physical indeed. It is easy to see how difficult it is for the sufferer to ascribe his suffering to emotional trauma. Yet many people have, as the result of emotional factors, developed symptoms which were serious enough to warrant urgent surgery, only to find afterward that there was no organic basis for their complaints.

The person who wishes to rid himself of anxiety must face the fact that his symptoms may be caused by underlying conflicts that he either does not, or will not recognize. Whether or not he believes this to be so, he should proceed as if it was true. This is the only way he can explore the possible basis for his anxiety. Of course, it is not always necessary to plumb the deepest sources of anxiety. The mind has many defenses and reparative mechanisms that can help repress or eliminate anxiety. The causes of anxiety may be so profoundly rooted in the individual's personality structure that they may be impossible to eliminate without extensive psychiatric treatment. This may not be practical for many reasons, such as limited finances, the absence of qualified psychiatrists, etc. It may suffice to arrive at a general idea of the causes of anxiety and then attempt to live around or master these. This is the objective in supportive psychotherapy.

Hypnosis may be of help here, and the doctor who is willing to co-operate with his patient to the extent of advising him in what areas he should use self-hypnosis will be pleasantly surprised with the results. It is not even necessary for the doctor to be expertly versed in hypnotic techniques. In fact it is better for him to leave this up to his patient. By assuring the patient that he is in good health—if this is so—and then, if the patient wishes to use self-hypnosis, mentioning the psychologic factors that he feels may be inhibiting emotional well-being, the doctor may have a patient who is motivated toward helping himself. The doctor who will gently guide his patient in his desire to use self-hypnosis, while at the same time he prescribes his regular medical treatment for the patient's symptoms, will be helping most effectively.

If anxiety is involved, the use of tranquilizers should be minimized to the fullest extent the doctor deems advisable. The efficacy of self-hypnosis as a supportive modality should be tested to avoid the side and after-effects of the tranquilizers.

Once the physical condition of the patient has been intelligently evaluated, and reasonable measures are under way to correct any mal-function, other measures may be taken to reduce anxiety-responses. In some instances the physician may seek to regulate the patient's diet, since psychologic as well as physical well-being is associated with the food and drink a person consumes. Self-hypnosis may help the individual to follow a proper diet, should he lack motivation to do so.

Irritating external circumstances may prevent resolution of anxieties and these should, if possible, be controlled. Financial problems, for example, are rampant, and the patient should be encouraged to resolve them. Serious consideration should be given to items such as luxuries that may seem important but actually are only stirring up more anxiety because of their cost. The person who insists on remaining in debt because of his need for luxurious trivia will have great difficulty in eliminating anxiety. A decision must be made as to which is more important: peace of mind or unneeded possessions. Lack of friends and companionship tends to stimulate tension. The individual with emotional problems often avoids other people, and this will exaggerate his diffi-culties. It is important for such a person to ventilate his ideas as well as listen to the problems of others. Frequent opportunity to give expression to emotions and opinions and to listen to those of others will go a long way toward making one feel he is not alone. To realize that others have problems too can often be reassuring. Externalization of one's interests is a good way of diverting anxiety. Sports or hobbies serve also as a means of meeting people and of beginning to think outside one's self. One of the best ways of diverting attention from inner conflict is to seek some way to help others. Volunteer work with children, invalids and handicapped people may result in excellent benefits to the anxious individual.

If indecision of any kind is involved as a factor in anxiety, an attempt should be made to resolve it. The inability to make up one's mind can be most destructive. Many people are able to arrive at decisions once they realize that, right or wrong, it is important to mobilize action. Mistakes can be corrected in the doing. Anticipating difficulties tends to paralyze thinking and fills the individual with catastrophic expectations, thus enhancing his anxiety. If necessary, the advice of a trusted person may overcome inertia. If indecision persists, putting the problem aside until a more relaxed attitude prevails may provide a more suitable answer later on.

In dealing with the anxiety-responses themselves, consideration should be given to whether they are pervasive or specific or both. The over-all anxiety pattern should be studied after writing down the various factors and revising the notations:

First, a period of time must be selected that is typical of one's daily activities and includes several episodes of anxiety. For instance, if anxiety occurs only once or twice each month, a span of six months to a year must be taken as the evaluation period. If the anxiety is experienced two or three times each week, then one or two months would be sufficient. If it is more frequent, or continuous, then perhaps one week, or even one day will be enough to obtain proper data. The purpose is to determine, if possible, what proportion of the total period is associated with anxiety. The period of time under consideration should be as close to current as possible, that is, if details of each episode can be remembered and reported accurately as to time of day, day of week, etc. Notation should be made of the intensity of each episode together with any ideas as to what might have caused it, how the person felt and acted, of what he was thinking, who else was present at the time, where it happened, how much it may have interfered with other activities and, if possible, any random associated circumstances, no matter how remote they may seem.

The person should then compile a careful list of events, situations or individuals who evoke anxiety or "nervousness" in any way. This list should include consideration for all activities of the person and those around him as well as for any happenings in his environment. It should include the effects of all stimuli: For example, starting from the time he awakens, notations should be made of how he feels upon awakening and of anything he feels, sees, smells, hears, tastes or thinks that evokes any anxiety-response from then until he goes to sleep.

If after investigating several days of activity in this way nothing can be found associated with the anxiety-responses, then the anxiety may be considered as "pervasive". If there are things that can be connected with the episodes, these " specific" things should then be listed. If the person feels anxious all the time, and everything he experiences seems to keep his anxiety going, no elements being discovered that seem to increase it more than usual, this also should be classified as "pervasive". If, on the other hand, the anxiety is continuous but increases upon exposure to certain special stimuli, then the frequency and intensity of these increases should be compared with the over-all anxiety pattern and those particular episodes considered "specific". A person can have both pervasive and specific anxiety, and some determination should be made as to which is more severe.

Pervasive anxiety must be controlled and diminished before attention can be directed toward the specific anxieties.

Let us now make the assumption that relaxation-responses are antagonistic to anxiety-responses. Experience has shown that when we are able to relax, the anxiety level diminishes. Therefore it is desirable to bring about relaxation as often and to as profound a degree as possible. If the person learns to relax, pervasive anxiety will diminish in direct proportion to the degree of relaxation obtained. Self-hypnosis is in itself a direct means of obtaining relaxation, and this can be utilized to the point where pervasive anxiety can be diminished and perhaps even completely eliminated during the entire day and night while awake or asleep, active or inactive, in trance or out of trance. There may, however, be some persons who cannot develop sufficient ability to induce relaxation. The anxiety itself may inhibit this development. In such cases other things may be done not only to decrease the anxiety significantly but also to improve the trance ability. We will explore these procedures first in order to help overcome resistance and to expedite self-hypnotic techniques.

Most everyone has some anxiety-responses that are conditioned to stimuli in their surroundings, but, unlike the person with pervasive anxiety, the "normal" person continuously extinguishes these responses. The major difference is that the non-anxious person has a response pattern that is not so generalized as to evoke anxiety-responses by realistically non-threatening stimuli. This is why a change in environment is sometimes beneficial. It is quite likely here that many of the stimuli in the new environment will not have anxiety-evoking potential. A change of scene then can be an excellent means of reducing anxiety, provided it can be made without developing other anxieties such as increased financial obligations, concern regarding the mode of travel, etc. Increased activity is also excellent. A program suitable for the individual can be arranged to increase muscular activity by walking, horseback riding, weight-lifting or any appropriate exercises. If advisable, there should be a temporary decrease of food intake for a specific period each day. This may serve to increase fatigue and hunger to the extent that resting and eating become significant as relief-responses.

A program of this sort must be carefully devised in accordance with the physical ability and personality structure of the anxious person. The major objective is to find some way of inducing relaxation-responses with increasing frequency and intensity, thereby diminishing the frequency and intensity of anxiety-responses. There are a great number of items from which to select in working up such a program, which is best tailor-made. What would be ideal for one person is not necessarily so for another. The basic principle here is one of finding stimuli that will evoke relief-responses of sufficient intensity to dominate the total response pattern of the individual to such an extent that anxiety-responses are diminished to the maximum degree.

Let us at this point briefly review the stimulus-response mechanism possibly responsible for the development of pervasive anxiety. We will then, with the underlying principles in mind, be in a better position to attempt to devise stimulus-patterns that will diminish or counteract these responses. So that the review will be clear and as easy to remember as possible, it will be in outline form with no further elaboration on each point.

First of all, a stimulus of a physical nature or in the form of imagery evokes anxiety. Anxiety is always associated with imagery that may include recognition of some undesirable situation. Anxiety evokes anxiety-responses which may be in the form of further imagery, physiologic reactions, or both. Any random stimuli present at the time of the original episode may take on the ability to evoke anxiety and the resultant anxiety-responses. Any anxiety-responses of a physiologic nature may then serve to reinforce the associated stimuli toward evoking anxiety-responses. The original stimulus then may be no longer necessary. At this point we have anxiety-responses conditioned to known stimuli even though these stimuli may not be considered or recognized in themselves as objectionable. If this process continues to the point where anxiety-responses are strongly conditioned to random stimuli, these responses are then automatic, and we are burdened with pervasive anxiety. Physiologic reactions have been conditioned to stimuli that are no longer recognized as having been present originally.

According to these same principles then, the first objective would be to establish relief-responses in any way possible. Once these have been established we should try to condition them to stimuli in the person's environment so that they will as completely as possible dominate or replace anxiety-responses. Once this conditioning process is established to the extent that the person is experiencing more feelings of relief than of anxiety, his ability to cope with life situations should then allow him to continue on his own.

Another concept that is extremely important to the reduction of anxiety is that of a method of selecting and controlling stimuli that will evoke relief-responses of sufficient intensity to dominate anxiety-responses. There is also the question of which anxiety-responses should be considered first in the attempt to diminish or replace them.

This concept evolves from consideration of a number of factors related to conditioning, anxiety and personality structure. First of all, it would seem reasonable to assume that there exists a high correlation of anxiety-level to coping ability. That the individual with a high level of anxiety is being exposed or has been conditioned to anxiety-evoking stimuli of a frequency and/or intensity exceeding that of relief-evoking stimuli seems self-evident. If this is so, it follows that, if the anxiety-responses could be diminished to the level of intensity of the relief-responses, or if the relief-responses could be raised to the level of the anxiety-responses, the individual's coping ability would then be sufficient to maintain equilibrium. Any further decrease in anxiety-level or increase in coping ability would then be considered as a reserve which would allow the individual to expend more energy in other ways and, if constructively expended, would conceivably result in increased happiness and better adjustment.

The problem then is not necessarily one of how to diminish the level of each anxiety-responses simultaneously, nor even one of attacking the most intense anxiety-responses. Those anxiety-responses that seem most trivial are generally the ones that should be considered first. These should be the easiest to desenitize because relief-responses of sufficient intensity to dominate them can more easily be discovered and controlled. By establishing small increases in relief-responses that may appear insignificant and by effecting desensitization of a number of seemingly trivial anxiety-responses, the total gain may well be sufficient to achieve equilibrium, and the individual may be better able to cope with the higher-level anxiety-responses even though little or no change has been effected in these.

An example of this procedure can be found in people who have suffered some major setback, such as the amputation of a limb. It would be difficult to find a single relief-response which would surely ensue from such an event. People do suffer such catastrophes, however, and may even recover with a better adjustment to life situations than they previously had achieved. It can usually be found that mobilization of sufficient emotional energy to offset such a traumatic event has come from a number of sources rather than from one single dominating source.

The higher the level of the lesser anxiety-responses, the more intense and the greater in number are the stimuli which must be selected for the anxiety-reduction program, keeping in mind, of course, the limitations of the individual involved.

The first consideration to be made is how to create new diversions that will distract the individual from his anxiety. It is desirable to develop some patterns which contrast with established ones. One of the reasons that many measures fail in attempts to reduce anxiety is that not enough diversionary contrast is utilized. Let us take, for example, the well-known expedient of rest as a therapeutic principle. The patient may have been trying to obtain rest for so long that simple mention of the word is upsetting. From what is he supposed to rest? His anxiety may have been keeping him from rest. The logical thing then to suggest is sufficient activity to bring about a state of genuine fatigue. Rest then will be welcome in bringing relief through contrast. Suppose it is known that the person is interested in music. To include music in the program may be a good idea, but not if he already has been trying to include it to little or no avail. It may be better for him to avoid any musical practice for a period of time or, if it is not too disrupting, to listen to music or sounds he *dislikes*. This acts as a contrasting principle, and satisfaction and relief will be much more significant to him upon hearing the music he prefers.

This technique of developing new tensions by contrast, under controlled conditions, may result in predictable relief-responses. It should be obvious that great care must be exercised in order to keep them under control. Simply adding new anxiety-responses to those already in existence would of course be most destructive.

The above material may be of little interest to the reader who wishes to reduce his own anxieties. It has been included mainly to help an assistant who wishes to understand some basic principles of anxiety control so that he can better help someone else.

We will now go on to practical applications, and, by analogy, attempt to show how these principles may be utilized. I have purposefully selected a case in which a supportive, reconditioning approach was employed rather than an analytical insight-approach.

REDUCTION OF A SEVERE ANXIETY-NEUROSIS

I first met Tim G. in March 1960. As a result of a conference with his parents and family physician, his father had brought him to my office, introduced us, then left after saying he would return in two hours to take him home.

Tim was extremely nervous. He sat down in the chair I had indicated and, as I busied myself for a few moments with preparations for taking notes, I noticed that he glanced around the room as if he were trapped and wished to escape. He started noticeably as I said, "Please excuse me for a minute or two. If you don't mind, I'd like to get better organized."

He looked at me, swallowed as if with difficulty, and then in a soft, well-mannered voice replied, "Oh, that's all right. Go right ahead." He then leaned back and seemed to relax or to at least appear somewhat less nervous.

Although casually dressed, his clothes were in excellent taste. He was a handsome young man, about nineteen years old, with black, slightly wavy hair. His features were what one might call "classic". His eyes were set well apart, and their darkness was accentuated by the extreme pallor of his face. His hands, too, were nearly white and possessed of a decided tremor, as I could see when I glanced at his long, graceful fingers. He had the curious appearance of one who, though perfectly healthy, was extremely fragile.

When I asked if he would mind answering a few questions, he replied, "No. Ask anything you like." Then, somewhat apologetically, "Do you mind if I ask you something first?"

I smiled and shook my head. "Not at all. What would you like to know?"

Frowning slightly, he asked, "Do you really think you can help me?"

Matching his serious mood, I hesitated and then replied, "I don't know. There is some routine information I need, and there are some tests I'd like to make, and then perhaps, if you would like me to, I'll try to tell you what I can about the techniques I use and how they may apply to you. This will be sort of a mutual effort. Once I have given you my ideas and opinions it will be up to you to decide whether or not you wish to proceed."

He started to speak, hesitated, and then leaning back in his chair he waved his hand in a gesture of assent and said, "Well, let's go."

Although I already had received a great deal of background material from his parents and his physician, I felt it would help to calm him down and give him an opportunity to become accustomed to my voice by going over the routine material again. We spent ten or fifteen minutes doing this, and then I instructed him on how I wished him to consider the questions on the Willoughby Personality Schedule before giving his answers. His score was 78, which is very high.

The balance of this session (approximately one and one-half hours) was spent listening to his description of his problems and the related events of the past two years. Here is a brief resumé covering the salient points of this material, plus some information as related by his parents:

Tim was the eldest of four children. He had a sister, one year younger than he, and two brothers, one fourteen, the other eight years old.

Although there had been some problems through the years related to marital difficulties and finances, his parents were apparently quite happy with each other and with their children. They were reasonably well-adjusted, intelligent and showed perhaps more concern over family matters than many people do today.

Tim, at the age of ten, had been stricken with poliomyelitis which fortunately had not been severe, but had left him with some incapacity in the function of his left leg. As a therapeutic measure his physician had suggested that some form of training, such as ballet, would be bene-ficial. His parents acted upon this suggestion with considerable under-standing and empathy for Tim by making arrangements for the *entire* family to take ballet lessons. In this manner they felt that Tim would not be made so much an object of attention. This apparently worked out well, at least to the extent that Tim's leg was strengthened. (There was, when I first met him, no evidence of any abnormality.) Some months later, however, Tim was subjected to considerable ridicule by his school-mates upon their discovery that he was taking "dancing lessons". This was extremely traumatic to him, as evidenced by his manner in relating it to me some nine years later.

Tim had always been considered a brilliant youngster. His teachers as well as his family and friends were proud of his accomplishments in music, history and art, which he particularly liked, and, in fact, most everything he studied or put his hand to. His talents were matched by his rapid progress in school, for he had entered college at 15 and was well into his second year, with excellent grades, when he began to manifest symptoms of anxiety.

He had been living in a rooming house, to be near the college, since the start of the second term. He enjoyed his life there and had developed a number of friendships with other students and with several older people with whom he enjoyed discussions, usually on subjects of music, art or philosophy. One such friendship was with a girl who was several years older than Tim. There was no romantic motivation on either side, apparently, as the girl was happily involved with an older man and Tim's interests lay solely in conversation. He had never had a sexual relationship of any kind, but he did express to me a fear of being a homosexual.

One evening, approximately two years before he first came to my office, he had been talking with this girl in her room. He could not remember the exact words of the conversation, but he recalled vividly that he had been midway through a sentence when she looked directly toward him and, as their eyes met, he felt a strange sensation of panic which momentarily paralyzed him. He never finished what he had been saying. He ran out of the house, boarded a street car and went to his home, which was several miles from there. During this time he began to shake uncontrollably. He remembered feeling slightly relieved, upon arriving home, to notice that the house was dark; everyone had gone to bed. He entered and went up to his room and lay quivering on his bed for the rest of the night. He remembered that the door of his room was ajar and, as the early morning light began to brighten his room, he got out of bed, went downstairs to the kitchen, drank a glass of milk and then went quietly back to his room, closed and locked the door and went back to bed. He was extremely upset because he could not imagine what had made him feel and act this way. He tried to reason it out, but the more he thought about it the more disturbed he became. He remembered that he had felt like screaming, but the thought of everyone rushing to his room prevented him from doing so.

Later that morning, when his mother knocked at his door and asked if he were coming down to breakfast, he had with considerable effort controlled his shaking sufficiently to ask if she would mind bringing him some toast and coffee. He remembered the tremendous relief he felt a few minutes later when she told him that she had left a tray for him on the hall table rather than, as he had feared she might, insisting on his opening the door.

From then until the time he was telling me this, he had left his room only a dozen times. For nearly two years he had been unable to meet or talk with anyone except his immediate family. He would on rare occasions go downstairs to join the family at a meal, but he would soon go back to his room. Once or twice he had been able to talk with visitors for a minute or two and then, with some urgency, return to the upper floor.

Only on three occasions had he left the house previous to the time he came to my office. On those days his father had accompanied him, and it was only with the greatest effort that he kept from running away to get back to his room at home.

Twice he had been taken to the office of a psychiatrist, and both times he had insisted upon leaving before the doctor could see him. He would not tolerate the suggestion, made several times by his mother, that the psychiatrist come to see him. It was not, he explained, that he did not feel he should see a psychiatrist. Quite the contrary. He fully realized that he needed help, but he simply could not bring himself to meet *anyone*, and he thought of attempting to explain his feelings was overwhelmingly repulsive and frustrating to him.

He had submitted to a thorough physical examination by the family physician only after it was agreed that it be conducted in his room. He was, the doctor stated, in perfect physical condition, except for being a few pounds underweight.

A number of tranquilizing regimes had been prescribed, but the end result had always been an increase in episodes of depression.

I had, at the request of the physician, talked with Tim's mother and father and, what surprised everyone, talked with Tim on the telephone when, during a conversation with his father. he had asked if he could speak with me. He wanted to know if it would be possible to find out, with the use of hypnosis, what had caused him to feel and act the way he did. I told him that it might be possible, but that it would not be advisable to probe for such answers until other measures were taken to reduce his anxiety and that even then it might not be necessary. I briefly explained some of the principles of conditioning, and the questions he asked regarding this and hypnosis were proof of exceptional perspicacity. He wanted to know if I would come to his house to talk with him. I told him that I would, but that if he could decide to come to my office I would feel much better about it. I suggested that he think about it for a while and then call me to let me know what he wished to do. He expressed no curiosity about this suggestion, and I got the impression that he had some idea of my reason and needed no further explanation. I feel that if a person is really motivated toward seeking help he should, unless it is absolutely impossible, express this desire by exercising some initiative. I made up my mind that I would go to see him if he personally requested me to, but that I would feel more optimistic about the outcome if he decided to come to my office.

Two weeks went by before I got a call from his father, who said that Tim had asked him to arrange an appointment.

During our second session, which lasted about an hour, I described to Tim some of the experiments listed in Chapter Two. Although he was very attentive and showed keen interest in what I was saying, he was unable to cooperate actively because of his tremor. This embarrassed and excited him to such an extent that I decided to go no further along these lines and to discuss relaxation techniques instead.

I discovered, upon asking him to imagine various scenes, that he had an excellent aptitude for mental imagery. His ability to conceptualize was amazing. He could repeat easily, forward and backward, lengthy series of numbers after hearing them only once, and upon listening to a description of two or three characteristics of geometric figures, he could immediately describe all of the possible combinations of characteristics necessary to complete each figure.

I noticed that during these mental gymnastics he would close his eyes and appear more relaxed, but upon completion of a problem his tremor would return in full force, his eyes would open, and his nervous, animated appearance would return.

I asked him to close his eyes and see how many ways he could imagine the number "1000-3", and to describe these thoughts to me as they occurred. To get him started, I gave him the ideas of imagining that he was looking at the electric signs of Times Square and then watching an airplane write the number across the sky. His creativity was immediately apparent. He described such scenes as these: a garden with the number growing in different colors of flowers; the number being engraved on the head of a pin by a man using an elaborate microscope; a giant bending the girders in a bridge to form the numerals. His imagery then tended toward weird and morbid scenes: a person being branded on the forehead with a red-hot iron in the form of the number; a machine gun cutting down mobs of people as it sprayed out bullets and formed the number on their dying bodies.

This was getting away from what I had planned. I found that if I detailed the imagery and specified each variation he would follow my direction, but if I gave him any latitude for utilizing his own creative ability, he tended toward, first, the unusual, and then the morbid.

At the conclusion of that session he was, if anything, more nervous than before. Although the next appointment had already been arranged, the thought crossed my mind that he probably would not keep it.

I was wrong. Three days later he walked in with his father, who simply nodded and left. Tim sat down and, looking at me with a frightened expression, asked, rather pitifully, "Do you think anything is going to help me?" Tears welled up into his eyes, and he bowed his head and started to cry. He said, "I'm sorry, I'm sorry . . ."

I kept quiet, trying to think of something to say that might help. I thought back over what he had told me about himself, and all I could think of was how frightened and lonely he must feel.

He stopped crying and, taking out a large, white handkerchief, dried his eyes. He then said, "For Christ's sake, don't tell me to relax. Everyone tells me I should relax." He then looked at me as if there were something that only he and I knew. "What in the hell do they think I've been trying to do for two years?" he said.

Somewhat startled at his outburst, the only thing I could think of to say was, "It's stupid, isn't it?"

Nodding in agreement, he said vehemently, "It sure is. It most certainly is." Then finally, "Well, what are you going to try today?"

"I'm not going to try anything today," I replied. He looked puzzled until I said, "You are. I'm going to explain something to you in detail, and I'm going to give you a task to perform. It is you who will do the trying."

I then told him that I wanted him to stare at a small, red disc and not to let his eyes waver from it for an instant, once we got started. I explained that the task I had mentioned was for him to think, starting with the number "one thousand", of each lower number by increments of two and one-half (I purposely made the task difficult to suit his mental capabilities) and to synchronize this counting with each breath.

He indicated that he understood and was ready to begin and then unexpectedly asked, "Are you going to hypnotize me?"

"No," I replied, "in fact, I'm not too sure that I dare mention the word that most aptly describes what we are going to do."

"Why?" he was genuinely puzzled.

"Well," I said, hesitating and then laughing, "I'm going to teach you how to...relax."

He looked somewhat sheepish, then muttered, "That'll be some trick, if you can do it."

"If *you* can do it," I corrected him. "Remember, I said it is you who must do the trying today. I'm just going to sit back and take it easy."

The red disc I had mentioned was a small "hypnodisc" made of a red fluorescent material with a black spiral imprinted on it. It was about three inches in diameter and revolved at approximately 20 r.p.m. I had found that this disc was excellent for quickly developing retinal fatigue. After staring at it for only a few seconds, anything else that one looked at, especially red objects, would evoke the strange perception of the object appearing to grow and yet remain the same in size.

I flipped on the switch and directed Tim to stare at it. I then got him started on his task of counting backward and instructed him not to pay any further attention to what I said until I touched him on the shoulder.

Once I was sure he was following instructions I spoke to him softly and said, "From now on you will relax easily. You will be more relaxed every day. When you see a *red rose* that appears to be growing, your eyes will close and you will relax. You will think only of the scenes I describe, and each time I work with you you will relax deeper and deeper." I was observing him very closely for any signs of increased agitation and particularly for any repetitive movement of his head or hands which would indicate a loss of control that might lead to hysteria. This did not happen. His eyes were nearly closed, and his eyelids were quivering, but the tremor in his hands had diminished noticeably. I had repeated the above suggestions three times when I held a tiny painting of a red rose before him and said, "Your eyes are closing, gently but firmly." This was true. Then, "In a few minutes, when I count from six to ten, your eyes will open, and you will be feeling better than you have for years You are relaxed, and you will remain relaxed." I mentioned the suggestions regarding his eyes in order to obviate any tendency to panic upon feeling that he could not open his eyes. I repeated all the suggestions several times and then added, "When you practice each day you will think only of the scenes I describe to you. You will be unable to think of any other scenes." I hoped also to obviate any tendency, such as he had already shown, toward fantasia of a weird or morbid nature.

I then went over the routine instructions for self-hypnosis, but only to the symbol "1000-3" for relaxation. I included the concepts of awakening at any suggested time, of eye-closure and of relaxation, but I also suggested that the sight or thought a red rose would evoke feelings of relaxation too.

I then touched his shoulder and told him that he could stop counting. I slowly counted from six to ten and, at the count of ten, asked him to open his eyes. His eyes opened with a slight start, which indicated that he had been in at least a light trance. He was smiling and very much relaxed, but I was disappointed to notice, a few minutes later, that his tremor had returned. This didn't seem to bother him. He was greatly pleased and said he felt certain that everything was going to work out well. He reported that he knew I had been talking to him, during the session, but that he was not aware of what I had said. He had kept his mind on the counting.

I again explained to him the self-hypnotic procedure, without mentioning the word "hypnosis". I told him it was simply a method of developing relaxation. I found later that he had suspected all along that this was actually hypnosis, but he didn't wish to embarrass me by questioning what I had said. I actually had felt that there was little possibility of his going into a trance, and had sincerely believed I was not misrepresenting my intentions—until I noticed his eyes quivering.

I asked him to go through the process once more by himself. This he did, and his eyes closed after approximately two minutes. With instructions to practice each day until our next session, that session was concluded.

Next time (he was coming into my office twice each week) I explained to Tim the process of desensitization of anxiety-responses through conditioning of dominating relief-responses. This discussion used up nearly the entire time, but I did get from him the promise that he would make a list of the things or thoughts that bothered him and bring it in the next time he came.

A representative hierarchy of Tim's anxiety-evoking stimulus-situations is shown below. There actually were nearly two hundred items on his list after we had worked for three weeks compiling it.

In order of increasing intensity:

1. Thinking of leaving his room to go downstairs for meals.
2. Actually going downstairs for meals.
3. Reading a book or newspaper.
4. Hearing the doorbell ring.
5. Hearing a friend or neighbor enter the house.
6. Hearing conversation about himself.
7. The thought of someone (including his family) coming upstairs.
8. Anyone actually coming up the stairs.
9. Thoughts of being a homosexual.
10. The sound of the phone ringing.
11. Being called to the phone.
12. Thoughts of being called to the door.
13. Thoughts of leaving the house with his father.
14. Leaving the house with his father.
15. Leaving the house with anyone in his family.
16. Leaving the house alone. (Extremely traumatic.)
17. Getting a haircut. (Very traumatic, either the thought or someone mentioning it. His hair had been cut for two years by his father.)
18. Thoughts of meeting old friends. (The last five items all seemed to have about the same intensity.)
19. Meeting old friends. (A group.)
20. Meeting a friend.
21. Meeting a stranger.
22. Being stared at by anyone.

It was interesting to note that Tim's list included many things that he had not done for two years, and although in many cases he considered the actual act as being of stronger intensity than the *thought* of the act, there also were items in which he considered the thought to be equally as anxiety-evoking as the act itself, yet both considerations were based only on imagery.

During the three weeks spent compiling the list, Tim had practiced the relaxation routine three or four times each day. He reported that, with only a few exceptions, he had been able to obtain some degree of relaxation, and this seemed to be increasing each time he practiced. He said, too, that he felt nearly as much at ease in my office as he did in his room, after he had a chance to calm down from the ordeal of leaving the house to reach my office.

Also during this period I had several consultations with the doctor. We decided that an attempt should be made to increase Tim's hunger-drive.

The doctor prescribed a diet so designed as to lower Tim's caloric intake at breakfast and lunch and to bring it up to his minimum requirements at the evening meal. Within a few days after this diet was put into effect, Tim reported feeling very hungry toward the latter part of each afternoon. He also found himself looking forward to the evening meal with pleasant anticipation. He was instructed to imagine "going downstairs" each time he had dinner.

During the sessions at the office I had him relax himself with imagery of the symbols "1000-1" to "1000-3" and then had him go through "fractional-relaxation" exercises several times. This procedure began to develop in him feelings of deeper relaxation and to strengthen his control to some degree. While he was deeply relaxed I described scenes to him in which he was performing physical activities such as digging in a garden or walking through a forest and climbing a hill. I emphasized the pleasant features of these activities, but also suggested that he feel tired and hungry. Then, although some incongruity was involved, I described a scene in which he was enjoying rest and satisfying his hunger at the family dinner table. I had him also practice these scenes during his sessions at home.

After one week of practicing these procedures he reported that imagery of "going downstairs for dinner" brought pleasant responses, and from then on he found that he could actually do this with no increase in his anxiety. After three weeks he was feeling more relaxed during the evening meal with the family than during any other period of activity.

Although Tim had once been an avid reader, he had read practically nothing since his anxiety had been triggered. There was, he told me, a book that he had started and had attempted several times to read further, but had been unable to get past the first chapter. Utilizing the same techniques of imagery involving reading during and after the evening meal, we soon found that he could actually do this with increasing pleasure and a lessening of anxiety. This was considered, by everyone concerned, excellent progress. The first three items on the list seemed to have been extinguished as far as anxiety-evoking potential were concerned. Then too, what seemed equally encouraging was the fact that stimuli which had formerly been anxiety-evoking were now evoking relief-responses.

Everything did not continue so smoothly, however. For example, there was a very discouraging setback when, during one evening meal, the *doorbell rang!* Tim was panic-stricken. He dropped his knife and fork and knocked over his chair in his haste to get to his room. Then, of course, he was completely shattered and discouraged for several days. I talked it over with him on the telephone, explaining that excellent progress had been made and would be easily reestablished. I also mentioned that his mother had invited me over for dinner that evening and that if *he* wished to he could practice imagery of joining us. Only if this imagery evoked no anxiety was he actually to go through with it. He had also been told that the doorbell had been disconnected and that during the meal one of his brothers would sit out on the porch to prevent any such unexpected event from happening again.

Tim did come down for the evening meal, and for the next few days the procedures were all devoted to strengthening the first three items on the list. The sound of the doorbell (the fourth item) had acquired a much higher anxiety-evoking potential, and it was thought best to postpone any attempt to desensitize it.

Over the next three months excellent progress was made in utilizing the same procedures and by instituting programs of reading. It was felt advisable that he avoid newspapers or any periodicals that might evoke imagery of the outside world. The books presented for him were carefully selected to stimulate his interest and to dissociate him as much as possible from environmental stimuli. *She,* by H. Rider Haggard, *Jurgen,* by James Branch Cabell and *The Right to Heresy,* by Stefan Zweig, were some of the books recommended. Music was also utilized, but we proceeded with extreme caution because we did not wish to evoke memories that might make him more aware of his incapacities. Fortunately there were many musical selections that, according to his mother, he had listened to only at his home. It was reasoned that these might evoke pleasurable responses associated with his home and family. Again, imagery was first utilized which evoked some mild increases in anxiety, but the simultaneous imagery of eating and resting soon began to dominate the anxiety-responses, and these were gradually extinguished. He then found that he could listen to music during his evening meals with no increase in anxiety, and shortly thereafter this became another source for evoking relief-responses.

During this three-month period Tim advanced to the point where most of those items on his list having to do with events within the home, were desensitized. We began to induce imagery of working in the garden near the house and of having lunch, first indoors, then outside in the back yard, after becoming tired and hungry. Another four weeks were required in order for Tim to actually work in the garden, but once he started he derived a great deal of pleasure from it, and, as had formerly been true, he did an excellent job. Compliments, first from his family and then relayed to him by members of his family from his neighbors, began to evoke pleasurable responses too.

We began to utilize the principles of "contrast" in the hope of intensifying the existing relief-responses.

Tim's mother began serving one "special" dinner each week with a menu that included items of particular appeal to Tim. The menus for lunch and breakfast on that day, and for all meals on the preceding day, were subtly diminished in such appeal. We intended to utilize the intensified relief-responses, evoked during this meal, to dominate Tim's negative responses to "poor" music. We then planned to exploit whatever degree of tolerance that could be developed for poor music by contrasting it with periods of "good" music. With the cooperation of Tim's sister it was arranged for music to be played, softly at first, during the "special dinner". These selections turned out to be slightly irritating to Tim, but by taking advantage of his sense of fair play, he began to tolerate this for the sake of his sister. We did not wish to condition Tim to experience relief-responses to "poor" music, but we did hope to establish a tolerance for it. Tim gradually developed the habit of playing records that he liked shortly after each "special" meal, and the relief he felt became significantly greater thereafter.

Over the next six months similar techniques were used to expand Tim's "world". His interest in learning foreign languages was utilized through such devices as having a local merchant stop by at the garden to have conversations with him in Spanish, having him imagine "going to the library" for foreign language records and, after some practice, actually doing so.

During this same period the self-hypnotic pattern was fully established, and direct suggestions were put into effect. These involved "deeper and more prolonged relaxation" and "intensification of interests, such as for music, reading and visiting away from home". A fair degree of time-distortion ability was developed which served to enhance and expedite the effects of conditioning through utilization of his imagery. Some difficulties were encountered here, as he still evidenced a tendency toward the weird and morbid whenever he was allowed to create his own imagery. This was an area that required strong, directive procedures.

For example, it was once suggested that he imagine, while in trance, a scene in which he was painting a portrait of a specific individual. He reported upon awakening that the canvas "kept turning away from him", so he couldn't get started. After several attempts, during which suggestions were made that the canvas would "remain still", he finally was able to "paint the portrait" to his entire satisfaction. Later, during that same session, it was suggested that he paint another picture of any subject of his own choice. Upon awakening he was noticeably disturbed while describing his painting of a scene at the beach. The painting had been nearly completed when a huge wave had come rolling out of the scene, engulfing everyone on the beach (in the imagined picture) and about to engulf him, too, by flowing out of the picture, when he escaped by awakening.

There were a number of episodes such as these, but in each instance, by means of carefully outlining and detailing suggestions, the imagery was brought under control. Although considerable importance was attached to these episodes, it was considered advisable to minimize their importance to Tim.

One of the most difficult items to desensitize was Tim's phobic reaction to getting a haircut at a barber shop. Nearly two months were required, with little or no progress being made, before he could go through this without tremendous feelings of anxiety. The procedure that seemed to be most effective was for someone to get him involved in a philosophical discussion and keep him thinking about it while going to the barber shop and while he sat in the chair. Imagery under hetero and self-hypnosis also helped when some new question was utilized as a means of keeping him preoccupied. Such questions were always discussed with him preceding the practice under hypnosis, and any opinions he formulated were the result of this pre-trance discussion. His preoccupation, under hypnosis, was in the nature of a review and consolidation of his previous thinking rather than a development of new and additional substantiation for his position on the question.

Another point of interest in this case was the fear Tim had that he might be a homosexual. It was explained to him that many men have this fear, but that a fear of this nature is far from being evidence that what is feared is true. I asked him to relate anything that came to his mind concerning this fear. He told me of three instances in which he had considered entering into such a relationship, but upon each occasion his ultimate reaction was one of revulsion. It became obvious to him that his fears were groundless, and this was further strengthened when his doctor reassured him that, physically, he was "normal". There was no indication at all of any hormonal, chromosomal, endocrine or anatomic abnormality, and our discussion had convinced him there was no psychological basis either.

A problem still did exist, however, that involved his feelings of masculine inadequacy. As he had never had a sexual relationship of any kind, his sexual drive was limited to biologic motivations and even these, apparently, had been repressed. There was little psychologic basis upon which to establish any program of conditioning. His boy friends had, as is natural, never tended to understate their prowess nor minimize their accomplishments in this area of human endeavor. This, of course, made him feel even more inadequate, and the possibility of ever being able to initiate a sexual relationship seemed to him to be very remote. This problem, though not completely resolved, was well under way toward such resolution during the last few observations of Tim in his life-situations.

One year from the time he first came to my office, Tim was working at an interesting job at one of the major universities. He was planning courses of study for the coming year. He had resumed his practices of music and art and was actively engaged in a number of social activities, not the least significant of which was his taking to lunch each day a young lady who, upon cursory observation, had no physical abnormalities either. It was further to be seen that her admiring stare did not disturb him—at least not in any negative way.

His Willoughby score at this time had dropped to 37. His renewed ability to assert himself in social situations was largely responsible for the improved rating and had probably also contributed to the reduction of the intensity of his over-all anxiety pattern.

Tim's anxiety was considered "specific". Even though the questions of what might originally have conditioned the anxiety-reactions and the triggering of them at that particular time have never been answered, the stimuli that evoked and maintained them after they were triggered were determinable. Since, therefore, the stimuli currently evoking the responses can be specified, the case under discussion clearly exemplifies specific anxiety.

Stimuli that have no ability to evoke anxiety-responses can often acquire such ability if they are affecting an individual in close temporal contiguity to stimuli that are evoking such responses. Stimuli from internal as well as external sources can condition responses in this manner, and what is more, this can occur without the individual being aware of it. This is the basis upon which anxiety-responses are conditioned, though the stimuli evoking them are indeterminable. The condition is called "pervasive" anxiety. It may be mild or severe, but no relationship can be found between it and other stimulus-response patterns. It may be episodic, cyclic or continuous, although the causes of cyclic manifestations generally turn out to be determinable and, upon sufficient investigation, associative stimulus-patterns are discovered.

The feelings accompanying pervasive anxiety are usually difficult for the sufferer to describe. He may state that he feels nervous, anxious, fearful or tense, or he may say he feels depressed or upset. In any case his description will invariably include an element of "mystification". This will be borne out by his facial expression during such attempts to describe his feelings. He can see no reason and, though he has undoubtedly sought for them, no events that he can associate with his feelings.

TREATMENT OF A MILD PERVASIVE ANXIETY-NEUROSIS

In the following case, which is typical of the treatment of a large number of such cases, self-hypnosis played a major role in establishing relief responses. There were, however, two other techniques utilized, apparently successfully, which were the major reason this particular case was selected for description here. These techniques involve the use of "assertiveness" and "noxious stimuli".

A middle-aged woman had been under treatment by her family physician for two years. Her major complaint was a feeling of "fear" which she had experienced, she said, for as long as she could remember. The physician, a man who had an excellent reputation for his handling of psychologic as well as physiologic aspects of his patient's problems, had mentioned her case with an air of resignation. He was an excellent hypnotist, having utilized successfully many specialized techniques himself. But he considered her a refractory subject for hypnosis, having tried to no avail over a long period of time to induce a trance. She "wouldn't sit still long enough," he remarked, and "Even though she will not admit it, she has a great deal of apprehension about hypnosis." Drugs too had had no significant effect.

"Do you think you could hypnotize her?" he had asked, one day a week or so after he had first mentioned the case.

"Well," I replied, "You know my theories. A patient essentially hypnotizes himself. If this woman will not cooperate," I continued, "I doubt if anyone could do much with her."

"It isn't that she won't cooperate," he said, frowning while thinking of how best to describe her behavior. Then, "She tries," he went on. "She really tries, I think, but she actually cannot control herself even for a few moments."

The use of "noxious stimulation" as a means of conditioning a dominating response came up in our conversation, as several instances of such procedures had been mentioned in recent texts. We decided to see if we could conceive of a way in which to utilize this technique to advantage in the treatment of the doctor's refractory patient.

Over the ensuing weeks we obtained a device that could safely induce a controllable electric current in the forearm or hand of a person by means of electrodes attached to the area. The stimulation, though extremely undesirable at the high point on the control knob of the device, would not injure the tissue even over a prolonged period, and it was also controllable from zero stimulation through an infinite number of intensities.

Contrary to our expectations, this patient expressed no resistance to submitting herself to experiments with this device. After explaining to her that we wished to see if we could condition a relief-response in this manner, her only remark was, "If you do, it will certainly be a relief to me."

The electrodes were attached to her left forearm, and she was instructed to turn the knob herself until she could just barely feel the stimulus. One of us kept his hand upon the toggle-switch in order to shut off the current immediately upon any residual build-up of stimulation, which sometimes happens. Even this would have no harmful effect other than startling the person, but we wanted to develop no further anxiety if we could possibly avoid it. Everything went along fine. When the indicator registered "five" on the dial she said she could feel a "needle-like" sensation and that it was easily bearable. As she slowly advanced the knob, the feeling changed, she reported, into a more "massive" sensation which was still bearable. She was then instructed to turn it back to zero and then to experiment by turning the knob up and down several times to see if she could establish an intensity that would "cause no anxiety and yet be sufficient to bring a feeling of relief upon cessation." This turned out to be number 12 on the dial. She said she could bear the stimulation fairly well for at least a couple of minutes and that she had marked feelings of relief upon shutting it off.

The next step was to see if we could condition these relief-responses to an imaginary symbol. This, we reasoned, might be done by having her imagine the symbol during the period that the current was being diminished and continue to think of it for a few seconds after the current was shut off. The problem then arose as to what she should think of during the period in which the current was being increased. We did not wish to condition a negative response to imagery during this period. The idea of a "neutral" type of imagery came to us over the next few days: in other words, imagery that had no emotional content or connotation whatever. The imagery we chose for this purpose was simply counting backward by increments of sufficient complexity to occupy the mental capacity of the individual for the interval during which the current would be increased. This idea is often used in inducing hypnosis. The difference here, we felt, was that a predictable relief-response was being utilized, whereas with such use in hypnotic induction the relief-response is dependent upon concomitant physiological factors which were not present in the case of our patient, notably those of relaxation due to dissociation, and various fatigue reactions contributing to progressive building of belief.

As all of us, including the patient, were extremely interested in the outcome of these experiments, we agreed to spend one hour each day in conducting them.

During these sessions either the doctor or I would attach the electrodes to the patient's arm, instruct her to count down from one thousand by fives, threes or sevens (we varied these increments in order to obviate familiarity factors), and as she counted out loud, the current would be turned up to the previously-agreed-upon maximum. We then would instruct her to think of a red rose, and we would sometimes show her a painting of a red rose, as the current was lowered to zero. If we intended to show her an actual object, we would have her close her eyes during the counting and open them upon the signal that the current was to be diminished. She submitted to from thirty to forty exposures during each daily session, and at the end of one week she had requested that the current be increased to 15. She had been advised to increase the limit as much as she could without increasing her anxiety or her tolerance. The major objective was to maintain feelings of relief.

We purposely used a red rose to establish a symbol that might also be used effectively in the induction of hypnosis. This turned out to be a good choice because at the end of the second week her relief responses were sufficiently conditioned to the thought or sight of a red rose to allow her to develop eye-closure to the symbols "1000-1" and "1000-2". From then on she progressed fairly well through the entire symbolic series, and though she did not develop significant ability to utilize suggestions, she did achieve excellent ability to relax at will and to remain relaxed during her practice sessions.

Up to this point we had been unable to discover any particular situations in which this patient's anxiety-level appeared to be affected either favorably or unfavorably. Even after considerable investigation of her background and current life-situation, neither she nor any members of her family could offer any significant suggestion as to specific stimulus-situations that either increased or decreased her anxiety.

As she developed her ability to relax, however, it soon became apparent that this ability was easily affected by factors involving her relationships with other people. A recognizable pattern began to form. Whenever she practiced self-hypnosis in the doctor's office or at home *alone* she reported experiencing much more pronounced feelings of relaxation than during practice sessions at her home when someone else was present or was expected to be present later. This reaction took place even when the other person was in another room.

This change in pattern was considered very significant. Whereas this patient's anxiety had, until now, been considered pervasive, it was now taking on all the aspects of specific anxiety. We now had a means by which various stimuli could be evaluated as to their ability to evoke anxiety.

The patient was instructed to compile a list of items from her thoughts or experiences which affected in any way her ability to relax. Over a period of three weeks she made notes regarding such occurrences, and after several revisions a list was made up which included 43 items that she felt were inhibitive to relaxation and eight that she felt facilitated this ability. All of the inhibitory items had to do, not with actual situations, but with her *thoughts* of how she looked to other people, or indecision as to certain courses of action she should take in order to avoid displeasing others.

The first three items, which were typical of the others on the list, were, in order of their increasing intensity:

1. Thoughts of how she should dress and otherwise arrange her appearance for greeting her husband upon his return from work each day.
2. Thoughts of serving different menus at the evening meal in order to minimize complaints or expressions of dissatisfaction on the part of her husband or any guests that might be present.
3. Thoughts of being secretly laughed at or held up to ridicule by her relatives, friends or strangers in matters pertaining to her attire, manners or speech.

Most of the items inducive to relaxation were related to thoughts of being in pleasant places alone or with an idealized image of her husband. These included imagery of dancing with her husband in a beautiful ballroom to strains of music provided by an invisible orchestra, serving a meal to her husband during which he complimented her after tasting each morsel, and walking alone through a beautiful garden which she had planned and cultivated herself. One item which she mentioned rather shyly involved the pleasure she experienced each day during her *toilette*. Although the thought had not occurred to her before, she now realized that during her daily routine of showering and elimination she felt much more relaxed than during most other activities.

It should be explained that this patient, though not extremely pretty, was a very striking woman who dressed well and spoke in a pleasant voice. She acknowledged the fact that neither her husband nor any of her acquaintances ever unduly criticized her in any way and that her feelings of anxiety resulted only from unrealistic *thoughts* that she might at some future time do something that would evoke such criticism.

It was explained to her that anxieties often result from thoughts of undesirable situations which are not likely to occur and which, even if they did occur, would not necessarily evoke the feared result. She was told that the items on her list of situations inhibitive to relaxation could probably be eliminated if she would work on them, one at a time, utilizing imagery while in the hypnotic state and systematic assertiveness in life situations. This she found to be so after several weeks of following the procedures recommended to her. During her daily practice sessions she developed imagery in which she planned a dinner menu of special appeal to her husband. She then visualized working in her garden (which was not yet a reality) and of becoming so engrossed in her work that she had no time to clean up or change her clothes if she were to have dinner ready by the time her husband arrived. She imagined her husband as being somewhat critical upon her greeting him in her dirty clothes, but then as kissing her and later on complimenting her on the meal she had prepared.

This imagery was designed to evoke pleasurable responses, such as those resulting from preparing a meal that would please her husband and from engaging in the gardening activity, that would dominate the anxiety-responses evoked by thoughts of her appearance when greeting her husband.

She reported that the first three practice sessions of this imagery resulted in no discernible change in her ability to relax, but during the end of that week she was able to relax somewhat more easily.

She began actual planning and working on a flower garden and found that this gave her a great deal of pleasure and also developed a strong hunger drive at lunch time each day. During lunch she utilized this drive to dominate the anxiety associated with imagery of her husband being critical of her appearance. She spent two or three minutes during each noon-time meal imagining her husband observing her in her work clothes. After several days of this she found that the imagery no longer evoked any anxiety, so she decided to see what his reaction would be to the actual situation. One evening she met him as he was walking up from the garage. He smiled when he saw her and, after kissing the tip of her nose, remarked about how nice she looked in her old clothes and showed interest in what she had done on her gardening project. Anxiety arising from the first item on her list was now extinguished. She realized that the criticism she had feared was not forthcoming even when she purposely arranged situations that she had thought would evoke it.

The anxiety aroused by the second item on her list was obliterated through the use of imagery in which she visualized herself serving meals to her husband in which one or two items were either poorly prepared or were known to be unappealing to him. The dominating part of each imaginary episode involved his pleasant reaction to another item on the menu and his ready understanding and acceptance of situations in which she had not performed perfectly. Upon putting this to actual test, she again found it to be true: Her husband did not expect her to be perfect in every way. In fact, he remarked several times that he felt more at ease and closer to her since she had become more relaxed.

During these weeks this patient had been instructed to purposely bring about situations associated with the first items on her list with the idea that repeated exposures to such situations would diminish her anxiety when she found that the critical response she feared did not occur. This is in keeping with the principles of conditioning. If a conditioning stimulus is repeatedly applied while at the same time the conditioned-response is inhibited by a stronger response being evoked by a dominating stimulus, the conditioned-response is weakened and can become extinct.

As this patient increased her ability to relax during her practice sessions, she also remained much more relaxed during life situations. As the anxiety caused by successive items on her list was extinguished, the rest of the items diminished in their intensity. By utilizing the relief and pleasurable responses evoked each day during her *toilette*, she was able to put an end to her anxieties owing to thoughts of how she appeared to other people. During her shower she would spend two or three minutes imagining her friends' reactions to lapses of courtesy or social graces on her part. Not only were her anxieties extinguished as far as these thoughts were concerned; she found herself smiling with some pleasurable anticipation at the thought of putting her new-found confidence to a test. In the follow-up over a four-year period, it has been found that this woman has acquired many new friends because of her little witticisms and her informalities which she formerly feared might evoke criticism and ridicule.

In many cases anxiety is evoked by thoughts of situations which are considered by the patient to be beyond his control. There is a fear of entering into situations from which he feels he cannot escape. This anxiety can be diminished if the patient can be brought to assert himself in situations that he can control, due to the fact that he initiates them himself, and if the situations contain only minor levels of anxiety. For example, a person with a strong phobic reaction to animals can quickly develop a tolerance for the imagery of an animal, perhaps some distance away, during imagery of a pleasurable episode, such as of watching a ball game, which will dominate the anxiety reaction because of the relative magnitude or intensity of the images. The phobic reaction can then be diminished further if the person will assert himself by purposefully approaching a confined animal, such as at a zoo or a race track, knowing that he can withdraw from the situation whenever he chooses to do so. The knowledge that he is in control of the situation will allow him to enter into it much further than when he has a feeling of being constrained. The utilization of additional dominating stimuli during this process will serve to enhance the extinguishing effect.

CHAPTER 13

ALLERGIES

SHARI'S MOTHER and I were sitting in the doctor's office. I was observing her reactions as the doctor explained how hypnosis often helps in the treatment of patients with asthma. She was short and stout, and her feet barely touched the floor as she sat in the straight "Captain's" chair, listening intently to the explanation. A Japanese, she had an attractive face and a high level of intelligence. Her voice was soft and had no trace of an accent as she questioned or answered the doctor. He had introduced us, and after giving a brief account of the case, had asked her to tell me about her daughter, Shari, the patient with bronchial asthma.

"What would you like to know about her?" she asked, smiling and turning to face me.

"Everything," I said. "Her age, her appearance, her likes and dislikes, her activities, when the attacks started, their frequency and intensity and anything else you feel I should know."

"She's very pretty," she started. Then she laughed and blushed slightly. It was obvious that she considered her own beauty the source from which her daughter's was derived. This she had every right to assume because, in spite of her full face and figure, she was a very striking woman with a radiant and lovely personality. She continued, "She is twelve years old, the oldest of five. She is slender but in very good health, except for her asthma. She is very smart in school. She's in the eighth grade and has always been an 'A' student. She plays the piano and just loves music. She has lots of friends." She stopped to think and catch her breath. Then, "She has had these attacks since she was a little baby. Let's see... about three, I think. Three years old when she had the first one. She has had them every since. Very severe." Turning to the doctor, "Don't you think so, doctor?"

He nodded. "Yes, they're severe all right. But I do think this is the answer." He looked at her as if he were expecting her to answer or agree with him, as he was slightly nodding his head up and down.

I smiled to myself. "He's using persuasion," I thought, "and only a couple of years ago he wasn't so interested in the use of hypnosis."

"I think so too," she finally said. "Shall I ask her to come in?" She stood up and went to the door as the doctor said "Yes," and then she turned and said, "I think I'll wait outside. Is that all right?" This I was happy to hear. It is always essential that a patient, especially an asthma patient, be interviewed without any relatives—particularly a parent—or acquaintances in the room.

Shari was one of the loveliest girls I have ever seen. She was slender and graceful, with erect carriage of body and head. Her eyes were unusually large and bright, her complexion exquisite. Very well-mannered, she bowed slightly as she greeted the doctor and acknowledged our introduction. She had a tendency to avert her dark eyes, an indication of shyness that seemed a little incongruous for one who carried herself so proudly. Her respiration was slightly accelerated, and I noticed some wheeziness each time she ceased talking. She had suffered a severe attack that morning, she said, and she felt there would be another before the afternoon was through.

She had no aversion whatever regarding hypnosis. And no questions. It seemed that anything the doctor ordered was perfectly all right with her. She was sitting very straight in her chair, but she settled down and leaned back as I directed her to do. She was interested and amused by the hand-clasp test. I had asked her to clasp her hands and hold them up in front of her face, fix her gaze steadily on them and imagine there were coils of strong rope that were squeezing her fingers and hands together. I said, "Imagine that I am pulling on the ends of this rope and, as I do, you can feel your hands being pressed together. Tighter...so tight that, when I count to three, you cannot take them apart. In fact, the harder you try, the tighter they will squeeze together." Her knuckles were white; her hands were pressing so tightly together that a slight tremor became noticeable. I then said, rather firmly, "One...you cannot take your hands apart." Most people do not try at this point. She tried but failed. Her hands, if anything, got even tighter. "Two...the harder you try, the tighter your hands lock together. You cannot take your hands apart until I touch the back of your right hand. Three...try...try hard. The harder you try, the more they squeeze together." She tried very hard, but her hands were locked.

I decided to carry this directly into a trance. I did, however, want to keep close control. A patient will feel and act, as they go into trance, the way they think they are expected to feel and act. I wanted this to be a pleasant experience for her. I quickly said, "Stop trying." I touched her right hand. Then, "Your hands and fingers are relaxing now. As they do, your entire body is relaxing. Your eyes are heavy...very heavy...they are closing. As your hands go back to your lap your eyes close and you feel very pleasant. Very comfortable. Completely relaxed. You hear my voice, and everything is exactly as I say. Pleasant. Relaxing...deeper... deeper."

She drifted into the trance perfectly. I then went through the suggested phenomena of arm-rigidity, hand-levitation, arm-heaviness and imagery of her first name being written across the sky by an airplane. I then suggested that the wind was blowing it away, and she would not be able to speak her name, after waking up, until I snapped my fingers. Before awakening her, I set up the self-hypnotic pattern, suggested she would go deeper each time and that she could easily talk and answer questions while in a trance.

She reported, with apparent surprise, that the experience had been very pleasant. She was delighted and astounded that she could not speak her name until I gave the signal. She laughed and said, "Shari," twice more, as if convincing herself she could really say it.

She remembered every word of the instructions and proved it by putting herself back into trance. The doctor and I then took turns talking to her and asking questions. We found, contrary to what her mother had said, that she did not like to practice on the piano and that trying hard in school was a source of anxiety for her. She also wished her mother would allow her more freedom—of action, and from surveillance.

When asked if there was anything that disturbed her, Shari replied that the sound of footsteps coming toward her room and stopping outside her door frightened her.

I set up the "fading star" technique by telling her she was lying on top of a hill watching the clouds go by. "The sky is getting darker as you go deeper," I said. "As I count from one to five, the sky will become very dark, and you will see a tiny star twinkling in the distance. As you see the tiny star, it will become brighter and brighter. When it is very bright you will raise your first finger of your right hand." Soon we saw her finger straighten out. I continued, "Five; the star is fading now, and when I count back to one it will have faded completely." I then explained to her that she had a good mind and a good body. That anything out of the past would not bother her ever again. "Everyone has things happen, from time to time, that frighten or disturb him. You are no different than anyone else. We all have things happen that make us feel guilty or fearful or frustrated. But these things are in the past. The footsteps you hear are your mother or father simply checking to make sure you are safe. They love you and want to make sure you are all right. You are learning now to relax yourself and to stay relaxed so you can feel better and think better. You will stay relaxed while studying, and you will find you are thinking and remembering better as you are relaxed. You will practice anything you wish while you are in this relaxed state, and it will help you to do everything better. Instead of avoiding things like a little girl, you will face the things you wish to change and you will bring your feelings out into the open. You are a big girl now and you will get the things you want by acting like an adult rather than crying for them like a baby."

I could detect no wheeziness after Shari woke up. She said she felt much better than she ever had before. She agreed to practice as instructed and to face up to her mother and anyone else if she wished them to act differently toward her. She appeared to be intrigued with the idea of practicing piano with time-distortion, so we agreed to teach her at the next session.

We had a brief talk with her mother, alone, before they left. She readily agreed to give Shari more responsibility and not to push her so hard in school and music practice. A changed attitude on the part of the parents is as important as the effect of hypnosis.

This was over three years ago. We saw Shari once a week for two months and then once a month up to the present time. She has had three very minor attacks in this time. She is still an honor student but enjoys her studies and is relaxed during examinations. She recognized that she had been rebelling against her mother by feeling choked up whenever her mother had asked her to do anything. Now she is doing practically the same things because she wishes to, rather than because she has to, and she has no ill effects. Shari, like many of us, does not mind being taught and guided, but resents being pushed.

I have yet to see an asthmatic who cannot be helped to some degree with hypnosis, and I have seen many in which the symptoms were completely alleviated. Although there are cases, such as those involving infants with asthmatic symptoms, in which the possibility of emotional factors seem remote, these factors usually exist and become more apparent as the person matures. These symptoms become conditioned as responses to undesirable stimulus-situations and are extinguished when dominating responses of an adaptive nature can be made to take their place or upon alteration of the environmental stimuli. This accounts, to a great extent, for the improvement experienced when an asthmatic moves to a different geographic location or changes jobs, social contacts, etc. This improvement is often short-lived, owing generally to a reversion to previous patterns of behavior or to stress.

One young woman had been suffering from severe attacks of asthma over a period of five years. Although only 25 years of age, she had seven children: four girls and three boys. She had been the youngest child in a large family and had become terribly upset and lonely as the older siblings had married and left home. She was aware that her desire to have a large family was motivated by a fear of being lonely. She did not realize, however, that her fear of her children growing up and leaving her was a basic stimulus in evoking responses similar to those she had had as a child. As a child she had cried in an attempt to keep her brothers and sisters from leaving her. As an adult she was doing the same things. She could not actually cry, because it would be unseemly for an adult. The asthmatic attacks were more "adult", and they apparently served the same purpose. This does not mean her symptoms were feigned; far from it. This woman was in a hospital very close to death, and the one thing she did not wish to do was leave her children stranded.

Under hypnosis the induced imagery of her oldest daughter getting married, moving into a house nearby and welcoming her mother with open arms when she came to visit proved to be a turning point in her illness. As she had more and more phantasies of all the wonderful events and expressions of love her future held for her, the symptoms disappeared and were replaced with relief and pleasure responses to stimuli that had previously evoked anxiety. Unless one has seen these changes taking place, one finds them hard to believe: the labored breathing; the anguished appearance; the physical and tangible evidence of bronchial passages blocked with phlegm. And then, upon suggestions of calmness and imagery of desirable situations, the breathing gradually eases, the wrinkled brow smooths out, and the patient finds other means for achieving aims and goals.

Constructive ends or goals may sometimes seem beyond reach to the patient. Feelings of hopelessness and despair are so often associated with one's symptoms. The patient may recognize only the two extremes: the undesirable situation that he feels exists and the seemingly impossible situation he considers ideal. The gap appears too wide to bridge. I often ask such a patient: "If you wished to go from this room to a room upstairs, would you expect to do so in one jump?" Upon the acknowledgement that this would be unreasonable, I then ask: "Is it not equally unrealistic to expect a sudden change from your present situation to one you consider ideal?" I try to point out that the patient's goals may not be unreasonable at all if some way can be found to progress toward them in easy stages. By projecting one's thoughts to some future time, one can obtain relief from phantasies of drives reduced and goals achieved. Satisfactions may also be derived, meanwhile, from attainment of each easy step. This, then, may make life more tolerable and enjoyable.

Various skin conditions often have a similar genesis. The stimuli, though, that condition these responses seem usually to be more highly correlated with situations that are or have been considered repellent, disgusting or sinful to the patient. Usually these people have a high galvanic skin response and a hypersensitive blushing-reflex. The "A-V capillaries" that would normally transport their blood at a level beneath the surface, respond too easily to emotional control. In certain situations these A-V capillaries are constructed, and the blood is forced to travel through the capillaries lying closer to the surface of the skin. This is the mechanism behind the blushing-reflex. Now, the same stimuli that evoke this response can also cause reactions to occur simultaneously in various internal organs and glands. It is easy to see how such a person can be abnormally susceptible to disorders of the skin.

It is not essential that a person interested in self-hypnosis become expert in physiology, but enough understanding to enable one to visualize the rudiments of the processes is helpful. It is not necessary, for instance, to become involved in a controversy over the irritating qualities of histamine in order to obtain benefit from imagery of improved circulatory conditions. This is the reason why many doctors who use hypnotic techniques on their patients cannot derive similar relief for their own problems. Knowing considerably more about anatomy and physiology, they cannot accept for themselves the same suggestions they successfully use with their patients. As a hypnotist called upon by physicians to help in certain problems, I have been able to observe reactions of both patient and doctor. The simple suggestion of imagining that "a tiny switch is being opened" may serve in developing anesthesia for the patient, whereas the identical suggestion to the doctor may have no effect at all. This block in some doctors often inhibits their use of suggestion and hypnosis. Their suggestions must make "sense" to them or they cannot talk and act as if they really expected them to be effective. Any uncertainty on the part of the hypnotist is easily detectable by the patient in trance, and this is reflected in his acceptance or lack of acceptance of the suggestions.

This reasoning has been substantiated many times in cases where the doctor is treating an allergic condition with medication and at some point decides to add hypnotic suggestion to the therapeutic procedure. The fact that he continues the medication is a strong suggestion to the patient that the doctor himself does not believe hypnosis will work. On the other hand, the hypnotist who must rely solely on suggestion will often be successful because his suggestions are not "watered down" by doubt or by overly critical evaluation of their "sensibility".

"Henry" had been under treatment by his physician for almost two years. His condition, described as atopic dermatitis, was severe, as evidenced by extreme redness and itchiness of the skin over his entire body. All areas were dry, cracked, and warm to the touch. He usually had to wrap himself in wet sheets at night in order to get to sleep. He was thirty years old, married and had two children. The onset of the condition was at the age of sixteen, and he had grown progressively worse with only slight and temporary alleviation upon moving to his present address from a Midwestern city and upon treatment by his doctor. His job was below his intelligence and capabilities, but his fear of social contact caused him to avoid living up to his potential.

He readily answered all questions and expressed a willingness to discuss his most intimate thoughts and behavior. He explained that over the years he had given the matter considerable thought, and he was certain that he knew what was causing his condition. He had recognized, he said, that the only thoughts he had and the only topics of conversation that made him feel uncomfortable were those pertaining to sexual matters. He had attempted, over the years, to obtain a thorough knowledge and acceptance of such things, and he felt that he had succeeded. He could understand how desires and behavior patterns developed and, within reason, could find nothing wrong nor sinful about his own activities, nor about those of most other people he knew or had read about.

Henry related several instances of his younger days in which he recognized a prudish attitude. One episode, at the time he was fourteen, involved being trapped in a hayloft by two girls, older than he, who had tried to seduce him. In his panic he had fled through an open door and landed in a pile of manure, unhurt but extremely embarrassed. "Given the same opportunity today," he laughed, "I think the outcome would be somewhat different."

He related several other episodes to illustrate that he knew he had once been overly sensitive, but that he now felt truly different about such things. The change of attitude had not been accompanied by similar change in responses.

Henry was "conscious" of all this. There had been little or no attempt to "repress" these episodes. The concept that "abreaction", "ventilation" and "insight" over an extended period could produce change is so often erroneous. It seemed, at least to me, that this condition reflected responses so thoroughly conditioned to known stimulus patterns that they had become automatic in nature. And no amount of conscious effort or will power would do anything but condition them more firmly.

If other, more desirable, responses could be made to occur upon evocation of the same stimuli, the new responses might dominate the old ones, weaken them and eventually replace them. This is called reciprocal inhibition. The interested reader who wishes more detailed information on this type of procedure may find other texts fruitful; for instance, the book by Dr. Joseph Wolpe.*

Self-hypnotic procedures made it possible for this patient to experience imagery of various upsetting situations while his body maintained a state of profound relaxation. This conditioned him to respond with feelings of relief to stimuli that formerly evoked anxiety-responses. Imagery was also utilized to condition sensations of "coolness" to stimuli that had formerly evoked blushing. The idea of his blood circulating much "easier" through these "limp muscles" and carrying off "waste products" much more efficiently, contributed to the total therapeutic "hypnotic environment."

After seven weeks, large patches of soft white skin began to appear and this continued to spread over his entire body. The patient obtained a better, more satisfying job; his entire life situation improved immensely; his circle of social activity widened, and he developed no other symptoms. To adopt the concept that this patient had wished to retain his symptoms as a means of avoiding a more undesirable reaction seems without foundation.

The associations between stimulus-patterns and responses are not always so easy to detect. Fortunately this is not always necessary, and may actually be inadvisable. The reliving and rehashing of traumatic experiences may only serve to further provoke the symptoms, and thus the stimulus-response patterns become even more obscured. Discovering, if possible, the current stimuli that evoke current responses is generally easier, less traumatic, less time-consuming, and apt to be more effective.

A young man was recently referred to me because of his symptoms of eczema. The condition was again one of long standing. The inner areas of his elbows, his arm-pits, and pelvic region were continuously in eruption, he said, in spite of a variety of treatments. He told me that he was an ambivalent homosexual and, as he mentioned this, he appeared to expect that I would attempt to dissuade him from this pattern of behavior. Instead, I told him he had been referred to me because of his eczema and, as far as I was concerned, his sexual interests were his own business.

---

* Joseph Wolpe, *Psychotherapy by Reciprocal Inhibition*, Stanford University Press, 1958.

Now this, in a way, was not truly what I believed. I felt rather certain, after he told me about it, that his sexual attitude was correlated with the symptom. My reasoning was that he had probably thought about this over a period of time, that others had probably attempted to change his behavior—apparently without success—so I would only increase his problems by letting him know I attached any significance to his sexual attitudes. Looking at him, I asked rather casually, "You're not interested in changing, are you?"

Surprised, he answered uncertainly, "No. I guess not. I'm getting along all right as it is."

"That's fine," I said, nodding. "I'll show you how you can learn to control your body to get rid of your eczema. You then, if you wish, can increase or decrease your other satisfactions."

I have found that homosexuals can be helped only if they themselves come to the decision that a change is what they want. Any attempt to influence their decision will only emphasize and reinforce the pattern and will likely increase any guilt responses to their behavior.

By making this patient feel that I saw nothing particularly wrong or unusual about homosexuality, he was helped to minimize his guilt feelings. And when I implied that he could use self-hypnosis to strengthen or weaken whichever of his drives he chose, the way was left open for him to work on this himself, if that was what he really desired.

This was one of those seemingly miraculous "cures" that all hypnotists effect, from time to time. Though it hardly seems possible, in three weeks there was not anywhere on this patient the slightest vestige of eczema. Whether or not his sexual behavior has changed, I do not know. His use of self-hypnosis, in any event, was instrumental, either directly or indirectly, in ridding him of his undesirable symptom.

There are many skin conditions in which itchiness plays a major role. The tendency to scratch and otherwise irritate the affected area can obviously prolong the condition. Hypnotic suggestions that the sensations of itchiness will cease or be altered to less disturbing ones will often be enough to enable the patient to refrain from scratching. This tends to keep the irritated area from spreading, and allows it to heal more quickly. Self-hypnosis seems to be more effective and longer lasting than hetero-hypnosis in these cases, but either will usually suffice.

Some cases of hay fever and rose fever respond extremely well to hypnotic suggestion. Others seem to be unaffected. Generally, though not always, the successful cases have shown less seasonal correlation and higher levels of anxiety-responses to environmental stimuli. Also, cases of more recent onset of symptoms seem more amenable to suggestion than those having been under treatment for long periods of time.

The conclusion most experimenters come to, after several years experience with the use of hypnosis in the treatment of allergies, is that hypnotic techniques should be tried in almost every case. Certainly no harmful result can come from their use, and the chances of improvement are high.

CHAPTER 14

SEXUAL DISORDERS

BECAUSE OF the intense drives involved, invariably there is an element of high-level anxiety, conscious or unconscious, associated with sexual disorders. Although this anxiety may be higher in one partner of a dual relationship, there is, of course, a strong interaction of affective and effective mechanisms which cannot exclude the other. Usually one of the partners in an unsatisfactory sexual relationship is more cognizant of the situation than the other, and often there is one who is more desirous of seeking help. To attempt desensitization of anxiety-responses or conditioning of new behavioral patterns with one partner without cooperation of the other, may result in little or no gain unless the one seeking help is the one who needs it most. To expect to help one person by working through another is to take on a difficult task; the attempt should not be made if there is any other alternative. The incidence of successful treatment of such cases is far greater when the understanding and cooperation of both persons are obtained.

In the event that both troubled partners are willing to cooperate, it is wise to treat them separately. Even history-taking should be done privately, and the only times the two should be seen together are during an attempt to obtain mutual consent for a cooperative effort and during educational sessions on topics of a general nature. When two people insist that they have no "secrets" from each other, this in itself may be indicative of some underlying problems. In any satisfactory hetero-sexual relationship there are always behavioral and motivational characteristics of each individual which are not known to the other and that should be considered separately. Otherwise many constructive elements lose their effectiveness. For instance, any word or act of expression on the part of one individual may be taken differently if the partner feels it is not spontaneously evoked by the other. Awareness that certain expressions are the result of advice given by another person may evoke responses entirely contrary to those intended.

When anxiety-responses have been conditioned to sexually associated stimuli, the performance of the individual in such situations may be drastically affected, often to the extent of partial or complete inadequacy. This situation may, in turn, serve to increase the level of anxiety. It is advisable, therefore, that the person be instructed to refrain from attempting sexual performance for a while except when prompted by an uncontrollable urge. Performance involving an attempt to meet a challenge or to prove something to oneself should be avoided. On the other hand, situations that evoke pleasurable responses may be encouraged. The cooperation of the partner should, if possible, be obtained to participate in situations which will evoke sexual excitement and yet not provoke a need to prove anything or to meet any particular standard of performance. In addition to this, a program should be planned by which anxiety-responses other than sexual may be systematically desensitized, the level of any pervasive anxiety being diminished.

There are often situations in which the male partner may become more active and excitable than the female and which may therefore result in his reaching a climax prematurely. This invariably will leave the women with feelings of frustration and, perhaps, diminished interest in participating the next time.

Such situations may sometimes be alleviated by encouraging the man to be more relaxed, to divert his attention from his performance to casual thoughts if possible, to halt in his movements when excitation gets strong and then, when it diminishes, to continue. When this counsel has been acted upon and the climax is still premature, another attempt an hour or so later may result in improvement. If emphasis is placed upon the significance of this second attempt, improvement will often invest future first attempts.

In cases where the sex drive evokes abnormal or bizarre behavior it may be possible to institute a program utilizing aversion-responses and so condition them as to dominate or replace the undesirable responses. In such cases the therapist may give the patient detailed instructions before, during and after the trance. Only upon thorough testing of responses to suggestions should any latitude be given the patient in selecting imagery. When the patient responds well to such suggestions with no tendency to deviate or elaborate, a narrowly delimited program of self-hypnotic practice may be utilized beneficially if close contact with the patient can be maintained.

IMPOTENCE

Mr. J., a 32 year old salesman, complained that he had been troubled for nearly one year by premature ejaculations. This period coincided exactly with the duration of his marriage. He had, he stated, always considered himself at least normally virile, and this belief had been shared by his wife, with whom he had had satisfactory sexual intercourse upon several occasions prior to their marriage. Their doctor, who had known both of them for years, attributed the unfortunate situation to circumstances related to the day of the wedding; his explanation, though probably correct, had served to enlighten them on the probable cause but had contributed little toward solution of the problem. The doctor had astutely observed that a unique combination of factors on this day had provoked in Mr. J. an undesirable response that was uncharacteristic. He had never before felt the need to prove his sexual adequacy. But he had never been so excited over such a prolonged period and had never before had quite so much to drink. On his wedding night he was too tired, too drunk and too excited to be physically capable of performing well. The realization that he had "failed" his wife made it imperative, in his mind, to remedy the situation as immediately as possible. This he had been trying to do ever since.

This type of situation occurs very frequently. A *temporary* physiologic incapacity often conditions a *permanent* psychological response: permanent only in the sense that a reinforcing mechanism is established whereby the increased incentive initiates excessive excitement which is inhibitive to the very act that is to be performed.

Desensitization of this excessive anxiety was accomplished by advising Mr. J. to refrain from actual sexual intercourse during the period that he took to learn self-hypnosis. Both he and his wife were also advised to participate in situations involving as much sexual excitement as possible as frequently as they wished, but under no circumstances to attempt actual coitus. The idea, of course, was to remove any need for Mr. J. to "prove" himself and, instead, to renew his feelings of pleasure as associated with the sex act.

Mr. J. proved to be an excellent hypnotic subject. He developed self-hypnosis to a high degree within three weeks. He reported that his ability to relax was proving beneficial to him in many ways and that he had begun to experience more relaxed and pleasurable feelings during the sessions with his wife. Upon appropriate suggestions his right arm would become very rigid, and in the waking state it would react only by becoming more rigid each time he attempted to bend it. Upon touching it with his left hand his arm would immediately relax. I noticed that

Mr. J. was attaching great significance to this control over his arm, and I assumed that he had already recognized that similar control would soon be suggested for other areas of his anatomy. This, I felt, would not be nearly so effective as what was planned, but the fact that he was thinking along such lines was a natural and constructive conclusion for him to make. I congratulated Mr. J. on his ability to control his arm so well and told him that we were now ready to take the next step. He seemed rather surprised when I advised him to make suggestions that even under the most exciting circumstances he would *not* have an erection! I explained that by working on control indirectly his tendency to become overly excited would not be so apt to interfere. This appeared logical to him, and he agreed to work on this for one week and also to continue, together with his wife, the program of experiencing exciting situations with no attempt at intercourse.

The following week, when he arrived for his usual session, he laughed and said his problems were over. During the previous week, he explained, he had experienced erections upon several occasions after having suggested that this would not occur. It had "dawned on him" that this was probably just what I had intended to have happen. During the next few days he had enjoyed increasing control over the sexual situation until he was certain he was "as good or better" then previously.

This was pretty much what had been expected, except that he did not ask the usual question: "How is it that excellent control is developed along various lines of suggestion but the technique 'fails' upon attempts to avoid an erection during periods of excitement?" The answer to this is a simple one. You must *want* the suggestion to go into effect or it is not likely to prove successful. This is another example of the effectiveness of "misdirection".

The follow-up on this particular case is only of six months duration, but it is so typical of a number of other cases, and Mr. J. is so firmly convinced that he is now over his problem, that the probability of there being no relapse is, in the writer's opinion, rather high.

A young man, 22 years of age, reported that he was extremely concerned about the following: Two months previously he had been out on a date with a girl whom he considered very attractive. After taking her to dinner at a picturesque restaurant several miles from the city in which they lived, they had gone on to another place where they danced and had two or three drinks. Upon returning to his car, which he had parked in an area obscured from view of the establishment, he had kissed her several times and she had returned his kisses passionately. He had become very much aroused sexually and believed that his friend was as anxious as he to proceed further. She had, however, mildly resisted him for a few moments, and then indicated her accedence. He found himself unable to go on. His original aroused condition had diminished, physiologically speaking, but his emotional ardor had remained unchanged. He became extremely provoked with himself, and although the girl stated otherwise, he was sure she was disappointed and that she considered him inadequate. During the ride back to the city he twice again became aroused. In each of these instances a sequence of events had occurred almost identical to those already described. The major difference was that on the third, and final, attempt there had been no resistance whatever on the part of the girl, but he still had been unable to perform. If he had had any doubts as to the girl's previous reaction there was, he said, little question left at this point—she was not only disappointed, but outspokenly disgusted with his lack of ability to finish what he started.

Since this unfortunate affair, he had attempted numerous other conquests with diminishing evidence of anything being left of his former ability. Having considered the possibility that his impotence might have been due to the liquor he had consumed, he had assured himself that this was not so by abstaining during a number of the above-mentioned trysts.

Upon questioning this young man regarding incidents prior to his reported failure, it was discovered that in nearly all previous sexual activities there had been several important factors which were not present on this particular occasion. Usually the girls had been better known to him and there had been longer periods of acquaintanceship leading to the first sexual encounter with each one. The occasion in question was the first in several years in which he had attempted actual intercourse in an automobile. There had been several instances in which preliminary advances were made under such conditions, but the finalities had occurred in greater privacy. Reflecting back with these factors in mind, he admitted to having had feelings of uneasiness that night regarding the possibility of being interrupted and, upon further thought, he remembered that this was the major concern expressed by the girl as her reason for her temporary resistance. One additional item he recalled that may have been a contributing factor was his reading of a newspaper account of a man who had been arrested after being found, in compromising circumstances, in a car with another man's wife.

We have here a case of psychogenic impotence conditioned by anxiety-evoking stimuli associated with a fear of being discovered in a compromising situation. The fact that he was unaware at the time of the true cause of his anxiety led this young man to attribute his failure to unknown causes which he associated with some physical disability. His fear of experiencing future inadequacies helped to more firmly condition his anxiety-responses to all situations involving sex instead of just those regarding the use of an automobile. His anxiety inhibited his sexual ability, and his inhibited sexual ability increased his anxiety.

The above conclusions were reached during the first session, which lasted two hours. The following week the young man reported that the insight he had gained had not altered his ability to perform as evidenced by three "tests" he had made during that interval. We discussed the possibility of developing self-hypnosis and utilizing imagery of his previous, satisfactory experiences to condition relief-responses to sex-associated stimuli. He said he would like to try it, and I explained to him the general procedures regarding his practice for the coming week. I had him stare straight ahead as I went over the explanation. He reacted well to the suggestions of eye-closure and relaxation, but as we had no more time for that session, we concluded it at that point upon his agreement to practice as he had been instructed to do.

At the start of the next session he told me that he had, contrary to my advice, attempted to relax himself by thinking of the symbols, while attempting sexual intercourse with a girl at his apartment. This, as was to be expected, had been completely ineffective. Cautioning him against proceeding too rapidly, I again explained that the responses to the symbols must first be conditioned and the manner in which suggestions were to be utilized was extremely important. He agreed to be patient and said he would, from then on, follow instructions implicitly.

I asked if he could arrange a number of specific situations with some girl with whom he had had satisfactory sexual relationships. He nodded rather confidently, so I explained that he must obtain her cooperation to the extent that she would agree to participate in a number of sexually stimulating situations with no expectation of being satisfied. He should, I continued, dismiss any thought of completing the sex act for at least two or three weeks, as this was too closely associated with his anxiety. Instead he was to concentrate on maintaining as profound a state of relaxation as possible during exposure to sexually stimulating situations.

During the rest of this session further progress was made toward development of the self-hypnosis pattern with special emphasis on suggestions that he could relax and stay relaxed during imagery of previous sexual encounters. He was instructed to imagine himself in a particularly satisfying situation after having suggested that he would remain completely relaxed during a period of five minutes. Upon awakening he informed me that he had experienced subjective imagery of performing perfectly and had felt only slight anxiety during the episode. I suggested that he practice this same imagery two or three times each day during the next week and arrange, if possible, two or three situations in his apartment with his girl friend, in which he would first spend ten or fifteen minutes making suggestions of continued relaxation and then continue to think of "1000-3" as frequently as possible while being exposed to the sexually-stimulating circumstances of being alone with the girl and free of any fear of being interrupted. The major objective, I told him, was to develop his ability to remain relaxed and not under any circumstances to attempt actual coitus.

Minor variations of this procedure were utilized during the next four weeks with a gradual increase in his ability to achieve erections accompanied by a diminution of anxiety during sexual excitement. Two weeks more showed such a marked improvement that he considered himself normal as far as sexual competence was concerned, but there still remained some degree of anxiety. It was considered that this anxiety, which had been conditioned by fear of being observed while in an automobile, could now be desensitized through practice of imagery of satisfying episodes in his apartment which also would include some stimulus-object associated with the incident in the automobile. We felt that the relief-responses experienced during intercourse were now sufficiently strong to dominate the anxiety-responses and any slight increase in them that might be evoked by a properly-selected stimulus-object being added to the imagery. The stimulus-object selected was that of the word "car". By first thinking of this word during imagery of satisfactory sexual episodes and then during the peak of excitement during actual participation in the sex act, the anxiety quickly subsided. The stimulus-object meanwhile went through the transition from "car" to "imagery of sitting in his car alone" to "sitting in his car with the girl" and finally "imagery of performing the sex act in the car".

The above procedures resulted in complete restoration of sexual ability and desensitization of all anxiety associated with sexual activity. There has been a close follow-up of this case with no relapse reported over a period of three years.

FRIGIDITY

A couple in their early thirties, married eight years and with two children, complained of unsatisfactory sexual relations. In every other way, they agreed, they were perfectly happy and considered themselves fortunate. There were no financial problems, and after some discussion it appeared that they were very considerate of each other's right as individuals but that there were also many things they enjoyed doing together. The first session was spent in obtaining routine information and explaining the various hypnotic techniques. Their problem, it appeared, mainly arose from a lack of enjoyable response, on the part of the wife, to sexual stimulation. In their eight years of marriage she had experienced only four or five mildly pleasurable episodes and had become resigned to the fact that she must be "frigid". The husband explained that this had bothered him at first, but that he was chiefly concerned about her happiness. There were so many other ways in which they enjoyed each other's love and companionship that they both felt they could continue to live a full and happy life if no way could be found to favorably alter this one problem.

It was agreed that they would each come to the office for one further session before any decision would be made as to subsequent procedures. Appointments were arranged to see the wife the following Tuesday and the husband two days later.

The information elicited from Mrs. C., as we shall call her, indicated that she was an apparently well-adjusted woman; her Willoughby score was 14, with no high-intensity in any one area. She had a broad and tolerant attitude toward life and no prudish or erroneous concepts regarding sex. She did, she explained calmly, become excited at the start of sexual approaches by her husband, she loved to have him caress her and speak to her of his love and affection, but upon realization that coitus was imminent, she would "tighten up" and, even when exercising as much control as she could achieve, she could not keep her husband from knowing that she disliked this part of the relationship and that it was often actually painful to her. She hoped so much to be able to please him, but this was one facet of her emotional pattern she could not change.

She recalled having had strong responses to sexually stimulating situations during her teens and, as a matter of fact, she still responded well to her husband up to the point of intromission. Only then did her excitement subside. Although she had never had sexual intercourse until after her marriage, there had been an incident during which a former boy friend had nearly forced her to submit to him. His caresses had excited her, and she remembered her passionate responses to his manual stimulation in the area of her clitoris. Upon his attempt to insert his finger into her vagina, however, she had panicked. She felt her reaction at that moment was due more to her feeling that this was a boy she did not intend to marry than to revulsion for the act itself. She had realized for years that this was probably the precipitating episode that had conditioned her avoidance reactions, but any attempt to think of this episode during sexual relations with her husband had only served to intensify her withdrawal. She had never mentioned this episode to her husband, as she had hoped to be able to overcome her reactions herself.

I suggested to her that self-hypnosis would help her to relax during these situations and that she should begin to develop the attitude that the sexual act could be *mutually* enjoyable. She should not, I told her, enter into such relationships with the sole idea of pleasing her husband. I pointed out to her that no woman can "put on an act" as if she enjoyed the intimate relationship. She would please her husband more by going only as far into the sexual episode as was truly enjoyable to her, and for the next few weeks this is what she should do. This, I continued, would desensitize her anxiety and eventually make the entire performance really desirable. Meanwhile, she could satisfy her husband by means other than coitus. She understood and agreed to follow these suggestions.

Two days later, during the private interview with Mr. C., it was determined that the best procedure for him to follow would be to refrain from any attempt at intromission until his wife indicated strongly that this would be desirable to her. During each episode, however, he was to caress her gently and stimulate her in every way possible but, upon reaching the climax himself, he should accept this as enjoyable and sufficiently satisfying for a while. Hypnosis, we concluded, would not be necessary in order for him to perform his part in the procedure. I also suggested that if his wife reached the point where she wished him to penetrate her, and expressed this desire strongly, that he should be very gentle, use some vaginal lubricant, and cease upon reaching climax himself. His attitude too, I explained, should be more toward self-satisfaction than toward pleasing his wife. Any attempt to please her should be expressed in words and gentle caresses. He too agreed that this approach appeared logical and that he would follow it as instructed.

The development of self-hypnosis to the point where she could relax easily was readily accomplished by Mrs. C. In less than two weeks she reported feeling more relaxed in every way. She found herself hoping that her husband would go further during each sexual episode and even began to notice feelings of considering him selfish. She also felt somewhat selfish herself, and realized that this was as it should be. Each should want the other, but only insofar as it was enjoyable to both.

During the third week she had expressed the desire for her husband to attempt intromission, but he had declined, feeling that her plea did not seem urgent enough. The next night, however, he acceded to her request which had then been voiced in no uncertain terms. Even then he was very gentle and careful to avoid hurting her. She said later that she was beginning to get a little provoked with his reluctance and had even stated that she did not expect any pain and that even if there were a little pain it would be better than "being left up in the air".

Life was fuller and richer for Mr. and Mrs. C. from then on. They were both happier with each other than they could express, and the term "frgiidity" is now strange to them and has been for more than eight years.

This couple could probably have achieved the same result without hypnosis, but it might have taken considerably longer. This is an example of why hypnosis should be considered as adjunctive to other therapeutic procedures rather than as a modality in itself. It can play a very important part or a very minor one. In either case, the procedures with which it is used should carefully be considered, and results—whether negative or positive—attributed to each in proper proportion.

TRANSVESTISM

Although in the experience of the writer these cases are somewhat rare, the method of treatment is similar to that of other cases in which abnormal sexual behavior is a major symptom. There is usually a gradual build-up of anxiety and feelings of frustration until the point is reached where the ritualistic behavior is triggered. This may occur in rather definite cycles, or there may be a specific set of circumstances involved in each triggering episode. There appear to be intense sexually associated drives that condition this compulsive form of behavior, and since these drives are never sufficiently reduced, the result is an increase in anxiety and feelings of guilt or shame.

Generally there is a strong and apparently genuine desire to overcome these compulsions which is often traceable to a fear of being observed or apprehended by relatives or authorities. The transvestite differs from the alcoholic in his willingness to continue treatment that appears to be affecting his compulsive behavior. Whereas the compulsive drinker will often disregard instructions and fail to keep appointments upon realization that improvement is being effected, the transvestite usually follows instructions, keeps his appointments and is willing to go through very stringent and noxious procedures to rid himself of his symptoms.

Mr. A., a good-looking and rather large man about 29 years old, was greatly concerned over his compulsion to dress in women's clothing and perform masturbatory acts. He had been performing this ritualistic behavior since he was ten years old and during the last three years had been observed and apprehended by the police on four different occasions. The frequency of this behavior was from four to eight weeks, and each episode would last from two to four days during which he would go through these acts two to four times each day. The fact that he had married at the age of twenty-two and had fathered two children had no effect on the cycle nor on the intensity with which the rituals were performed. His wife and mother knew all about his problem and had tried many procedures in attempting to help him, all to no avail.

This patient was referred by a psychiatrist who had been treating him for two years with no change whatever in his bizarre behavior. The doctor had described the symptoms and asked what procedures I would use in attempting to influence such symptoms. I explained to him the techniques of developing relaxation through self-hypnosis and suggested that if the patient turned out to be a good hypnotic subject, some form of aversion therapy might be effective. As a result of this conference it was decided that tests would be made to evaluate the patient's susceptibility to hypnosis and we would then decide on the best course to take as might be indicated by the outcome of the tests.

Mr. A. was very cooperative, and during the first session a deep trance was achieved. He was instructed to practice for a few minutes twice daily and to use only suggestions for obtaining deeper relaxation. The patient was informed before and during the trance that he would not be able to induce hypnosis himself except for the specific purposes, and in the exact manner, we described. This suggestion was tested by asking the patient to see if he could induce a trance while standing up and after having made some suggestion of his own choice. He was unable to do this although he could, as was demonstrated a few minutes later, easily induce a trance upon following the procedures as instructed.

We saw Mr. A. for two one-hour sessions each week. After three weeks he had developed an excellent ability to relax himself at will. He had then been asked if he could recall some incident which involved any feelings of nausea or revulsion. He immediately described such in incident as having occurred during a ride on some revolving device at an amusement park. He could remember very well the sensation of being whirled around at high speed and of becoming extremely sick upon stepping off the device. Upon having him review this scene under hypnosis, it was found that intense feelings of nausea and aversion were easily developed with appropriate suggestions. The next four sessions were then utilized in conditioning the nauseous response to the stimulus of the spoken words, "your dress". Repeated emphasis was given to these suggestions until he reported feelings of nausea each time the stimulus words were spoken while he was in trance.

During the following sessions Mr. A. was instructed to develop imagery of himself going through the ritual of dressing in women's clothing and to experience all the accompanying sensations, including his thoughts before, during, and after the performance.

After he reported that this imagery was vivid and instantaneously evoked each time it was suggested, we had him suggest this imagery to himself, induce the trance state, and then signal, by raising the first finger on his right hand, upon the start of the imagery. The stimulus words "your dress" would then be spoken to him and suggestions made that he feel nauseous and revulsed. The stimulus was evoked at different times as related to his imagery of going through the ritual for the purpose of conditioning aversion-responses to every element of the ritual. This was done several times before he gave the signal, with the idea that the repetition would affect his thoughts preparatory to the ritual itself.

During the time that Mr. A. was practicing self-hypnosis for relaxation, he reported having performed the ritual twice. From the time the aversion conditioning was started he performed it only once, about two weeks later, and has not performed it since. Conditioning was continued until he expressed revulsion, in the waking state, to any thought of the ritual or to his performance of it. This required nearly three months, during which the aversion continuously increased in intensity—a total of 35 hours. The permanence of this conditioning is by no means firmly established. The case is typical of four in which the major symptoms were nearly identical, as were the procedures utilized and the results obtained. The follow-up has been carefully conducted with no relapse apparent, but the longest symptom-free period to the time of this writing is only seven months. This, however, is considered very significant by all concerned, as it is the first procedure yet found that has favorably affected the behavioral patterns.

CHAPTER 15

BREAKING BAD HABIT PATTERNS

IN ORDER TO CONDITION responses that are more desirable than those associated with various habits, it is necessary to understand something about the factors that may have contributed to development and maintenance of the habit. These factors vary considerably, depending upon the nature of the habit, the length of time it has been established and the degree of resistance or acceptance indicated by the individual as to whether the factors are predominantly physiologic or psychologic. Nail-biting, for instance, is almost certainly attributable to psychologic factors, whereas drug addiction, although it may first have been instigated by psychologic factors, may become dependent upon physiologic factors for its continuation. Excessive smoking may be attributable in some degree to factors of physiologic addiction but is more apt to be based on psychologic factors, especially during the original conditioning.

ENURESIS

The problem of bed-wetting is often approached, with little or no success, by attempting to establish the sensation of a full bladder as a stimulus for awakening the patient and causing him to get out of bed to go to the bathroom. Most of these patients admit that they would rather stay in bed, even though it is wet, then get up during the night. Although they may not feel this way during the day, at night, when the decision must be made, this is their reported reaction.

Results are much more satisfactory when the idea of waking up during the night is not mentioned. Instead, emphasis is directed toward making the wet bed very uncomfortable and the dry bed very desirable and then, once these reactions are established, toward development of bladder control through the entire sleeping period.

Although direct suggestions through the use of hetero-hypnosis may be effective, the likelihood of long term results is much greater when the techniques of self-hypnosis are utilized. This is probably because the building of the patient's self-confidence, by means of his own suggestions, is related to his control over his bodily functions.

There are many theories as to the underlying causes of enuresis. One of the most prevalent of these involves the concept that the patient is, or at some time was, frustrated because of goals being set too high for him by over-attentive parents. The patient then is supposed to be reverting to infantile behavior in an attempt to obtain the attention and sympathy he feels he cannot obtain through achievement of impossible goals. Whether or not such theories regarding the underlying causes are true does not appear to be so important as the realization that this type of behavior can be conditioned to be repeatedly evoked even after the original causative factors no longer exist. This is evidenced by the fact that many such cases have been successfully treated and with no relapse over long periods of time, yet without investigation having been made into probable causes for the individual symptoms.

During the initial practice sessions in the development of self-hypnosis, the patient is told to do nothing whatever about his problem. He is first to develop self-hypnotic ability to the point where neutral suggestions such as arm-rigidity or hand-levitation bring appropriate responses in the trance state. He is then instructed to make suggestions and to develop imagery related to the discomfort and undesirability of lying in the wet bed. He is further instructed to drink a glass of water each night, one-half hour before retiring, and to make suggestions while going through the practice procedure in bed that he will urinate in bed before going to sleep. After several nights this should become highly undesirable to the patient, and when he strongly objects to continuing this uncomfortable practice, he should be instructed to begin the practice of interrupting urination each time during day or night that he empties his bladder. Each time he starts to urinate he should interrupt the flow of urine by tightening the sphincters for four or five seconds several times during the process until his bladder is empty. This, he should be told, will help him to develop control so that he can maintain a dry, comfortable bed through the entire night. Instructions are changed from purposely wetting the bed to going to the bathroom before retiring each night. It should be pointed out, in this connection, that he can control his bladder by urinating before going to sleep. It is rare for a patient to wake up during the night once he goes to sleep in the wet bed, and the chances are that he will go through the night without further micturition. From then on his practice sessions are devoted to suggestions and imagery related to the advantages of a dry bed.

Many patients find that the frequency with which they wet the bed has already diminished, and with a few weeks' practice the symptom completely disappears. Approximately thirty per cent report that upon starting the positive imagery the symptom no longer occurs, and their beds remain dry from then on.

There have been surprisingly few relapses in cases where these techniques have been utilized; in several of the cases, long-term results were obtained after resuming both negative and positive practice for several weeks.

A brief definition of the terms "negative practice" and "positive practice", as employed in the above discussion and in that to follow, may here be in order.

Positive practice includes the systematic attempt to refrain from performing the undesirable activity at times when the involuntary urge is present. This may be very difficult to carry out, especially if the patient is largely unaware of his undesirable performance until it is partially or completely executed or until some alteration of the associated stimulus-response patterns has been effected.

Negative practice may be the means by which such alteration can be accomplished. It is the *voluntary* systematic performance of the undesirable activity at times when the *involuntary* urge is *not* present. During this type of practice there are many factors that differ considerably from those associated with positive practice. There are differences in the type and intensity of motivation, imagery, environmental stimuli, response patterns and the sequence in which these factors occur during negative practice. The use of this technique may provide a basis for changes in the habit-pattern itself, changes that might otherwise be difficult to accomplish. Once these changes are effected, positive practice may then be successfully used where previously it had been ineffective.

STUTTERING

In the experience of the writer, the incidence of successful treatment of stutterers has been about fifty per cent. Those who were good hypnotic subjects and could develop vivid imagery while in the trance achieved far better results than did refractory subjects. It has also been noted that those patients whose stuttering ceased or diminished while talking in the trance state almost invariably made marked improvement.

The techniques most effective were those in which the patient was encouraged to learn self-hypnosis before attempting to attack the problem directly. Upon achieving this, the patient would be requested to talk frequently while in the trance, and complimentary remarks would be made upon the least sign of improvement. Having the patient repeat statements made by the hypnotist would save the patient from making any decisions, and this resulted in more frequent successful responses. The complexity of the statements would gradually be increased as improvement indicated. The next step was to give the subject a choice of which statement he wished to repeat. The reasoning here is that many such problems result from an inability on the part of patient to coordinate his speech with his thinking. There often seems to be a conflict in the mind of the patient between whether he should express what he truly feels or what he feels would be acceptable to the listener. This conflict is minimized by utilizing the process of preparing statements for him and then giving him two or more statements from which to choose, one of which is obviously correct so that he can choose easily. As improvement is evidenced, the statements may be made more difficult as to proper choice.

In addition to suggestive procedures while the subject is in trance, there are various techniques involving the use of imagery that the subject can practice daily at his own convenience and during a self-induced trance. Imagery in which the subject sees himself talking perfectly to one person may be productive; when he can do this easily, he should be encouraged to make simple statements to one person until this also is done easily.

Cases in which the stutterer has a high level of anxiety regarding his performance are usually more readily affected than those in which little or no anxiety or embarrassment is observed.

The use of time-distortion appears to be very facilitative to improvement if it is developed at first along lines not associated with the problem. This also seems to work out best if the type of practice, and the phrases used, are first brought under control without it. Time-distortion then is utilized mainly for consolidating gains already made through other means.

Another helpful technique is one in which the patient is instructed to select a person whom he feels talks very well and then to develop imagery of this person talking. There seems to be a tendency for the patient, under such circumstances, to project himself into his imagery of the other person and, in acting as if he were the other person, he dissociates himself to the point where he can talk more easily.

The confidence the stutterer builds up in experiencing the effect of his own suggestions is another important factor. When he learns to place more emphasis on *what* he is saying rather than on *how* he is saying it, improvement invariably follows.

TICS

While tics are not completely a "bad habit", they are classified as such for convenience, since they are subject to the conditioning process. The incidence of successful treatment of tics is somewhat higher than that for stuttering. The use of hypnotic techniques is similar to the way they are applied in cases of stuttering. There are, however, some additional applications that may be helpful.

In cases where the patient is largely unaware of the tic-like movement, he can be made aware of it by conditioning the movement as a stimulus that evokes awareness. Once this is accomplished, relief responses can then be conditioned to the start of the movement, and completion of the act becomes no longer necessary. This method, of course, can only apply to movements that are extensive enough or of sufficient duration to enable a distinction to be made between their start and cessation. Those tics caused by degeneration or malfunctioning of neural pathways would not be amenable to such procedures.

One young man had a tic-like habit of repeatedly moving his head as if his collar were too tight. This occurred only when he was engaged in conversation. The movement was most pronounced as he prepared to speak, its magnitude and frequency then diminishing as he talked and, as he reached his conclusion, disappearing until the next time he prepared to speak. He was more aware of this movement immediately after starting to speak than he was during the formulation in his mind of what he intended to say or after he got started saying it. If someone interrupted him or if the opportunity for him to speak did not immediately arise coincidentally with the formulation of his thoughts, the frequency and intensity of the tic would become greatly increased.

After this patient developed self-hypnosis and practiced imagery in which he visualized himself speaking without the tic, there was some slight improvement. As this small gain was considered insufficient, it was decided that a more stringent type of conditioning would be required.

The movement-pattern of this tic consisted of a jutting-out of the chin and then a downward motion of the chin toward the right shoulder. The patient's head would then go quickly through a circular motion back to a normal position.

The patient, while in the trance, was instructed to visualize writing on a blackboard a question asked by the hypnotist and to signal when he had done so by a straightening out of the first finger of his left hand. (In his imagery the patient wrote with his right, so it was felt more desirable for him to signal with the other hand.) He was then instructed to write out his answer to the question in the same manner. Since he visualized this writing as being on a blackboard placed straight in front of him, his attention was so directed as to tend to keep his head facing in that direction. He was advised to formulate his thoughts in this manner during waking conversations; after practicing these procedures for two weeks, both in and out of trance, there was a marked improvement. We then decided to utilize noxious stimulation for negative conditioning in an attempt to eliminate the last vestiges of the tic. This worked out very well. The procedure involved the induction of a mild electric current into the forearm of the patient each time his head moved to the right during practice while in trance. Each time he visualized writing a question and answer with no motion of his head, there would be no current applied, and a relief response was established. If there was the slightest movement of his head toward the right, the current was induced for the duration of the movement. This procedure was followed for the major portion of seven one-hour sessions at the end of which time there was no further tendency for the patient to move his head. The patient then reported that he could talk easily in all sorts of situations and that he formulated his thoughts "externally" as if they were on an imaginary blackboard placed in front of him. He had no tendency whatever to perform the tic-like movement. The habit evidently had been altered. There has been no recurrence of the symptom in 18 months.

Variations of these techniques have been used successfully in dozens of similar cases in which the symptoms ranged from slight localized movements such as muscular twitches around the eyes to gross movements of the head or arms. Developing the ability to relax during manifestation of the tic seems to help. Imagery designed to condition both negative and positive responses, such as relief upon performing well and an avoidance response to poor performances, appears to be additionally facilitative to improvement. Most effective of all is the utilization of these techniques plus the conditioning procedures involving noxious stimulation. In some cases it has been found that the negative reaction to electric stimulation can be conditioned to the touch of a finger, after the patient has felt the actual stimulation while in the trance, and from then on the results are no different than when the current is actually applied. In a few cases in which the patients were superior hypnotic subjects, the actual application of the noxious stimulus was eliminated from the procedure, and excellent avoidance responses were conditioned simply through the use of suggestion.

Another technique which has been used very successfully involves the conditioning of the tic-reaction to a new and controllable stimulus and then extinguishing it through negative-conditioning procedures. A typical case was one in which the patient's tic consisted of a movement of his right hand to the back of his neck, a slight movement of his head and, after a moment or two, the dropping of his arm back to his lap. This behavior would occur every minute or so during conversation or intense thinking. The patient developed only a slight ability to relax through self-hypnotic suggestion, and there was no observable change in the frequency or intensity of the symptom after several weeks of practice.

Improvement was fairly rapid, however, after the movement was conditioned to a new stimulus and then extinguished. This was done by attaching electrodes to his left forearm and then instructing him to perform the movements of the tic each time he heard the signal of two taps on the desk with a pencil. Immediately following the signal a mild current was induced simultaneously with his performance, and the current was shut off only after his arm dropped back to his lap.

Forty such exposures were given during each of five sessions spaced two to three days apart, a total of two hundred conditioning episodes with no trials in between. Upon the first trial session five signals were given at two-minute intervals, and each time the response of the tic-movement was made spontaneously, even though no current was induced. The patient was then instructed to *try* to perform the movement upon each signal of *one* tap of the pencil after being told that the current would be increased in proportion to the degree of movement of his arm. Dual exposures were then made during which random signals of one or two taps were given. When the signal was one tap, the current would be induced only if he raised his arm. He was told to magnify and emphasize his feelings of relief when he did not raise his arm, and the noxious stimulation was therefore not induced. Upon the signal of two taps, however, the only way he could minimize the noxious stimulation was to quickly perform the movement.

One hundred and twenty exposures were then given during three sessions until conditioning was well established to the signals: no movement of the arm at one tap and rapid movement at two taps. Desensitization was then achieved through one hundred and twenty exposures to signals of one tap only with the time interval between taps being gradually decreased to the point where it approximated that of the two-tap signals. The patient then reported the experiencing of significant relief responses to the signals when he refrained from raising his hand. These were due to the fact that toward the end of the conditioning period the only time current was induced was upon observation of his starting the movement, regardless of which signal was given. During the final three sessions the tic gradually disappeared, and the only effect of a tapping sound was the evocation of feelings of relaxation.

NAIL-BITING

This type of behavior appears always to be associated with some form of anxiety, especially when it is first conditioned. It can, however, develop into an automatic response to stimulus situations of which the subject may be totally unaware. It also can become a compulsive reaction which the subject recognizes but still cannot control. Treatment procedures are identical to those utilized for tics, so there would be little value in repeating them here. The incidence of successful treatment is much higher in these cases than in any other area of undesirable habits. This is due to the fact that there rarely are any "drop-outs". These patients most generally follow procedures recommended to them until the symptoms completely disappear.

ALCOHOLISM

Only three out of the twenty most recent cases of alcoholism referred to this writer showed significant, long-term improvement even though all twenty patients gave every indication of being good hypnotic subjects. The major reason for this low incidence was the refusal on the part of 15 of these patients to continue treatment after two or three sessions. There are strong indications that if the treatment had continued the data would have been much more encouraging.

The degree of motivation evidenced by the patient appears to be extremely important. Those patients who are urged by someone else to seek treatment rarely cooperate. This becomes apparent when the patient is directed to look in a specific direction and, though he claims to be doing so, actually focuses his eyes elsewhere. Immediately upon any indication of progress these patients will often find some excuse not to show up for the next appointment. They do not really wish to be helped, but they do not want anyone else to know they are avoiding it.

Another difficulty in such cases is that because there are so many environmental factors contributing to the problem, the therapist must enter into many more phases of the patient's life-situations than is practical or possible due to time limitations or a desire to avoid such an intimate patient-relationship.

These and many other factors point to the desirability of some form of confinement. In this way the many variables may be brought under adequate control.

In each of the three cases that showed improvement the patient had sufficient motivation to seek help without being urged to do so by some other person. The procedures utilized were essentially the same in all cases.

It was considered inadvisable to teach self-hypnosis at the beginning of treatment. Instead, a trance was induced by direct suggestion using the hand-levitation method. The trance was then deepened by suggestions of arm-rigidity, arm-heaviness and lightness and continuous suggestions over a period of approximately one-half hour. The patient was then instructed to visualize several instances in which he had experienced nausea due to drinking, and this imagery was developed by repeated suggestions to the point where the patient reported, while still in trance, that the scenes were vivid and the associated sensations were being intensely re-experienced.

It was then suggested that each time he thought of taking a drink containing alcohol these scenes and sensations would immediately be evoked and would grow even stronger until he decided not to take the drink. An average of one hour was spent in building the "negative image" in which the patient visualized himself as experiencing the most revulsive sensations related to drinking. A glass of whiskey was then placed in his hand and he was instructed to "try" to drink it. During his attempt to lift the glass to his lips, emphatic suggestions were made that he experience "ten times as much" nausea and revulsion, but each time the effort to lift the glass diminished he would be strongly urged to try harder. This procedure continued until no further effort was made toward raising the glass.

"Positive conditioning" was then begun by suggesting imagery in which the patient visualized himself as looking and feeling perfectly well and happy. Great detail was utilized in these suggestions, and the attempt was made to describe every possible benefit to the patient that would ensue from *not* taking the drink or from drinking a non-alcoholic beverage. A glass of water was then placed in the patient's hand, and he was told that each time he drank a glass of water he would think of the positive imagery and feel the pleasant sensations associated with it. These negative and positive conditioning procedures were continued alternately until the patient strongly refused to lift the whiskey glass but easily lifted and drank from the glass of water. The final suggestions were made that each morning thereafter the patient would drink a glass of water or milk, and this would give him the strength to maintain his positive image through the next 24 hours.

In each of these cases arrangements were made for increasing the constructive activities of the patient. Two were advised to take up hobbies and sports. Appointments were made with a dentist to have one patient's dental problem corrected. Consideration was given to as many details as could be thought of which might build confidence and pride and keep the patient productively occupied. The initial sessions required approximately four hours with each of these patients, and they were seen for one hour each day for the following two weeks. A checklist was made for each patient in order to evaluate and record the degree to which each suggestion was being followed. During each session the positive and negative conditioning was reinforced by direct suggestions.

A considerable amount of time was spent with the friends and relatives of each of these patients and in conferences with their individual physicians. Many decisions were made for them which ordinarily would have been considered an encroachment upon their private affairs. A much greater intimacy of the patient-therapist relationship was developed than in any other type of case in this writer's experience. After two or three weeks, during which time none of these patients expressed any desire to drink, the frequency of the sessions was changed to twice weekly and then, after another four weeks, to once weekly. The conditioning of limited self-hypnosis was begun at this point with suggestions that the ability could be used only for practicing the positive and negative imagery and for improving the ability to relax.

The follow-up on two of these patients was carefully conducted for slightly more than two years with no evidence of a recurrence of symptoms. The third patient had one serious relapse about six months after treatment started, but he then recovered. During a four-year follow-up there was no evidence of any desire to drink, and the patient's life-situation had improved tremendously.

SMOKING

There appears to be a rather widespread belief that smoking and a number of other habits can be quickly and easily altered by using hypnotic techniques, with little or no desire or effort on the part of the subject. This unrealistic attitude is typified by frequently-heard remarks such as, "So you are a hypnotist? I must drop by sometime and have you *make me* stop smoking." Such lack of appreciation of the true state of affairs is understandable in view of the publicity given to dramatic "cures" in various publications. Unfortunately it is only the successful cases that are so reported. The fact that these cases may represent only a small number of the total cases treated or that many such cases show a relapse at some later date is rarely included in the report.

Adding to this confusion are the demonstrations of hypnotic phenomena seen on television screens, in night-clubs and in lecture halls. Those observing these demonstrations may not realize that they are perceiving only a few of the total number of factors required for a true appreciation and understanding of what is going on. For example, one who is witnessing the performance of an accomplished hypnotist may be misled into thinking that the hypnotist is capable of immediately inducing a trance in any subject who steps upon the stage.

This is an understandable conclusion, but it is far from being true. If one reviews what actually happened, he will find that the hypnotist had ample opportunity to observe the reactions of several members of the audience to subtle suggestions included in his opening remarks. When he invites "volunteers" to participate in the performance he is actually selecting those persons who responded favorably to these suggestions. The hypnotist's smiling nod toward the individual he selects and his casual, "Would you like to volunteer for this interesting experiment?" is *not* a random selection of *volunteers* at all. It is instead a very careful process of selecting some of the most highly suggestible persons from his audience. The hypnotist makes further refinements in his selection of subjects by inviting several persons to the stage, making further tests by observing reactions to his instructions and then working with only one or two persons from the total selected. Since the hypnotist knows from experience that he can count on two or three persons out of every ten as being good subjects, he develops his ability to select these good subjects in order to assure an interesting performance.

The hypnotist working in a clinical atmosphere is faced with an entirely different set of problems. If he is to do his job properly, he must work with each person upon whom the use of hypnotic techniques has been deemed advisable. He cannot select his subjects. He must therefore expect to work with subjects of varying degrees of susceptibility. He, too, will find that two or three out of ten will respond quickly to suggestion, but that the other seven or eight will not be so amenable.

The person who desires to effect some alteration of habit patterns must reach an understanding of these limitations of the use of hypnosis. It is true that some speedy results are obtained, and it is also true that some of these cases maintain long-term benefits. But for the individual to expect that he is necessarily in the high-susceptibility group is unrealistic. Such a person should be given correct information before any therapeutic procedures are instituted, or his erroneous beliefs may be inhibitive to favorable results.

There are some favorable factors in the clinical situation that do not exist in the stage or demonstration procedures. These make the incidence of successful uses of hypnotic techniques higher in cases that otherwise might be, to some degree, refractory. Time, for example, is not generally so important in the clinical situation, as it is in demonstrations. The clinical hypnotist may (and generally does) take many hours in his careful induction of trance states because he is more interested in the *certainty* of his results than in the time or dramatic manner in which they are achieved.

These observations lead us to the realization that proper understanding of the effectiveness of hypnotic procedures and sufficient degrees of motivation are essential to successful alternation of habit patterns.

In cases in which the desire to stop smoking is high, the use of self-hypnosis can be very effective. Conditioning of the self-hypnotic pattern can start during the first session and, upon evidence of the appropriate responses to neutral suggestions, conditioning of relief-responses to stimuli associated with "not smoking" and of aversion-responses to stimuli associated with smoking can be initiated. This may be accomplished by developing imagery in which the subject visualizes himself starting to reach for a cigarette (or whatever form of tobacco he uses). This movement then becomes the stimulus to which responses of aversion are conditioned, while the movement of the hand in the opposite direction (not going through with the original movement) becomes the stimulus to which relief responses are conditioned. Repeated emphasis should be placed on the benefits to be derived from not smoking as well as on the negative aspects of the habit itself. The effectiveness of these negative aspects can be greatly enhanced through the use, during the early conditioning stages, of negative practice. This procedure should only be used after careful consideration and upon approval of the person's physician. In making use of negative practice, the individual would, in the performance of his normal activities, increase the practice of his habit to a frequency of at least twice the established rate. For example, the person who smokes a cigarette on an average of two per hour is instructed to smoke one *every ten minutes* without fail during all his waking hours. Only upon developing an intense revulsion is he allowed to cease this practice, and he then is instructed to utilize these feelings, which are generally very intense, to increase the vividness of his imagery during the subsequent conditioning episodes.

In cases of excessive smoking in which low motivation is evidenced, it is not advisable to institute treatment procedures until motivational intensity is increased. This may often be accomplished through discussions in which physiologic factors are explained and the cost and other undesirable aspects of excessive smoking are brought to the person's attention. When this is found to be necessary, it is advisable to spend at least one or two sessions in which direct suggestions are made toward increasing the motivation. If significant motivation cannot be developed, then self-hypnosis, for this particular purpose, is quite apt to be useless.

The number of sessions required for successful utilization of these procedures, in the case of a person who smokes from one to four packages of cigarettes per day, averages between twelve and fifteen on the basis of one hour per session. The incidence of success has been approximately sixty-four per cent, not counting drop-outs.

OTHER UNDESIRABLE HABITS

Most all undesirable habits and mild compulsive acts respond in some degree to hypnotic suggestion. The infinite numbers of individual habit-patterns and the wide variety of environmental and personality characteristics make detailed procedures impractical to explain. The utilization of hetero- and self-hypnotic procedures to provide a measure of relaxation and to develop an increase in feelings of relief for the patient is generally productive. Further than this, there is a certain amount of perceptive ability required for determining procedures best suited to affect the individual symptoms, and the ingenuity with which these procedures are applied may well determine the outcome.

A stimulus that is found to evoke favorable responses in one patient may have the reverse effect upon someone else. An imaginary scene that is highly pleasing to the hypnotist may evoke revulsive reactions in the patient. With a careful and gentle approach these factors can be determined and evaluated as to the advisability of incorporating them into therapeutic procedures. Fortunately there appears to be an unlimited source of stimulus-objects that may be so utilized in "custom-planning" of procedures to suit the individual problem.

REFERENCES

Although there are few, if any, direct quotations in this book, there are a number of texts which contributed considerably to the theoretical and practical concepts presented herein. The reader interested in obtaining more detailed information regarding these concepts will find the following list helpful:

Arons, Harry: Handbook of Self-Hypnosis. Power Publishers, 1959.

Bramwell, Milne: Hypnotism—Its History, Practice, Theory. The Julian Press, Inc., 1956. (Re-issue of Grant Richards edition, 1903.)

Dunlap, Knight: Habits, Their Making and Unmaking. Liveright Publishing Corp., 1949.

Erickson, Milton H., Hershman, Seymour, and Secter, Irving I.: The Practical Application of Medical and Dental Hypnosis. The Julian Press, Inc., 1961.

Hull, Clark L.: Hypnosis and Suggestibility. Appleton-Century-Crofts, Inc., 1933.

LeCron, Leslie M.: Experimental Hypnosis. The Macmillan Co., 1956.

Moss, Aaron A.: Hypnodontics. Dental Items of Interest Publishing Co., 1957.

Pavlov, Ivan: Lectures on Conditioned Reflexes. Perfecting of English rendition by Walter B. Cannon, 1928. Liveright Publishing Corp., 1928.

Salter, Andrew: Conditioned Reflex Therapy. Creative Age Press, 1949.

Shaffer, L. F.: The Psychology of Adjustment. Houghton Mifflin Co., 1936.

Weitzenhoffer, Andre M.: General Techniques of Hypnotism. Grune & Stratton, Inc., 1957.

Wolberg, Lewis R.: Medical Hypnosis. Vols. 1 and 2. Grune & Stratton, Inc., 1957.

Wolpe, Joseph: Psychotherapy by Reciprocal Inhibition. Stanford University Press, 1958.

Zoethout, William D., and Tuttle, W. W.: Textbook of Physiology. The C. V. Mosby Co., 1958.

INDEX

MELVIN POWERS SELF-IMPROVEMENT LIBRARY

ASTROLOGY

____ ASTROLOGY: HOW TO CHART YOUR HOROSCOPE *Max Heindel*	5.00
____ ASTROLOGY AND SEXUAL ANALYSIS *Morris C. Goodman*	5.00
____ ASTROLOGY MADE EASY *Astarte*	3.00
____ ASTROLOGY MADE PRACTICAL *Alexandra Kayhle*	3.00
____ ASTROLOGY, ROMANCE, YOU AND THE STARS *Anthony Norvell*	4.00
____ MY WORLD OF ASTROLOGY *Sydney Omarr*	7.00
____ THOUGHT DIAL *Sydney Omarr*	4.00
____ WHAT THE STARS REVEAL ABOUT THE MEN IN YOUR LIFE *Thelma White*	3.00

BRIDGE

____ BRIDGE BIDDING MADE EASY *Edwin B. Kantar*	10.00
____ BRIDGE CONVENTIONS *Edwin B. Kantar*	7.00
____ BRIDGE HUMOR *Edwin B. Kantar*	5.00
____ COMPETITIVE BIDDING IN MODERN BRIDGE *Edgar Kaplan*	4.00
____ DEFENSIVE BRIDGE PLAY COMPLETE *Edwin B. Kantar*	15.00
____ GAMESMAN BRIDGE—Play Better with Kantar *Edwin B. Kantar*	5.00
____ HOW TO IMPROVE YOUR BRIDGE *Alfred Sheinwold*	5.00
____ IMPROVING YOUR BIDDING SKILLS *Edwin B. Kantar*	4.00
____ INTRODUCTION TO DECLARER'S PLAY *Edwin B. Kantar*	5.00
____ INTRODUCTION TO DEFENDER'S PLAY *Edwin B. Kantar*	3.00
____ KANTAR FOR THE DEFENSE *Edwin B. Kantar*	5.00
____ KANTAR FOR THE DEFENSE VOLUME 2 *Edwin B. Kantar*	7.00
____ SHORT CUT TO WINNING BRIDGE *Alfred Sheinwold*	3.00
____ TEST YOUR BRIDGE PLAY *Edwin B. Kantar*	5.00
____ VOLUME 2—TEST YOUR BRIDGE PLAY *Edwin B. Kantar*	5.00
____ WINNING DECLARER PLAY *Dorothy Hayden Truscott*	5.00

BUSINESS, STUDY & REFERENCE

____ CONVERSATION MADE EASY *Elliot Russell*	4.00
____ EXAM SECRET *Dennis B. Jackson*	3.00
____ FIX-IT BOOK *Arthur Symons*	2.00
____ HOW TO DEVELOP A BETTER SPEAKING VOICE *M. Hellier*	4.00
____ HOW TO SELF-PUBLISH YOUR BOOK & MAKE IT A BEST SELLER *Melvin Powers*	10.00
____ INCREASE YOUR LEARNING POWER *Geoffrey A. Dudley*	3.00
____ PRACTICAL GUIDE TO BETTER CONCENTRATION *Melvin Powers*	3.00
____ PRACTICAL GUIDE TO PUBLIC SPEAKING *Maurice Forley*	5.00
____ 7 DAYS TO FASTER READING *William S. Schaill*	3.00
____ SONGWRITERS' RHYMING DICTIONARY *Jane Shaw Whitfield*	6.00
____ SPELLING MADE EASY *Lester D. Basch & Dr. Milton Finkelstein*	3.00
____ STUDENT'S GUIDE TO BETTER GRADES *J. A. Rickard*	3.00
____ TEST YOURSELF—Find Your Hidden Talent *Jack Shafer*	3.00
____ YOUR WILL & WHAT TO DO ABOUT IT *Attorney Samuel G. Kling*	4.00

CALLIGRAPHY

____ ADVANCED CALLIGRAPHY *Katherine Jeffares*	7.00
____ CALLIGRAPHER'S REFERENCE BOOK *Anne Leptich & Jacque Evans*	7.00
____ CALLIGRAPHY—The Art of Beautiful Writing *Katherine Jeffares*	7.00
____ CALLIGRAPHY FOR FUN & PROFIT *Anne Leptich & Jacque Evans*	7.00
____ CALLIGRAPHY MADE EASY *Tina Serafini*	7.00

CHESS & CHECKERS

____ BEGINNER'S GUIDE TO WINNING CHESS *Fred Reinfeld*	5.00
____ CHESS IN TEN EASY LESSONS *Larry Evans*	5.00
____ CHESS MADE EASY *Milton L. Hanauer*	3.00
____ CHESS PROBLEMS FOR BEGINNERS *edited by Fred Reinfeld*	2.00
____ CHESS SECRETS REVEALED *Fred Reinfeld*	2.00
____ CHESS TACTICS FOR BEGINNERS *edited by Fred Reinfeld*	4.00
____ CHESS THEORY & PRACTICE *Morry & Mitchell*	2.00
____ HOW TO WIN AT CHECKERS *Fred Reinfeld*	3.00
____ 1001 BRILLIANT WAYS TO CHECKMATE *Fred Reinfeld*	4.00
____ 1001 WINNING CHESS SACRIFICES & COMBINATIONS *Fred Reinfeld*	4.00

_____ SOVIET CHESS *Edited by R. G. Wade* 3.00

COOKERY & HERBS

_____ CULPEPER'S HERBAL REMEDIES *Dr. Nicholas Culpeper* 3.00
_____ FAST GOURMET COOKBOOK *Poppy Cannon* 2.50
_____ GINSENG The Myth & The Truth *Joseph P. Hou* 3.00
_____ HEALING POWER OF HERBS *May Bethel* 4.00
_____ HEALING POWER OF NATURAL FOODS *May Bethel* 5.00
_____ HERB HANDBOOK *Dawn MacLeod* 3.00
_____ HERBS FOR HEALTH—How to Grow & Use Them *Louise Evans Doole* 4.00
_____ HOME GARDEN COOKBOOK—Delicious Natural Food Recipes *Ken Kraft* 3.00
_____ MEDICAL HERBALIST *edited by Dr. J. R. Yemm* 3.00
_____ NATURE'S MEDICINES *Richard Lucas* 3.00
_____ VEGETABLE GARDENING FOR BEGINNERS *Hugh Wiberg* 2.00
_____ VEGETABLES FOR TODAY'S GARDENS *R. Milton Carleton* 2.00
_____ VEGETARIAN COOKERY *Janet Walker* 4.00
_____ VEGETARIAN COOKING MADE EASY & DELECTABLE *Veronica Vezza* 3.00
_____ VEGETARIAN DELIGHTS—A Happy Cookbook for Health *K. R. Mehta* 2.00
_____ VEGETARIAN GOURMET COOKBOOK *Joyce McKinnel* 3.00

GAMBLING & POKER

_____ ADVANCED POKER STRATEGY & WINNING PLAY *A. D. Livingston* 5.00
_____ HOW NOT TO LOSE AT POKER *Jeffrey Lloyd Castle* 3.00
_____ HOW TO WIN AT DICE GAMES *Skip Frey* 3.00
_____ HOW TO WIN AT POKER *Terence Reese & Anthony T. Watkins* 5.00
_____ WINNING AT CRAPS *Dr. Lloyd T. Commins* 4.00
_____ WINNING AT GIN *Chester Wander & Cy Rice* 3.00
_____ WINNING AT POKER—An Expert's Guide *John Archer* 5.00
_____ WINNING AT 21—An Expert's Guide *John Archer* 5.00
_____ WINNING POKER SYSTEMS *Norman Zadeh* 3.00

HEALTH

_____ BEE POLLEN *Lynda Lyngheim & Jack Scagnetti* 3.00
_____ DR. LINDNER'S SPECIAL WEIGHT CONTROL METHOD *P. G. Lindner, M.D.* 2.00
_____ HELP YOURSELF TO BETTER SIGHT *Margaret Darst Corbett* 3.00
_____ HOW TO IMPROVE YOUR VISION *Dr. Robert A. Kraskin* 3.00
_____ HOW YOU CAN STOP SMOKING PERMANENTLY *Ernest Caldwell* 3.00
_____ MIND OVER PLATTER *Peter G. Lindner, M.D.* 3.00
_____ NATURE'S WAY TO NUTRITION & VIBRANT HEALTH *Robert J. Scrutton* 3.00
_____ NEW CARBOHYDRATE DIET COUNTER *Patti Lopez-Pereira* 2.00
_____ QUICK & EASY EXERCISES FOR FACIAL BEAUTY *Judy Smith-deal* 2.00
_____ QUICK & EASY EXERCISES FOR FIGURE BEAUTY *Judy Smith-deal* 2.00
_____ REFLEXOLOGY *Dr. Maybelle Segal* 3.00
_____ REFLEXOLOGY FOR GOOD HEALTH *Anna Kaye & Don C. Matchan* 4.00
_____ 30 DAYS TO BEAUTIFUL LEGS *Dr. Marc Selner* 3.00
_____ YOU CAN LEARN TO RELAX *Dr. Samuel Gutwirth* 3.00
_____ YOUR ALLERGY—What To Do About It *Allan Knight, M.D.* 3.00

HOBBIES

_____ BEACHCOMBING FOR BEGINNERS *Norman Hickin* 2.00
_____ BLACKSTONE'S MODERN CARD TRICKS *Harry Blackstone* 3.00
_____ BLACKSTONE'S SECRETS OF MAGIC *Harry Blackstone* 3.00
_____ COIN COLLECTING FOR BEGINNERS *Burton Hobson & Fred Reinfeld* 2.00
_____ ENTERTAINING WITH ESP *Tony 'Doc' Shiels* 2.00
_____ 400 FASCINATING MAGIC TRICKS YOU CAN DO *Howard Thurston* 4.00
_____ HOW I TURN JUNK INTO FUN AND PROFIT *Sari* 3.00
_____ HOW TO WRITE A HIT SONG & SELL IT *Tommy Boyce* 7.00
_____ JUGGLING MADE EASY *Rudolf Dittrich* 3.00
_____ MAGIC FOR ALL AGES *Walter Gibson* 4.00
_____ MAGIC MADE EASY *Byron Wels* 2.00
_____ STAMP COLLECTING FOR BEGINNERS *Burton Hobson* 3.00

HORSE PLAYERS' WINNING GUIDES

_____ BETTING HORSES TO WIN *Les Conklin* 3.00
_____ ELIMINATE THE LOSERS *Bob McKnight* 3.00

MARRIAGE, SEX & PARENTHOOD

_____ ABILITY TO LOVE *Dr. Allan Fromme*	6.00
_____ GUIDE TO SUCCESSFUL MARRIAGE *Drs. Albert Ellis & Robert Harper*	5.00
_____ HOW TO RAISE AN EMOTIONALLY HEALTHY, HAPPY CHILD *A. Ellis*	5.00
_____ SEX WITHOUT GUILT *Albert Ellis, Ph.D.*	5.00
_____ SEXUALLY ADEQUATE MALE *Frank S. Caprio, M.D.*	3.00
_____ SEXUALLY FULFILLED MAN *Dr. Rachel Copelan*	5.00

MELVIN POWERS' MAIL ORDER LIBRARY

_____ HOW TO GET RICH IN MAIL ORDER *Melvin Powers*	15.00
_____ HOW TO WRITE A GOOD ADVERTISEMENT *Victor O. Schwab*	15.00
_____ MAIL ORDER MADE EASY *J. Frank Brumbaugh*	10.00
_____ U.S. MAIL ORDER SHOPPER'S GUIDE *Susan Spitzer*	10.00

METAPHYSICS & OCCULT

_____ BOOK OF TALISMANS, AMULETS & ZODIACAL GEMS *William Pavitt*	5.00
_____ CONCENTRATION—A Guide to Mental Mastery *Mouni Sadhu*	5.00
_____ CRITIQUES OF GOD *Edited by Peter Angeles*	7.00
_____ EXTRA-TERRESTRIAL INTELLIGENCE—The First Encounter	6.00
_____ FORTUNE TELLING WITH CARDS *P. Foli*	4.00
_____ HANDWRITING ANALYSIS MADE EASY *John Marley*	5.00
_____ HANDWRITING TELLS *Nadya Olyanova*	7.00
_____ HOW TO INTERPRET DREAMS, OMENS & FORTUNE TELLING SIGNS *Gettings*	3.00
_____ HOW TO UNDERSTAND YOUR DREAMS *Geoffrey A. Dudley*	3.00
_____ ILLUSTRATED YOGA *William Zorn*	3.00
_____ IN DAYS OF GREAT PEACE *Mouni Sadhu*	3.00
_____ LSD—THE AGE OF MIND *Bernard Roseman*	2.00
_____ MAGICIAN—His Training and Work *W. E. Butler*	3.00
_____ MEDITATION *Mouni Sadhu*	7.00
_____ MODERN NUMEROLOGY *Morris C. Goodman*	3.00
_____ NUMEROLOGY—ITS FACTS AND SECRETS *Ariel Yvon Taylor*	3.00
_____ NUMEROLOGY MADE EASY *W. Mykian*	4.00
_____ PALMISTRY MADE EASY *Fred Gettings*	5.00
_____ PALMISTRY MADE PRACTICAL *Elizabeth Daniels Squire*	4.00
_____ PALMISTRY SECRETS REVEALED *Henry Frith*	3.00
_____ PROPHECY IN OUR TIME *Martin Ebon*	2.50
_____ PSYCHOLOGY OF HANDWRITING *Nadya Olyanova*	5.00
_____ SUPERSTITION—Are You Superstitious? *Eric Maple*	2.00
_____ TAROT *Mouni Sadhu*	8.00
_____ TAROT OF THE BOHEMIANS *Papus*	5.00
_____ WAYS TO SELF-REALIZATION *Mouni Sadhu*	3.00
_____ WHAT YOUR HANDWRITING REVEALS *Albert E. Hughes*	3.00
_____ WITCHCRAFT, MAGIC & OCCULTISM—A Fascinating History *W. B. Crow*	5.00
_____ WITCHCRAFT—THE SIXTH SENSE *Justine Glass*	5.00
_____ WORLD OF PSYCHIC RESEARCH *Hereward Carrington*	2.00

SELF-HELP & INSPIRATIONAL

_____ DAILY POWER FOR JOYFUL LIVING *Dr. Donald Curtis*	5.00
_____ DYNAMIC THINKING *Melvin Powers*	2.00
_____ GREATEST POWER IN THE UNIVERSE *U. S. Andersen*	5.00
_____ GROW RICH WHILE YOU SLEEP *Ben Sweetland*	3.00
_____ GROWTH THROUGH REASON *Albert Ellis, Ph.D.*	4.00
_____ GUIDE TO PERSONAL HAPPINESS *Albert Ellis, Ph.D. & Irving Becker, Ed. D.*	5.00
_____ HELPING YOURSELF WITH APPLIED PSYCHOLOGY *R. Henderson*	2.00
_____ HOW TO ATTRACT GOOD LUCK *A. H. Z. Carr*	5.00
_____ HOW TO DEVELOP A WINNING PERSONALITY *Martin Panzer*	5.00
_____ HOW TO DEVELOP AN EXCEPTIONAL MEMORY *Young & Gibson*	5.00
_____ HOW TO LIVE WITH A NEUROTIC *Albert Ellis, Ph.D.*	5.00
_____ HOW TO OVERCOME YOUR FEARS *M. P. Leahy, M.D.*	3.00
_____ HUMAN PROBLEMS & HOW TO SOLVE THEM *Dr. Donald Curtis*	5.00
_____ I CAN *Ben Sweetland*	7.00
_____ I WILL *Ben Sweetland*	3.00

____ LEFT-HANDED PEOPLE *Michael Barsley*		5.00
____ MAGIC IN YOUR MIND *U. S. Andersen*		6.00
____ MAGIC OF THINKING BIG *Dr. David J. Schwartz*		3.00
____ MAGIC POWER OF YOUR MIND *Walter M. Germain*		5.00
____ MENTAL POWER THROUGH SLEEP SUGGESTION *Melvin Powers*		3.00
____ NEW GUIDE TO RATIONAL LIVING *Albert Ellis, Ph.D. & R. Harper, Ph.D.*		3.00
____ PROJECT YOU *A Manual of Rational Assertiveness Training Paris & Casey*		6.00
____ PSYCHO-CYBERNETICS *Maxwell Maltz, M.D.*		5.00
____ SCIENCE OF MIND IN DAILY LIVING *Dr. Donald Curtis*		5.00
____ SECRET OF SECRETS *U. S. Andersen*		6.00
____ SECRET POWER OF THE PYRAMIDS *U. S. Andersen*		5.00
____ STUTTERING AND WHAT YOU CAN DO ABOUT IT *W. Johnson, Ph.D.*		2.50
____ SUCCESS-CYBERNETICS *U. S. Andersen*		6.00
____ 10 DAYS TO A GREAT NEW LIFE *William E. Edwards*		3.00
____ THINK AND GROW RICH *Napoleon Hill*		5.00
____ THINK YOUR WAY TO SUCCESS *Dr. Lew Losoncy*		5.00
____ THREE MAGIC WORDS *U. S. Andersen*		5.00
____ TREASURY OF COMFORT *edited by Rabbi Sidney Greenberg*		5.00
____ TREASURY OF THE ART OF LIVING *Sidney S. Greenberg*		5.00
____ YOU ARE NOT THE TARGET *Laura Huxley*		5.00
____ YOUR SUBCONSCIOUS POWER *Charles M. Simmons*		5.00
____ YOUR THOUGHTS CAN CHANGE YOUR LIFE *Dr. Donald Curtis*		5.00

SPORTS

____ BICYCLING FOR FUN AND GOOD HEALTH *Kenneth E. Luther*		2.00
____ BILLIARDS—Pocket • Carom • Three Cushion *Clive Cottingham, Jr.*		3.00
____ CAMPING-OUT 101 Ideas & Activities *Bruno Knobel*		2.00
____ COMPLETE GUIDE TO FISHING *Vlad Evanoff*		2.00
____ HOW TO IMPROVE YOUR RACQUETBALL *Lubarsky Kaufman & Scagnetti*		3.00
____ HOW TO WIN AT POCKET BILLIARDS *Edward D. Knuchell*		5.00
____ JOY OF WALKING *Jack Scagnetti*		3.00
____ LEARNING & TEACHING SOCCER SKILLS *Eric Worthington*		3.00
____ MOTORCYCLING FOR BEGINNERS *I. G. Edmonds*		3.00
____ RACQUETBALL FOR WOMEN *Toni Hudson, Jack Scagnetti & Vince Rondone*		3.00
____ RACQUETBALL MADE EASY *Steve Lubarsky, Rod Delson & Jack Scagnetti*		4.00
____ SECRET OF BOWLING STRIKES *Dawson Taylor*		3.00
____ SECRET OF PERFECT PUTTING *Horton Smith & Dawson Taylor*		3.00
____ SOCCER—The Game & How to Play It *Gary Rosenthal*		3.00
____ STARTING SOCCER *Edward F. Dolan, Jr.*		3.00

TENNIS LOVERS' LIBRARY

____ BEGINNER'S GUIDE TO WINNING TENNIS *Helen Hull Jacobs*		2.00
____ HOW TO BEAT BETTER TENNIS PLAYERS *Loring Fiske*		4.00
____ HOW TO IMPROVE YOUR TENNIS—Style, Strategy & Analysis *C. Wilson*		2.00
____ PLAY TENNIS WITH ROSEWALL *Ken Rosewall*		2.00
____ PSYCH YOURSELF TO BETTER TENNIS *Dr. Walter A. Luszki*		2.00
____ TENNIS FOR BEGINNERS, *Dr. H. A. Murray*		2.00
____ TENNIS MADE EASY *Joel Brecheen*		4.00
____ WEEKEND TENNIS—How to Have Fun & Win at the Same Time *Bill Talbert*		3.00
____ WINNING WITH PERCENTAGE TENNIS—Smart Strategy *Jack Lowe*		2.00

WILSHIRE PET LIBRARY

____ DOG OBEDIENCE TRAINING *Gust Kessopulos*		5.00
____ DOG TRAINING MADE EASY & FUN *John W. Kellogg*		4.00
____ HOW TO BRING UP YOUR PET DOG *Kurt Unkelbach*		2.00
____ HOW TO RAISE & TRAIN YOUR PUPPY *Jeff Griffen*		5.00
____ PIGEONS: HOW TO RAISE & TRAIN THEM *William H. Allen, Jr.*		2.00

*The books listed above can be obtained from your book dealer or directly from
Melvin Powers. When ordering, please remit 50¢ per book postage & handling.
Send for our free illustrated catalog of self-improvement books.*

Melvin Powers
12015 Sherman Road, No. Hollywood, California 91605

WILSHIRE HORSE LOVERS' LIBRARY

_____	AMATEUR HORSE BREEDER *A. C. Leighton Hardman*	5.00
_____	AMERICAN QUARTER HORSE IN PICTURES *Margaret Cabell Self*	3.00
_____	APPALOOSA HORSE *Donna & Bill Richardson*	5.00
_____	ARABIAN HORSE *Reginald S. Summerhays*	4.00
_____	ART OF WESTERN RIDING *Suzanne Norton Jones*	5.00
_____	AT THE HORSE SHOW *Margaret Cabell Self*	3.00
_____	BACK-YARD HORSE *Peggy Jett Pittinger*	4.00
_____	BASIC DRESSAGE *Jean Froissard*	5.00
_____	BEGINNER'S GUIDE TO HORSEBACK RIDING *Sheila Wall*	2.00
_____	BEGINNER'S GUIDE TO THE WESTERN HORSE *Natlee Kenoyer*	2.00
_____	BITS—THEIR HISTORY, USE AND MISUSE *Louis Taylor*	5.00
_____	BREAKING & TRAINING THE DRIVING HORSE *Doris Ganton*	10.00
_____	BREAKING YOUR HORSE'S BAD HABITS *W. Dayton Sumner*	5.00
_____	COMPLETE TRAINING OF HORSE AND RIDER *Colonel Alois Podhajsky*	6.00
_____	DISORDERS OF THE HORSE & WHAT TO DO ABOUT THEM *E. Hanauer*	5.00
_____	DOG TRAINING MADE EASY & FUN *John W. Kellogg*	4.00
_____	DRESSAGE—A Study of the Finer Points in Riding *Henry Wynmalen*	5.00
_____	DRIVE ON *Doris Ganton*	7.00
_____	DRIVING HORSES *Sallie Walrond*	5.00
_____	EQUITATION *Jean Froissard*	5.00
_____	FIRST AID FOR HORSES *Dr. Charles H. Denning, Jr.*	3.00
_____	FUN OF RAISING A COLT *Rubye & Frank Griffith*	5.00
_____	FUN ON HORSEBACK *Margaret Caball Self*	4.00
_____	GYMKHANA GAMES *Natlee Kenoyer*	2.00
_____	HORSE DISEASES—Causes, Symptoms & Treatment *Dr. H. G. Belschner*	6.00
_____	HORSE OWNER'S CONCISE GUIDE *Elsie V. Hanauer*	3.00
_____	HORSE SELECTION & CARE FOR BEGINNERS *George H. Conn*	5.00
_____	HORSEBACK RIDING FOR BEGINNERS *Louis Taylor*	5.00
_____	HORSEBACK RIDING MADE EASY & FUN *Sue Henderson Coen*	5.00
_____	HORSES—Their Selection, Care & Handling *Margaret Cabell Self*	5.00
_____	HOW TO BUY A BETTER HORSE & SELL THE HORSE YOU OWN	3.00
_____	HOW TO ENJOY YOUR QUARTER HORSE *Willard H. Porter*	3.00
_____	HUNTER IN PICTURES *Margaret Cabell Self*	2.00
_____	ILLUSTRATED BOOK OF THE HORSE *S. Sidney* (8½" × 11")	10.00
_____	ILLUSTRATED HORSE MANAGEMENT—400 Illustrations *Dr. E. Mayhew*	6.00
_____	ILLUSTRATED HORSE TRAINING *Captain M. H. Hayes*	5.00
_____	ILLUSTRATED HORSEBACK RIDING FOR BEGINNERS *Jeanne Mellin*	3.00
_____	JUMPING—Learning & Teaching *Jean Froissard*	5.00
_____	KNOW ALL ABOUT HORSES *Harry Disston*	3.00
_____	LAME HORSE Cause, Symptoms & Treatment *Dr. James R. Rooney*	7.00
_____	LAW & YOUR HORSE *Edward H. Greene*	7.00
_____	MANUAL OF HORSEMANSHIP *Harold Black*	5.00
_____	MOVIE HORSES—The Fascinating Techniques of Training *Anthony Amaral*	2.00
_____	POLICE HORSES *Judith Campbell*	2.00
_____	PRACTICAL GUIDE TO HORSESHOEING	5.00
_____	PRACTICAL GUIDE TO OWNING YOUR OWN HORSE *Steven D. Price*	3.00
_____	PRACTICAL HORSE PSYCHOLOGY *Moyra Williams*	4.00
_____	PROBLEM HORSES Guide for Curing Serious Behavior Habits *Summerhays*	4.00
_____	REINSMAN OF THE WEST—BRIDLES & BITS *Ed Connell*	5.00
_____	RIDE WESTERN *Louis Taylor*	5.00
_____	SCHOOLING YOUR YOUNG HORSE *George Wheatley*	5.00
_____	STABLE MANAGEMENT FOR THE OWNER-GROOM *George Wheatley*	4.00
_____	STALLION MANAGEMENT—A Guide for Stud Owners *A. C. Hardman*	5.00
_____	TEACHING YOUR HORSE TO JUMP *W. J. Froud*	2.00
_____	TRAINING YOUR HORSE TO SHOW *Neale Haley*	5.00
_____	TREATING COMMON DISEASES OF YOUR HORSE *Dr. George H. Conn*	5.00
_____	TREATING HORSE AILMENTS *G. W. Serth*	2.00
_____	YOU AND YOUR PONY *Pepper Mainwaring Healey* (8½" × 11")	6.00
_____	YOUR FIRST HORSE *George C. Saunders, M.D.*	5.00
_____	YOUR PONY BOOK *Hermann Wiederhold*	2.00

The books listed above can be obtained from your book dealer or directly from
Melvin Powers. When ordering, please remit 50¢ per book postage & handling.
Send for our free illustrated catalog of self-improvement books.

Melvin Powers
12015 Sherman Road, No. Hollywood, California 91605